PENGUIN BOOKS

THE NEW PENGUIN FREUD
GENERAL EDITOR: ADAM PHILLIPS

Beyond the Pleasure Principle and Other Writings

Sigmund Freud was born in 1856 in Moravia; between the ages of four and eighty-two his home was in Vienna: in 1938 Hitler's invasion of Austria forced him to seek asylum in London, where he died in the following year. His career began with several years of brilliant work on the anatomy and physiology of the nervous system. He was almost thirty when, after a period of study under Charcot in Paris, his interests first turned to psychology; and after ten years of clinical work in Vienna (at first in collaboration with Breuer, an older colleague) he invented what was to become psychoanalysis. This began simply as a method of treating neurotic patients through talking, but it quickly grew into an accumulation of knowledge about the workings of the mind in general. Freud was thus able to demonstrate the development of the sexual instinct in childhood and, largely on the basis of an examination of dreams, arrived at his fundamental discovery of the unconscious forces that influence our everyday thoughts and actions. Freud's life was uneventful, but his ideas have shaped not only many specialist disciplines, but also the whole intellectual climate of the twentieth century.

John Reddick was born in 1940 and educated at Oxford University. He has held lectureships at Edinburgh and Cambridge universities and chairs at Sydney University and Liverpool. His publications include *The Danzig Trilogy of Günter Grass* (1974) and *Georg Büchner: The Shattered Whole* (1994), which won the J. G. Robertson Prize. John Reddick also translated Georg Büchner's *The Complete Plays, Lenz and Other Writings* for Penguin (1993).

Mark Edmundson is Professor of English at the University of Virginia. He is the author of *Towards Reading Freud* (1992), *Literature against Philosophy, Plato to Derrida* (1995), *Nightmare on Main Street* (1997) and *Teacher* (a memoir) (2002). He is a contributing editor for *Raritan* and *Harper's Magazine*.

Adam Phillips was formerly Principal Child Psychotherapist at Charing Cross Hospital in London. He is the author of several books on psychoanalysis including *On Kissing, Tickling and Being Bored, Darwin's Worms, Promises, Promises* and *Houdini's Box*.

SIGMUND FREUD

Beyond the Pleasure Principle and Other Writings

Translated by John Reddick
with an Introduction by Mark Edmundson

PENGUIN BOOKS

PENGUIN BOOKS

Published by the Penguin Group
Penguin Books Ltd, 80 Strand, London WC2R 0RL, England
Penguin Putnam Inc., 375 Hudson Street, New York, New York 10014, USA
Penguin Books Australia Ltd, 250 Camberwell Road, Camberwell, Victoria 3124, Australia
Penguin Books Canada Ltd, 10 Alcorn Avenue, Toronto, Ontario, Canada M4V 3B2
Penguin Books India (P) Ltd, 11 Community Centre, Panchsheel Park, New Delhi – 110 017, India
Penguin Books (NZ) Ltd, Cnr Rosedale and Airborne Roads, Albany, Auckland, New Zealand
Penguin Books (South Africa) (Pty) Ltd, 24 Sturdee Avenue, Rosebank 2196, South Africa

Penguin Books Ltd, Registered Offices: 80 Strand, London WC2R 0RL, England

www.penguin.com

'Zur Einführung des Narzissmus' first published 1914 in *Jahrbuch der Psychoanalyse*
'Weitere Ratschläge zur Technik der Psychoanalyse: II. Erinnern, Wiederholen und
Durcharbeiten' first published 1914 (Leipzig) in *Internationale Zeitschrift für ärztliche
Psychoanalyse*, 2 (6)
Jenseits des Lustprinzips first published 1920 (Leipzig, Vienna and Zurich: Internationaler
Psychoanalytischer Verlag)
Das Ich und das Es first published 1923 (Leipzig, Vienna and Zurich: Internationaler
Psychoanalytischer Verlag)
Hemmung, Symptom und Angst first published 1926 (Leipzig, Vienna and Zurich:
Internationaler Psychoanalytischer Verlag)

Sigmund Freud's German texts collected in *Gesammelte Werke* (1940–52)
Copyright © Imago Publishing Co. Ltd, London, 1940, 1946, 1948

This translation published in Penguin Classics 2003

026

Translation and editorial matter copyright © John Reddick, 2003
Introduction copyright © Mark Edmundson, 2003
All rights reserved

www.greenpenguin.co.uk

Contents

Introduction

Freud in Love

Sigmund Freud is Western culture's laureate of unhappy love. He is our prose-poet of the heart's endless desire to break. The heart breaks time and again and, Freud insists, it is prone to do so in the same fashion. Freud, as the works gathered in this volume demonstrate, put the idea of erotic repetition at the centre of his thought. He believed that we are all inclined – many of us are doomed – to repeat, and what we repeat is disaster, erotic disaster and political disaster as well. We fall in love not only with 'sexual objects' (as Freud charmingly calls them) but, individually and collectively, with power. Though badly in need of sane and measured authority, we swoon before the authoritarian. For most people, there is not much to be done about these sad tendencies. Through experience, Freud believed, most of us learn nothing, unless it is to repeat our own worst experiences.

Life, from Freud's perspective, frequently circles from romance to disillusionment, then does so again and again. We seek perfect love, perfect truth, perfect protection. We believe that we once had those things (though we never did) and we continually sight them, glowing, on the far side of a noisy room or dispensing truth from a banner-draped stage, Klieg- or torch-lights flaring. We are drawn into the golden circle, abase ourselves, submit, and for a while enjoy an extraordinary sense of well-being. It is as though we have attained a long-sought completion. We never feel so strongly as then, in the midst of love, that we live in the present. (Though the truth is that in love, more than at any other time, we are dwelling in the past.)

But soon our idealizations dissolve, the honey-glow disappears, and we're tolled back, as Keats has it, to our sole selves. We find ourselves then disillusioned, void of life (illusion, whatever its pitfalls, is to Freud the great energizer), and waiting for the next irresistible falsehood, the next narcissistic ploy, to come along. For once the period of disillusion – or mourning – is over, Freud says in a memorable phrase, we pursue the next 'object' the way a starving man pursues bread.

Perfect love and perfect authority are not available to mortals. Yet to write that sentence now, to think that usefully demystifying thought, will not save one from losing everything in a futile quest for sublime love, sublime authority. In fact, the ability to articulate this Freudian wisdom may induce us to lower our guards, making ruin all the more likely. As soon as we feel that we have finally learned Freud's lessons, we are ripe for another fall.

Among his detractors, Freud is known as an erotic reductionist. He takes the worlds of love and power, with their marvellous iridescent shades, and swabs them with his dun-coloured brush. But perhaps Freud is not so much a reductionist as he is someone who brilliantly exposes the state of the psyche when it is at its most minimal and besieged. Maybe Freud is not, strictly speaking, a reductionist but someone who aptly describes us when we are at our most reduced.

Happy men and women (the enchanted, mystified ones, Freud would generally say) look at the psychoanalytic account of love and sneer. It's all too simple, too cut and dried. But in times of crisis, erotic or political, they may return to Freud's purgatorial map for a stark overview of the terrain, and some hints about how to traverse it. Yet Freud's map, even at its best, can only lead one to equanimity – to irony, detachment, poise. Philip Rieff in *The Mind of the Moralist* (University of Chicago Press, 1979) suggests that there is something Eastern in the Freudian ethos. The quest for equanimity through psychoanalysis is akin to Buddhist attempts to attain relative calm through yoga and meditation. The way to live beyond delusion, for Freud, is to achieve sceptical distance from one's desires – though without ever suppressing them.

Can we ask for more than this? Is it possible to conceive of love and power in ways that, while taking Freud's strictures seriously, still propel us past the ethics of irony and renunciation that Freud overall commends?

I think so. Though, to be sure, there are risks in such a quest: as Freud always insisted, the better is often the enemy of the good. Freud derided civilization for asking too much of people. In general he thought that the middle classes were victimized by their own attempts to live beyond their psyches' means. Despite such prudent warnings, I want to turn to Shakespeare, from whom Freud learned a great deal but perhaps not enough, to describe some possibilities for renewal that pass beyond Freud, but that also contain some of his harshest wisdom about power, love and the compulsion to repeat.

The simplicity at the core of Freud's thoughts about power and Eros is scandalous. But then, simple, abrupt diagnosis is part of the psychoanalytic ethos. In psychoanalysis, the road to humility often runs through repeated humiliation. The neurotic believes that she is special: no one has ever felt precisely this way before. No one has ever suffered like this. But Freud insists that neuroses don't individualize us. On the contrary, they rob us of whatever singularity we may possess. Therapy, then, becomes an encounter with the distinct possibility that whoever you are, whatever you've achieved, you've become no more than a cliché, a walking tired and tiring figure of speech: anally retentive, orally fixated, Oedipally tied. Perhaps the fear of being a lifelong solecism incarnate helps jolt patients into recovery. They don't want to be an embodied diagnosis, the realization of some array of principles gleaned from a textbook, so they rebel and begin to change.

In any event, Freud's diagnosis of collective humanity is simple and potentially humbling. To a Freudian mind, all the stories of Eden, Nirvana, the Blessed Fields, Valhalla and the rest reduce to one primary experience, the experience of blissful union that most of us have just after we enter the world. We come into life absurdly unfit for it. We're small, shivering and afraid, squalling at our fate, swimming in phantasmagoria, drawn forth from time to time by a flashing or familiar object, only to sink back into primal flow. One baby in the room, says Emerson, makes a dozen more of the adults in attendance, who bend to the child's every whim. There is probably no perfume more disarming than the infant's natural scent. It's fortunate that Emerson is right. Human babies need all the fawning and protection that they can get.

In only a few weeks, the calf that was tottering unsteadily beside its mother is running through the pasture. The human infant, born the same day, has learned to raise its head and fix a stare for five or so seconds, not much more. In a decade's time many other mammals have run through the course of their lives. We are relatively defence-less still. Dickens shocked his huge audience, as Blake did his much smaller one, by depicting wretched children, ten or eleven years old, marooned in the midst of city life. The Artful Dodger, Oliver, and Blake's chimney sweepers, are little more than babes making their way through a slag-heap world. We stay too short a time in the womb and we are mere children for a very long time after that – Freud would say most of us remain children to the end. To the experienced psychoanalyst, there are very few grown-ups.

In the early period of deep dependency a rich inner life begins: the child's complex human character starts to take shape. The infant – etymologically, the one who cannot speak – lives in a world of images and desires, great pleasures (he is, potentially, a polymor-phous pervert) and body-wrenching wants. Giant figures, godlike in their power (as proportionately grand as the figures on the movie screen that bring these grown-up demi-gods themselves back to thrilling infancy) loom over the child, capable, it seems, of satisfying all wants. Where they are, dressed out in their full potency, is Eden, a world of perfection. Filled up with mother's milk the baby experiences a blissful satisfaction that will be a standard for all requited love to come. In the father's voice, the child senses a power that unerringly protects and guides. That voice will return later in life with every experience of what the eighteenth century called the sublime – in Wagner and Beethoven, say, thunderously assertive, as though they were rendering the thoughts of Jove and, too, in the voice of every plausible purveyor of Truth, each subject (as Lacan has it) who is supposed to know.

But gaps open up too. Mother is distracted and looks away; father fails some elementary test. And into the gap between desire and delivery come fantasy, wish, yearning, and resentment as well. So like all paradises, this one is eventually lost. But to Freud, the psyche is profoundly conservative. He says over and over that we will never willingly give up a satisfying libidinal position once we have inhabited it. If we lose such a position, we will strive to restore it in dreams, in fantasy, through neurosis, or – with every semblance of probity – in what appears to be well-ordered adult life. We regress where and when we can, and what we regress to is the dream of perfect authority and love. We do so again and again, for reality, even the best-made reality, is too poor for our hopes. In his attempt to surrender unconditionally to the primal dream, the opium-eater is the prototype of all humanity.

Love, says the narrator of Céline's *Journey to the End of the Night*, is a poodle's chance of attaining the infinite – 'and frankly I have my pride'. Freud would concur in the general denigration of love, I suppose, but he would doubt that much of anyone, even the rancid Céline, could always sustain his pride in the face of Eros. Perhaps Freud's most unpleasant remark on love comes in his paper on the transference. 'It is true', Freud writes there, 'that the love [that the patient develops for the therapist] consists of new editions of old traits and that it repeats infantile reactions. There is no such state which does not reproduce infantile prototypes. It is precisely from this infantile determination that it receives its compulsive character, verging as it does on the pathological. Transference-love has perhaps a degree less of freedom than the love which appears in ordinary life and is called normal; it displays its dependence on the infantile pattern more clearly and is less adaptable and capable of modification; but that is all, and not what is essential.' ('Observations on Transference Love', *Standard Edition*, vol. XII, p. 168).

So the obsessive love that arises in therapy is a little bit madder than the love that arises in everyday life, but not very much. In saying so, Freud seeks to explain a peculiar situation that occurs all the time in experience, but that we often take in our stride. The fact that people of all sorts do the most bizarre and unexpected things for love, that they live in a haze, abase themselves, act in outlandish ways, is something we simply accept as normal. In *The Symposium*, Plato's great dialogue on love, it's suggested that someone who has fallen in love is really little different from one who has fallen physically ill.

Freud sees this domesticated madness and does what he can to explain it. He says that when we fall in love, all of the infantile fantasies about power and pleasure are reactivated. They have been dormant, but they have never died, and they are resurrected, a little like the horror-movie spooks who rise up when their burial ground is accidentally disturbed. The old wishes come once again to the fore and they dominate life. Love is pathology, at least romantic love. Married love, which takes place under the reign of that sour deity, the Reality Principle, is far less interesting to Freud. So Freud would disabuse us of our erotic illusions and make us more sober, or at least capable of some measure of irony at the point when we are once again about to drown ourselves in Eros.

An effective, flexible super-ego (assuming that such a thing exists) is, one might hypothesize, the source of whatever ironic vision we can apply to our own experience. Super-ego irony entails distance, detachment, a sceptical sense that we are not so different from anyone else, that we are as ripe for humiliation as the next person. And, more than that, such irony suggests the possibility that we are, despite protestations, not so different from our former selves: that we are likely to behave as disastrously in the present as we have in the past.

In love, the reigning super-ego suffers usurpation. In love, Freud says in *Group Psychology and the Analysis of the Ego* (1921), the lover puts the beloved in the place of the Over-I. The lover becomes the standard for judgement. What the beloved finds admirable, or interesting, or just noteworthy, is splendid behaviour. Like being drunk, which also suspends the super-ego, at least until the next morning when it can assert itself with redoubled force (the great essay on the psychology of the hangover is yet to be written), being in love lets us displace our own internal monarch and put a lord of temporary, blissful misrule on the throne. Alas, when we remember our various erotic abasements, it is through the unforgiving agency of the true super-ego, the one based on harsh parental prototypes, which has retaken the seat and glares bitterly at the past. Love, too, has its morning after. (Sometimes it lasts for years.) But for a while, ludicrously, absurdly, exaltingly, we feel free.

To love, according to Freud, is to 'over-estimate the erotic object'. What is the nature of this so-called over-estimation? To over-estimate someone is, presumably, to see them as larger than they are in themselves, or to others – or (maybe more to the point) than they would be to Freud, who was, to say the least, a rather harsh judge of character. And naturally the first over-magnified figures in life were the parents, the mother in particular, who looms over the child. 'The mother's face,' says Wallace Stevens, 'is the purpose of the poem' and, Freud would add, of much more besides. We, males and females alike, seek her, according to the Freudian wisdom, from one end of our lives to the other. So we are anxious and dissatisfied when monogamous – the sole object that we invest in is never the right one, the original one. But we tend to be equally unhappy with promiscuity. For here the original object is pursued in a series of substitutes, none of whom brings full satisfaction. As Philip Rieff puts it: 'Freud acutely understood the intimate connection between libertine and ascetic behaviour. Both are excesses, deriving from an imperfect emancipation from childhood's insatiable love for authority figures . . . If from Freud we may infer that monogamy is not a very satisfactory arrangement, the results of his science may also be taken to show that man is a naturally faithful creature: the most inconstant sexual athlete is in motivation still a toddler, searching for the original maternal object.' (p. 166)

So, erotically, we repeat. We continue time and again trying to regain an illusory former happiness. And too, perhaps, we repeat our former humiliations as punishment. If the incest wish informs every desire, then desire must be chastened time and again. Every erotic hope is a hope for the mother or the father, and such hopes require retribution. The super-ego, Freud's often depraved agency of inner authority, may even push us towards erotic failure and suffering so as to confirm its harsh rule. Thus we repeat out of libidinal desire, and repeat out of a desire for punishment; the Over-I and the It assert themselves at the expense of the bewildered self.

Near the end of the third chapter of *Beyond the Pleasure Principle*, Freud describes a scene from Tasso which, he says, illustrates the repetitive nature of erotic wounding. Tancred, the hero of *Gerusalemme Liberata*, unknowingly kills his beloved Clorinda in a duel when she is disguised in an enemy's armour. After she is buried, Tancred makes his way into a magical forest, which fills his army with fear. He slashes with his sword at a tree, but blood rather than sap flows from the cut and the voice of Clorinda, whose soul is imprisoned in the tree, cries out that he has wounded her again.

We inflict erotic wounds, inadvertently, unconsciously, as Tancred does. And we feel them to the quick, in Clorinda's way. Try as we might, the Freudian wisdom says, we can never find a love that does not set the wheel of primal ambivalence in motion. In love, we reopen the narcissistic wound again and again, as each new object does to us what the parent has done, falls short of perfection, or thrusts us aside for another. And because we activate primal fantasies in others, we probably wound as often as we are wounded.

Is all of this reduction back to the mother and the father too simplistic to sustain belief? If so, one might look at Freud's thoughts on Eros from another perspective. One might consider them as a sort of mythology of origins. Imagine that, rather than trying for some empirically reliable vision, Freud looked around him at what he took to be human erotic folly, and tried to find a metaphor that would capture what he saw. Thus he might be taken to be saying something like this: 'People act *as if* they're still in love with their parents. They act as though in some fundamental way they're still infants. Only a myth that is that grotesque and that hyperbolic will get you close to seeing how strange and disturbing the situation really is.'

What makes an object lovable in the most obsessive way? What makes us compelled to over-estimate it? Narcissism. The narcissist is the one who can transport us away from our standard vision of the day-to-day and convince us that extraordinary things are possible. The narcissist, says Freud, in the great essay 'On the Introduction of Narcissism' included in this volume, is the one whose satisfaction comes not from loving, but from being loved. When such a figure is beautiful or powerful, then his sway over those around him is boundless. He returns them to the dream of perfection.

The narcissist exudes charisma, in the secular rather than the sacred sense. He needs nothing and no one but himself. The narcissist sends off a glow of sheer inviolability. Nothing gets to him. Nothing daunts him. His being is unified, coherent and composed: the narcissist has transcended all painful self-division; he is never prey to ambiguity and anxiety. Of the incomparable Alcibiades, a paragon of narcissism, Plutarch writes that 'In the midst of [his] displays of statesmanship, eloquence, cleverness, and exalted ambition, [he] lived a life of prodigious luxury, drunkenness, debauchery and insolence. He was effeminate in his dress and would walk through the marketplace trailing his long purple robes, and he spent extravagantly . . . He had a golden shield made for him, which was emblazoned not with any ancestral device, but with the figure of Eros armed with a thunderbolt . . . The people's feelings towards him have been very aptly expressed by Aristophanes in the line: "They long for him, they hate him, they cannot do without him."'

It is magical, the sense of perfection the narcissist brings, and we believe that by gaining the narcissist's love or at least his recognition, we might share in his numinous life. As Freud observes, '[I]t seems clearly apparent that narcissism in an individual becomes magnetically attractive to those who have altogether relinquished their own narcissism, and who are casting around for object-love. The fascination of the child rests to a great extent on its narcissism, on the fact that it is sufficient to itself and impervious to others; so too does the fascination of certain animals that appear to show no interest in us, such as cats and the great beasts of prey.' ('On the Introduction of Narcissism', p. 18). From the Homeric gods to our current celebrities, the centrality of narcissistic personalities to culture is beyond debate. Without them we might all die from hopelessness, perish of boredom. With them, we alternate from intoxication, sometimes mild, sometimes not, to rank disillusion. Is there any crowd as disconsolate as the one seeping from a starlit Hollywood movie into the sad light of the everyday?

The narcissist exploits our longing to be bewitched. They enchant us with the possibility that we are the one who will really share in their glow, or break it down and turn them, as though through a reverse enchantment, once again into a common mortal like ourselves. But alas, narcissism in another, which initially is so exhilarating, is over time demoralizing. It provokes despondency, as we recognize that the glowing one doesn't need us at all. Beautiful women, great criminals, superb jesters, Helen of Troy, Balzac's Vautrin, Groucho, never seem to be defeated – or inevitably turn gap into gain, trump defeat with their wit or beauty. But they do so alone and independently. They do not require our assistance in the least.

When the narcissist does break down and show need, then he is one of us, and his fascination is gone. At the moment when the narcissist becomes human and returns the love of one of his worshippers, he turns from prince to frog, no longer fit for worship. A narcissist, void of self-love, tends to *be* void, in that he has never had to cultivate anything but the capacity to fascinate. Inwardness is not part of his game. When the narcissist enters erotic life, he creates the quest, the romance, poems, humiliations, great deeds, and rank unhappiness. When what the narcissist captures is political power, the result is tyranny.

The narcissist is one of Freud's great archetypes, memorable and illuminating. Yet are absolute narcissists to be found in experience? Is it possible that the narcissist is simply an illusion sustained by the lover, the one who wants the old perfect archetypes to reappear in life, and will work to create them out of whatever promising material comes to hand? To Freud, we weave our dreams whenever we have the chance, awake or asleep. Can't narcissists themselves fall under the spell of others, and be turned into dependent or anaclitic lovers by the presence of this or that more apparently self-contained and self-delighting being? Emerson tells us that we create perfection in others by being afraid to own up to our own powers. Not recognizing our particular genius, we project it outside. The presence of the narcissist as an absolute type in Freud, rather than a projection, a creation by wishful illusion, suggests that Freud, the most severe interpreter, may have been himself taken in by the kind of glowing promise and perfect love that he also seeks to debunk.

The narcissist, even if doomed to be merely a walking illusion created by others, a sex symbol as it were, which is actually a mere signifier until it is invested with meaning from outside, is a crucial element in our imaginative lives. The narcissist testifies to the human hope that life will not be all drab continuities and predictable expenditures. And yet, because we seek transformation from another, outside ourselves, we're doomed to disillusion.

But is it possible to liberate the erotic drive from the demands of the past, and to be either a monogamist or an inconstant sexual athlete without the obsessive hunger that's never slaked and that makes every erotic affair fall so far short of expectation? Freud was once moved to remark that satisfaction, upon some examination, proves to be unsatisfying. (How happy can human Eros be, a Freudian might ask, if some of us can substitute buying experience, consumerism, for sexual experience and be identically unhappy with both?) If the possibility for erotic happiness exists, it is not one that Freud, preoccupied as he was with regression and the past, ever succeeded in envisioning. But we should pursue the question ourselves, keep it on our horizon: what would it mean to loosen the erotic drive, if not to detach it fully, from the old obsessions? Perhaps there is no free love, no Eros without human cost, but can love ever, through exertion or through canny realization, be liberated from the compulsion to repeat the past?

To Freud, sexual love always entails love of authority. In love, the object after all takes the place of the super-ego. If the extreme form of anaclitic or dependent erotic love is an infantilization of the self, then the extreme form of love for authority comes when the subject is willing to abase himself to the tyrant. The sycophant and the follower are the political incarnations of the prostrate lover. Freud's theory of sex is also a theory of politics. When the narcissist is hungry for power, we submit, but erotically. When he drives for erotic domination, we swoon; courtly lovers speak of monarchs of the heart. The sado-masochist, debased by uniforms, badges and rank, is, alas, an active sexual prototype that looms before us all.

Love for authority sublimates Eros, makes it less immediately perceptible, often because Eros, under such conditions, is homosexual and therefore anxiety-provoking. Yet Hitler said it himself: he made love to the masses who came to him in waves. All of those serried ranks at Nuremberg, lovingly filmed by Leni Riefenstahl, stand at firm attention, but their hearts are blazing away. They are being wooed and won by one of the great lovers of all time.

We yearn for erotic absolutes and political absolutism. Dictatorship, the rule of the talker who never stops, the super-ego so sure of itself that it never needs to brook contradiction, or pause for an answer, resonates so fully with our childhood fantasies about a protective force far greater than ourselves that it can hypnotize us, make a whole nation into sleepwalkers.

Democracy, American style, which Freud despised, supposedly inverts the longing for the father, repudiating what we most desire, without understanding what is at stake in that repudiation. We replace obeisance to the rule of the leader with obeisance to the rule of the crowd and think highly of ourselves for it. In America, we invert, and repeat by reversal. We never learn to remember and to work through our primary fixations.

Who is the tyrant? The tyrant is the political equivalent of the common day-to-day narcissist. Fired by a love for public power and a wish to sway the masses to action rather than to Hollywood-style adoration, the authoritarian figure capitalizes on the same needs as does a diamond-cold beloved. He is the omnipotent father resurrected. Freud believed that the murder of the primal father had begun civilization. After that deed, guilt attached us all to various father substitutes. But one does not have to concur with the fable to see how the roots of religion, and also of most forms of politics that revolve around the leader, might go back to the first investments in authority.

For Freud, politics in their essence are authoritarian politics;

reaction will always assert itself after any revolution, for we yearn to live within a system of total control. As Blake knew, but disliked knowing, tyranny and sycophancy are very nearly the standard state of human life, the default conditions to which we tend by a gravitational force. What Blake called the Orc Cycle, the circuit from rebellion to tyranny and back again, is to Freud the way of the world.

The essential leader, whose reign recurs interminably through time, is the latterday descendant of the primal father, whom Freud describes this way: 'his ego had few libidinal ties; he loved no one but himself, or other people only in so far as they served his needs. To objects his ego gave away no more than was barely necessary . . . Even today the members of a group stand in need of the illusion that they are equally and justly loved by their leader; but the leader himself need love no one else, he may be of a masterful nature, absolutely narcissistic, self-confident and independent.' (*Group Psychology and the Analysis of the Ego, Standard Edition*, vol. XVIII, pp. 123–4)

Everything that matters is past, according to the psychoanalytical theory of the unconscious, says J. H. van den Berg, 'and there is nothing new'. One might add that, from Freud's perspective, any attempt at the new will probably stretch the resources of the psyche too far and compel us to lapse back into the lowest ebb, a regressive phase of the repeating cycle of submission and revolt. Rebellion is beside the point: rebellion, in Freud, is a tribute to the power of the wish for domination, in that trying to rid ourselves entirely of that wish is little different from capitulating entirely and embracing it. The Freudian humanist seeks a disabused middle state.

Although Freud wrote during the period of Nazi ascendancy and was eventually forced to leave Vienna to save his life (his sisters, who stayed behind, died in concentration camps), Germany is not the nation that comes in for the most Freudian invective. That distinction belongs to America. Whenever there is an occasion to say a bad word about the United States, Freud takes it, and when an occasion isn't manifest, he's inclined to fabricate one. Freud disliked America because all of the principles on which the nation is founded are affronts to deep human truths, at least as Freud conceived them.

America, the proud democracy, is distinctive and distinctly foolish, for having tried to do away with hierarchy. Its people assumed that everyone was a king, that all were equal. But to Freud, the only way that a people can develop, or even maintain stability, is by accepting individuals of the leader type who tap into the old Oedipal fantasies, but who, not being exclusively narcissistic, can guide the masses to higher ways of life. In sane politics, as in sane love, the old archetypes still preside, though in sublimated forms.

Fascism and communism, or what we might summarily call transference politics, have perhaps a degree less freedom than the liberal, enlightened politics that evolve in the world and are called normal; they display their dependence on the infantile pattern more clearly, and are less adaptable and capable of modification; but that is all, and not what is essential.

Non-transference politics, to be effective, cannot stray too far from the old patterns. Without authentic leaders, societies devolve into mediocrity and, when under pressure, into barbarism. It is clear that Freud saw himself as one such leader. How Americans could be so interested in psychoanalysis without a corresponding sense of how far they'd strayed from its basic lessons was something that continually puzzled him.

The result of throwing off, or pretending to throw off, the addiction to the leader, is that one will hunger for authority and will seek it, without self-awareness, in odd places. The American becomes a crowd animal, starved of order and truth and finding them in consensus. (Freud provides psychological explanations for much of what de Tocqueville thought he saw in America.) But because he does not know that subjection is what he seeks, there is no opportunity to submit the drive for authority to critical scrutiny and to do what Freud commends in his central paper 'Remembering, Repeating, and Working Through' – to recall and diagnose love for the authoritarian rather than simply repeating it in displaced forms. The psychiatrist, says Freud, 'prepares himself for a constant battle with the patient, in order to keep within the psychic domain all those impulses that the patient would prefer to divert into the motor domain, and regards it as a therapeutic triumph when he successfully uses the remembering process to resolve an issue that the patient would rather get rid of in the form of an action' ('Remembering, Repeating, and Working Through', p. 39).

Freud even goes so far as to denigrate American love affairs for their lighter than air quality. Nothing is risked, nothing can be lost. The American in love, presumably, cannot have primal hopes engaged, at least at the outset, and by the time that he does, it is too late. Then he's fallen all the way and is lost in the glorious authoritarian world that is regressive Eros. In America there is no psychological mean, no area where we can engage the primal fantasies and also put them at a distance. One of the many reasons that Freud so admired England may have been that in its constitutional monarchy, all the primal fixations are there to remember and to work through, manifest as they are in harmless ceremonial forms. The monarchy is theatrical, peopled with surrogates, and thus allows a sort of free national psychoanalysis to be ongoing. Citizens can displace political fantasies onto the royal family in much the way that patients displace them onto the therapist through the transference. Is it possible that in America people displace their psychodramas onto their celebrities and thus leave the politicians a little more unenchanted space in which to work? Freud would never have allowed as much: to him America is an eternal disaster.

What could be done for a psyche, or for a culture, in love with oppressive authority, or with outmoded fantasies about Eros? How can you bring the cycle of illusions and vastation to an end, if not for the masses who are by Freud's account bound to be lazy and stupid, then at least for promising individuals, those who need to bear the burdens of civilization, and whose health is, accordingly, most precious?

Freud attacked this problem from as many sides as he could. In his writings he tried to direct people away from crippling religious beliefs, from the longing for the primal father, who would take the place of a richer and more complex super-ego, and for the longing for the mother, which, in *Civilization and its Discontents* (1930), Freud implicitly equates with the 'oceanic feeling', the sense of being overwhelmed by an enveloping presence – a regression, in other words, back to the undifferentiated world of the id and the womb. The sublime and the beautiful are primary aesthetic experiences because they arise from – and with some luck transform – the first fantasies of authority and of love.

In *Group Psychology and the Analysis of the Ego* (1921), Freud reflected on hypnotism and taught us – W. H. Auden praises him for looking deeply into the most common things – how close this apparently harmless diversion was to being enthralled by the fascist orator, by the general or by the charismatic teacher. He showed in that book how difficult it is to sustain the later acquisitions of the psyche, ideals and rationality. He argued that we want to sink back into easy pleasures and easy hates by letting a masterly object take the place of the super-ego, and acquiescing to what appears to be discipline, but is really the indulgence of early and brutal desires. To Freud, the greatest human pleasure conceivable would perhaps be found in committing barbarous deeds with the full approval of the Over-I. To destroy the Jews, the gypsies, the queers, and to do so not with an aching conscience, but in the name of the Father and Fatherland, what human pleasure could exceed that?

For the individual caught in erotic repetition, there was of course therapy. In therapy, Freud plays with fire. For in order to disabuse us of our reliance on authority in its most overbearing form, Freud, and the therapists who followed him, assuming the role he composed for them, effectively masquerade as that authority. The therapist puts on a disguise which can easily corrupt the wearer, that of omniscience, of the subject who is supposed to know. The result can be that the man comes to be defined by the mask. It shapes and distorts, or maybe simply confirms, the contours of his face. The authoritarian pose never left him, says Auden, in part because within the drama that is therapy, Freud was willing to be what he most feared and despised – the figure who promised complete truth and endless love. The result of activating primal fantasies was the transference, a state of emotional vertigo not unlike falling in love. There was then the work of allowing the patient to aim her richest hopes and fears at the analyst and showing her that none of them, ever, could be realized in experience and that she would have to accept the Freudian compromise: half truths, partial pleasures.

The therapist, in this understanding, becomes whatever the patient needs and wants him to be. To maintain his own emotional health, the therapist has got to recognize that in therapy he is not himself; his godly status is a hallucination shared by all of his most adept patients, but pertaining in no way to the facts of the case. What rich dissonances between the world of the consulting room and that of the street must then arise. How can even the most self-aware analyst not occasionally succumb to the desire that Sartre thought was at the fulcrum of bad faith, the desire to be god?

At one point, in an analysis that seemed to be sinking into failure, Freud cried bitterly to his patient: 'We are getting nowhere because you do not think it worth your while to love an old man.' Perhaps the old man was too palpably mortal for this patient, not a deity who lives forever. He was simply a grumpy, undernourished codger, with bandages on his jaw from all the cancer operations, with two chows and a bourgeois living room and too many books.

If Freud's myths of love and power and repetition have some bearing on experience, then questions remain: is there anything to do about this distress save for reading Freud scripturally, or entering therapy, save, that is, for finding an old man worthy of love and becoming a good deal like him? The problematic of love and authority and of the hunger to repeat is Freud's great legacy to us; and his solutions are manifold, but they all take us back under the rule of the grey deity, the Reality Principle. He leaves us without charisma, without anything akin to the glowing world that the myths and the movies both in their ways deliver. Do we have to give up all glories and live the nobly stoical Roman life that Freud seemed finally both to accept himself and to commend for others?

Rosalind and Falstaff are two of Shakespeare's most adored characters, figures with whom audiences habitually fall in love. Both of these figures are great entertainers and vital presences, but can they also be great teachers, beloved for their wisdom? (Can they, perhaps, do the old man's job better than he could himself?) They are both flawed, of that there's little doubt. Falstaff leads men to their deaths so as to line his pockets. Rosalind can be a vaunting egotist who has trouble remembering that the other people around her are real.

What binds the two together is wit, a particular kind of wit that enlarges the contours of experience, letting us feel that there is more to know and relish about life than we had imagined. Instead of authority and succour, the truth and the cure, they give us variety: not cohesion, but expansion, not contraction and concentration, but extemporaneous performance.

Both are, like their creator, master play-makers. Rosalind plays for and with her beloved, Orlando; Falstaff for and with his beloved, Prince Hal, who in the end bitterly spurns him. By playing they expand the interpretations of reality, they show us that it could be many other ways than it is commonly conceived. They show that what is taken seriously by all of the serious-minded people can also be laughed raucously away. And they suggest the corollary too, a truth that Freud knew very well: that what the sensible people commonly laugh at or ignore can be invested with enriching sense.

The Falstaff of *Henry IV* Parts I and II is a great jester, a player like no other, but in his jest at least he is entirely benevolent. As he says, he is witty in himself and the cause of that wit is in other men. Hal, the future King of England, who thinks that he is Falstaff's pupil and that he has learned all the fat man has to teach, has a rancid wit, is prone to cruelty and is aiming for control. Falstaff's humour is expansive: he gets people around him to say and think things they never would have without him. Hal's humour contracts and reduces. He skewers people on the point of a word, insisting that all that matters about Falstaff can be summarized in his rather self-serving use of one word, 'instinct', or that Frances, the apprentice tapster, is no more than a walking linguistic hitch, the infinite repetition of the word 'anon'. Hal tries to force people back in the direction of repetition, because that is where he can know and manipulate them. And, Freud would say, because back to repetition is where they, and we, all wish to go.

In the tavern scene, a magnificent psychoanalysis that exceeds every analysis yet attempted, Falstaff jumps gaily into the Oedipal circle, filling the role of Hal's father. 'Do you stand for my father,' says Hal, attempting to precipitate and control his own transference, 'and examine me upon the particulars of my life.' Will Hal remember or repeat? Work through or stay clutching the past?

What ensues is a splendid dialogue between Falstaff and the Prince; at issue is who will be the Prince's true father, Falstaff or the cold usurper, Bolingbroke. On some level, every psychoanalyst, no matter how humane, must hope for some level of benign influence over the patient. Falstaff being Falstaff, that is a man who has no repressions, and who makes what is latent in others overt in himself, drives directly and humorously for that power. He sets in by trying wholly to displace Bolingbroke, the merely natural father. Thus Falstaff takes the part of the old usurper: 'That thou art my son,' he says to Hal, 'I have partly thy mother's word, partly my own opinion, but chiefly a villainous trick of thine eye, and a foolish hanging of thy nether lip that doth warrant me.'

Beneath the Groucho-style abuse, there's a point. Who could know – before DNA testing, at least – who his biological father was? And if the identity of the biological father is up for grabs, then surely the role of spiritual father is open to competition as well. So Falstaff sets about advertising himself as a better ideal for Hal than his own father. There is, says Falstaff, 'a virtuous man whom I have often noted in thy company, but I know not his name' (*Henry IV*, Part 1, II, iv).

Prince: What manner of man, and it like your Majesty?
Falstaff: A goodly portly man, i' faith, and a corpulent; of a cheerful look, a pleasing eye, and a most noble carriage.

But the prince is having none of it. He's afraid to take the exchange further, afraid even to toy with the idea that Falstaff is putting into play. Quickly – we see where the power lies in this analysis – he usurps Falstaff's position and takes the role of his own father. All of a sudden, the space of extemporization – 'it is a real lived experience', says Freud of the transference, 'but one made possible by particularly favourable conditions, and purely temporary in nature'

('Remembering, Repeating, and Working Through', p. 41) – where identities are in flux, closes down. And when it does, Hal shows that he is truly Bolingbroke's son, for he is just as cold and ruthless and cruel as his father. 'Wherein is he good,' Hal says of Falstaff, 'but to taste sack and drink it? wherein neat and cleanly but to carve a capon and eat it? wherein cunning but in craft? wherein crafty but in villainy? wherein villainous but in all things? wherein worthy but in nothing?' (II, iv).

Falstaff, never outdone, comes back with his most plangent lines: 'If sack and sugar be a fault, God help the wicked! If to be old and merry be a sin, then many an old host that I know is damn'd; if to be fat be to be hated, then Pharaoh's lean kine are to be lov'd' (II, iv).

Falstaff is self-serving here: he wants to be in favour when Hal takes the throne. But he is more than self-serving, too. For if Hal could actually imagine the situation that so revolts him, that he finds so unbearable, the one where he disowned Bolingbroke and took Falstaff for a father, then he might offer an entirely different sort of rulership.

Falstaff demystifies Bolingbroke: in the mock-play, Hal's father is not an omnivorous god out of Freud's *Totem and Taboo*, but a man in jeopardy, elevated beyond his prowess, whose situation can be seen humorously, ironically. Rather than play the father as heavy primal man, the hoarder of women and the slayer of sons, Falstaff offers the vision of a father who is himself confused, flawed and mortal. Underneath, he suggests, all fathers may be so. They are not to be maligned for their weakness, but understood, forgiven, laughed at and then laughed with. As Falstaff plays the role of Bolingbroke, we understand, so Bolingbroke merely plays the role of king.

Hal takes in only a part of this beautiful lesson: he sees that all authority is based on playing, and he resolves to continue as a master player of the primal role. Made wholly sane by Falstaff, he might have tried to make his constituents sane by blending authority and humour in one personage, proving that they need not be separable.

But Hal's mind is too small to encompass this kind of therapy, this inspired breaking and remaking of the paternal imago. In Shakespeare, children are all too much like their parents and all too little like their lovers and friends. Hal insists at the end on turning the tables. He assumes the role of his father, and with a meanness that he, mistaking Falstaff utterly, takes for wit, he assumes his father's old cruel, domineering role, the legacy of the Bolingbroke clan. He turns Falstaff's jest into invective.

Socrates showed that a man could both jest and wield authority – and it is the promise of this capacity that makes Falstaff into the Elizabethan Socrates. Says Montaigne of Socrates, 'He was seen, unmoved in countenance, putting up for twenty-seven years with hunger and poverty, with loutish sons, with a cantankerous wife and finally with calumny, tyranny, imprisonment, leg-irons and poison. Yet that very man, when the dictates of courtesy made him a guest at a drinking match, was, from the entire army, the man who best acquitted himself. Nor did he refuse to play five-stones with the boys nor to run about with them astride a hobby horse. And he did it with good grace: for Philosophy says that all activities are equally becoming in a wise man, all equally honour him' (*The Complete Essays of Montaigne* (trans. Screech), p. 1261). It's the inability to become that kind of philosopher king, not a Platonic but a Socratic monarch, that makes Hal so sad a figure.

The man who kills his prisoners in France and who hangs poor Bardolph is the son of the grotesque father whose cycle Falstaff, the inspired psychoanalyst, tries to break. Perhaps Shakespeare can imagine no other kind of effective king – if so, he is deeply Freudian, not responsive to his larger and better Falstaffian self. Freud's account of the successful leader is remarkably apt for Bolingbroke and, sadly, for Hal as well: 'His ego had few libidinal ties; he loved no one but himself, or other people insofar as they served his needs. To objects his ego gave away no more than was barely necessary.' (*Group Psychology and the Analysis of the Ego*, 1921) Maybe that is the best we can hope for; but in the centre of what is perhaps Shakespeare's most striking meditation on rulership, there is a force that undermines this hard wisdom and a hope for something better.

Rosalind in *As You Like It* is, like Falstaff, an enemy of reduction. In the tavern scene, Falstaff assaults political reduction; all through her play Rosalind contends against reduction of the erotic kind. She comes to life as a character after she hears Touchstone the jester proclaim that erotic love is nothing more than an affair of rutting, wiping clean, and rushing away. Touchstone doesn't have anything to do with turning base metals into gold, as his name suggests, but rather takes what men and women have concurred in finding precious and exposes its sordid underside. Touchstone is a wild Freudian analyst whose nose is always ready to sniff out sex and scat. Touchstone is Hal's jester cousin.

Rosalind has been swooning over Orlando's very conventional love poems, poems that are petrified Petrarch, at best. Touchstone, always obliging, pops up to enlighten her: 'I'll rhyme you so eight years together,' he says, then quickly hits stride:

> If a hart do lack a hind,
> Let him seek out Rosalind.
> If the cat will after kind,
> So be sure will Rosalind.
> Wint'red garments must be lin'd,
> So must slender Rosalind. (III, ii)

Despite all the refined sentiment on display in the Forest of Arden, Touchstone insists, what it all comes down to is simple instinct, sweating and rutting and the two-backed beast.

To which Rosalind says, eventually, yes. Yes, but. She takes in all that Touchstone knows and, with a lightning celerity – Rosalind is one of Shakespeare's quickest thinking figures – begins compounding a version of erotic love that includes sexual desires but isn't bound and defined by them.

In her mock dramas with Orlando, in which she's disguised as a boy, Rosalind, goaded by Touchstone, grows candid about her own shifting sexual desires. But she doesn't stop there. For, to her, shifting erotic desire is the inspiration for shifting human identity and for the playful exercise of wit. Without sex, life would be insupportable, but without self-willed changes of identity, shifting, theatrical improvisation, life would be impossible as well. Sex is finite, the affair of an hour. But play, pure extemporization, is endless, at least when the player is Rosalind (and Shakespeare). So, Rosalind avers, Orlando is going to have to put up with someone who never wants the same thing twice, and never is the same person on any two occasions: 'I will be more jealous of thee than a Barbary cock-pigeon over his hen; more clamorous than a parrot against rain; more new-fangled than an ape; more giddy in my desires than a monkey: I will weep for nothing, like Diana in the fountain, and I will do that when you are dispos'd to be merry; I will laugh like a hyen, and that when thou art inclin'd to sleep' (IV, i).

In short, Rosalind asserts, 'make the doors upon a woman's wit, and it will out at the casement; shut that, and 'twill out at the key-hole; stop that, 'twill fly with the smoke out at the chimney' (IV, i). What Rosalind promises, in short, is a life of Shakespearean variety and largesse (and tribulation) – a life she might never have had the wherewithal to conceive, had not Touchstone sent her flying into her own broadening fields of play.

The woman of Orlando's mawkish poetry is simple and clichéd. What Rosalind seeks to do in her erotic education of her wooer is to complicate this standing version. The woman behind Orlando's facile fiction is the archetypal woman, who stands in for the mother, and who, looked for, will be found and found unsatisfying. Orlando, in quest of simplicity, will be inclined to find it, or make it where it is not easily found. Rosalind puts all of her energy and humanizing, therapeutic force into teaching Orlando that love is more than anything one can readily comprehend, at least once the exercise of wit has taken it beyond Freudian-style reductions. Imagination, Rosalind suggests, can push us past the desire for the old parental imagos, even though such desires may still abide at the core of erotic need.

Rosalind approaches Orlando disguised as a young man, as Ganymede. Orlando, self-enclosed, and enclosed in easy rather than demanding fictions about love, needs the transitional stage of a narcissistic attraction in order to be drawn out, very slowly, from himself. Surely on some level the figure of Rosalind shows through the disguise – she is there and not there. But that is all Orlando, the man, can bear: to be confronted immediately by a woman whose wit makes her exceed his libidinal stereotypes would send him screaming away in terror. Rosalind engages Orlando's narcissism to help him to pass beyond it into something else. She hopes to help connect Orlando, however undeserving he may be, to something that is more complex and finer than he is.

Our love for Falstaff is inseparable from the fact that he would deliver us from the regressive super-ego which compels life to take place under the aegis of outworn authority and the easy inversion of that authority. Under the role of the standard super-ego we dream of uniting ourselves with a great sublime form – the father, or the metaphysical truth, or the state – and basking there for all time. Our love for Rosalind is inseparable from her attempt to deliver us from an id which would make life take place in the realm of pure wish-fulfilment. Tempted by the oceanic feeling, we dream of perfect immersion, for the easy erotic bliss of the maternal sublime. Falstaff and Rosalind might help save us from these urges, but they would not do so by taking us to the world of ironic stoicism that Freud commends. The realm that they open up is the realm of imagination. It is a place of plenty and pleasure, where we are anything but perfect, but where we enact perpetual enriching change – what Emerson thought of as the shooting of the gulf, the darting to an aim, the making and breaking of circles. Through the exercise of imagination, we may find an alternative to a more secure state of being in which everything is past and there is nothing new.

If we read with an open heart and mind, despite whatever socialization we have had, art can – if only for short stretches – remove us from the harsh reductions that Freud eventually took all too much relish in describing. Unable to defeat them grandly enough, being allowed only the provisional victories of therapy, Freud cast his lot with what he took to be the forces of fate, hoping to share its awful power. Shakespeare teaches us that we need not join him in this surrender.

Mark Edmundson, 2003

Translator's Preface

It is a curious and remarkable fact that Sigmund Freud's ideas have entered and conditioned modern consciousness not in their original German form, but mainly through English translations, most notably those enshrined in the *Standard Edition*, under the general editorship of James Strachey, and the ever jealous guardianship of the Institute of Psycho-Analysis. This circumstance would be enough in itself to justify new English versions even if the *Standard Edition* were flawless, since no translation, however good, can ever render the shapes and shades of an original text in all their subtlety; but in fact the *Standard Edition* is deeply, systematically flawed, making new translations all the more imperative. Take the opening paragraph of the *Narcissism* essay, for instance, which in the *Standard Edition* reads as follows:

ON NARCISSISM: AN INTRODUCTION

I

The term narcissism is derived from clinical description and was chosen by Paul Näcke in 1899 to denote the attitude of a person who treats his own body in the same way in which the body of a sexual object is ordinarily treated – who looks at it, that is to say, strokes it and fondles it till he obtains complete satisfaction through these activities. Developed to this degree, narcissism has the significance of a perversion that has absorbed the whole of the subject's sexual life, and it will consequently exhibit the characteristics which we expect to meet with in the study of all perversions.

If this were handed in by a student as a translation exercise, it would end up covered in red pencil, with everything from light squiggles to heavy underlinings and multiple exclamation marks, for it is so full of slips and shifts and omissions as to be a travesty of Freud's original. At the less serious end of the spectrum, 'attitude' would merit at least a squiggle: Freud's word is *Verhalten*, 'behaviour'; so, too, would 'developed to this degree': Freud's *in dieser Ausbildung* simply means 'in this form' or, more loosely, 'in this sense'; the phrase 'has the significance of' would also elicit a tut-tut and a squiggle, since the German translates quite simply as 'means' or 'signifies' (the second sentence would thus more crisply and more correctly begin 'Narcissism in this form means . . .'). We can also cavil at 'absorbed', as it loses the force of Freud's graphic metaphor *aufgesogen*, which in this context means 'sucked up' or 'swallowed up'; while 'exhibit[s] the characteristics' is an unduly loose rendering of words that more strictly mean 'is subject to the expectations . . .' (*unterliegt den Erwartungen*). A more serious distortion lurks in the words 'a person who treats his own body in the same way in which *the body of a sexual object is ordinarily treated*': what Freud's German unambiguously says is that the narcissist (in Näcke's sense of the term) treats his own body in the same way in which he – *the narcissist himself* – might treat that of any other sexual object.

Whilst none of these infelicities makes much difference on its own, their cumulative effect is to alter the whole tone and thrust of the passage (and we find similar shifts if we take almost any paragraph in Freud's original German and compare it with the translation offered in the *Standard Edition*). They are as nothing, however, by the side of the two quite startling mistranslations that reveal themselves in these few lines. One of them is in fact much worse than a mistranslation – it is a flagrant case of bowdlerization. No one reading the first sentence of the *Standard Edition* could possibly divine that in Freud's original the narcissist is said to stroke and caress and gaze at his own body *mit sexuellem Wohlgefallen*, 'with sexual pleasure': this oh-so-explicit phrase is quite simply excised – and thus another bit of Freud's characteristic oomph and colour is obliterated. Much more serious, however, is the garbled title: the wording 'On Narcissism: An Introduction' is a grave misrepresentation of Freud's heading *Zur Einführung des Narzissmus*, which unarguably refers to the introduction *of* narcissism, and not to any kind of introduction *to* narcissism. This may conceivably have been ignorance on the part of the *Standard Edition* translators (they commonly misunderstand Freud's German) – but it is much more likely to have been a case of deliberate spin: Freud's choice of words clearly reflects the *newness* of his narcissism theory and a concomitant sense that it therefore needs a good deal of explaining; the *Standard Edition* (mis-)title, however, implies that the theory is soundly established, and that the novice reader is about to be introduced to it, rather as a first-year undergraduate might be introduced to macro-economics or human anatomy. The agenda here (and elsewhere) is clear, and not a little pernicious: Freud's writing is to be presented not as a hot and sweaty struggle with intractable and often crazily daring ideas, but as a cut-and-dried corpus of unchallengeable dogma.

This agenda is what also underlies the gravest and most pervasive defect of the *Standard Edition*, and that is its wilfully turgid and often obfuscatory style. Even the very best-educated English-speakers are likely to reach for their dictionary in the face of 'the *thaumaturgical* power of words', for example, whereas any German-speaking child of eight or nine would readily understand Freud's own plain-speaking description of the *magical* power of words: 'die *Zauberkraft* des Wortes'. Freud is often said to be a great prose-writer, but while this is plainly a nonsense if we compare his prose with that of Goethe or Nietzsche or Grass, he certainly writes with unmistakable verve and punch, particularly in the derring-do period when he was boldly carving out his more radical ideas – the period so powerfully reflected in this volume. The *Standard Edition* fed Freud through a kind of voice-synthesizer to make him sound like a droning academic; one of the main aspirations of this present translation is to render not only his meanings, but also the mercurial flavour of his style, so that his sometimes combative, sometimes diffident, sometimes solemn, sometimes mischievous voice can be clearly heard in all its registers.

It has to be admitted, however, that while it is easy enough to criticize other people's translations, it is far from easy to make one's own – especially in the case of Freud, whose particular patterns of thought and language are sometimes hard even to construe, let alone render into satisfactory English. But the very fact that Freud's ideas have permeated world culture chiefly through the medium of the *Standard Edition* and the English terminology there enshrined, adds a whole extra dimension of difficulty: on page after page the re-translator faces the challenge of whether to retain or reject the old, often dubious, but now universally accepted terms invented by the earlier translators. In some cases the decision was easy: 'anaclitic', for instance, is a preposterous neologism founded on plain ignorance of Freud's German (*Anlehnung*), and was rejected with relish and relief; 'frustration' was likewise rejected as a startlingly inept misrendering of the important term *Versagung* ('refusal' is used instead). It was easy, too, to discard 'instinct' and 'satisfaction' as translations of *Trieb* and *Befriedigung*, and to use 'drive' and 'gratification' in their place. Other terms, however, often provoked months of head-scratching. In the end, '(super-)ego' and 'id' – latinisms quite devoid of the earthy punch of Freud's (*Über-)Ich* and *Es* – were reluctantly retained, for want of any practicable alternatives; so too, with even greater reluctance, was Strachey's opaque and ugly word 'cathexis', together with the associated verb 'cathect': other translators in the new Penguin Freud Library have opted for plain-English alternatives to these rebarbative inventions, but all such alternatives seemed to me to have misleading connotations. In general, specific terms of Freud's are consistently translated (thus for instance *Abfuhr* is always rendered as 'release', in preference to 'discharge' as used in the 'Standard Translation'), but in some cases his vocabulary renders any such laudable consistency impossible. A particularly fascinating instance of this is Freud's word *Instanz*, a metaphor he deploys again and again to describe the various processes of surveillance, admonition, censorship, control to which, in his view, every human psyche is enduringly subject. Borrowing the term from the forbidding realms of the law (where it is a standard term for 'court', 'tribunal' etc.), Freud applies it to the whole panoply of – literally – forbidding forces that bear upon individuals almost from the moment of their birth, firstly from without in the persons of their parents and, in due course, their teachers and the larger community, then from within in the form of internalized control mechanisms – chiefly hypostasized by Freud in the 'pleasure principle' and, above all, the 'super-ego'. The sheer frequency of the word *Instanz* turns it into an integrative and (discomfitingly) evocative cypher in Freud's original texts – but this distinctive effect cannot be reproduced in English, which simply has no equivalent word or concept, so that we are forced to use a whole gamut of different makeshift terms, from 'parental voice' (*Elterninstanz*) through to 'entity', 'agency', 'matrix', 'arbiter' – and numerous others besides. (One wonders whether Freud could ever have arrived at his vision-cum-analysis of the human psyche if he had been born and brought up in, say, France or England, since it so clearly derives – like the poetic visions of Franz Kafka – from a specifically Austro-German matrix of notions and assumptions.)

Various traps and chicanes await the translator of texts from an earlier age. One of these is the lure of anachronisms. In general this particular lure has been resisted throughout the present volume – though it has to be admitted that the alert reader might find a handful of words and idioms that were not yet current in English in the period when Freud wrote the relevant essays (no prizes for their discovery . . .). Another inveterate problem, rendered all the more acute by the prevailing fashion for political correctness, is that of gendered language. Sharing as he did the premises and predilections of his age, Freud's perspective is of course overwhelmingly phallocentric. In general, this perspective has been faithfully transferred into English (to do anything else would be to practise a modern form of bowdlerism). Furthermore, it has been applied by extension to those situations where the rules of German grammar required Freud to use the neuter – most conspicuously in references to children, the noun *Kind* in German being neuter (*das Kind*). In such contexts grammatically neuter pronouns and possessive adjectives are assumed to refer to males unless there is specific evidence to the contrary.

Finally, a word on dictionaries. One of the major disadvantages suffered by earlier translators of Freud was that they didn't have at their disposal the plethora of excellent German–English dictionaries now available. Chief amongst these is the multi-volume set produced in the 1960s and early 1970s under the wonderful editorship of Trevor Jones at Jesus College, Cambridge – though if the assiduous reader spots weaknesses in my translation of German words beginning with S through to Z, then they should please direct their brickbats at Oxford University Press, who have signally failed to publish the missing volume(s)! On the other hand, the OUP certainly deserve the warmest possible plaudits for their *Oxford English Dictionary*: no one could wish for a better resource than this matchless work, and having plundered its riches several times daily for many months, I happily close by offering grateful obeisance to what is surely one of the mightiest achievements of English culture.

On the Introduction
of Narcissism[1]

I

'Narcissism' originated as a term of clinical description, having been chosen by Paul Näcke in 1899 to define that form of behaviour whereby an individual treats his own body in the same way in which he might treat that of any other sexual object, by looking at it, stroking it and caressing it with sexual pleasure[2] until by these acts he achieves full gratification. In this formulation the term 'narcissism' means a perversion that has swallowed up the entire sexual life of the individual, and consequently entails the same expectations that we would bring to the study of any other perversion.

Psychoanalysts were then struck in the course of their observations by the fact that individual elements of narcissistic behaviour are encountered in many people suffering from other disorders, for instance – according to Sadger – in homosexuals, and finally the supposition inescapably presented itself that a form of libido lodgement[3] definable as narcissism may occur on a far larger scale, and may well be able to lay claim to a role in the normal sexual development of human beings.[4] The difficulties encountered in the psychoanalytical treatment of neurotics led to the same supposition, for it looked as if just such a narcissistic pattern of behaviour on their part was one of the factors limiting their amenability to influence. One might say that narcissism in this sense is not a perversion, but the libidinal correlative of the egoism of the self-preservation instinct, an element of which is rightly attributed to every living creature.

Compelling grounds for entertaining the notion of a primary and normal form of narcissism arose when the attempt was made to apply the libido theory to our understanding of dementia praecox (Kraepelin) or schizophrenia (Bleuler). Those suffering from this condition, for whom I have proposed the term paraphrenics, display two fundamental characteristics: megalomania, and withdrawal of interest from the external world (people and things). The latter development makes them unamenable to psychoanalysis, it makes them incurable no matter how hard we try. The paraphrenic's withdrawal from the external world, however, needs to be more precisely characterized. The hysteric and the obsessional neurotic likewise abandon their relationship to reality, assuming their illness develops to that point. But analysis shows that they by no means forsake their erotic relationship to people and things. They hold fast to it in their imagination, on the one hand replacing or mingling real objects with imaginary ones drawn from their memory, whilst on the other not initiating in respect of those objects any of the motor activities needed for the attainment of their goals. For this condition of the libido alone, and for no other, should one use the term indiscriminately applied by Jung, namely *introversion* of the libido. With the paraphrenic, however, the position is quite different. He really does seem to have withdrawn his libido from the people and things of the external world without replacing them with any others in his imagination. In cases where he *does* so replace them, this appears to be a secondary process, and to form part of an attempt at recovery that seeks to lead the libido back to the object world.[5]

The question then arises as to the subsequent fate of the libido in schizophrenia once it has been withdrawn from objects. The megalomania characteristic of this condition points the way. We can assume that it arose at the expense of object-libido. The libido, having been withdrawn from the external world, is channelled into the ego, giving rise to a form of behaviour that we can call narcissism. However, the megalomania itself is not a new entity, but, as we know, only a magnified and more distinct form of a pre-existing state. This in turn leads us to think that the form of narcissism that arises as a result of the incorporation of object-cathexes[6] is a secondary one that develops on top of a primary one rendered obscure by a variety of different influences.

Let me stress once again that I am not seeking here either to resolve or further to complicate the schizophrenia problem, but am merely bringing together what has already been said in other contexts, in order to justify introducing the concept of narcissism.

A third factor contributing to this, in my view legitimate, extension of the libido theory arises from our observations and interpretations of the inner life of children and primitive peoples. In the latter we find traits which, if they were to occur individually, could be classed as megalomania: an overestimation of the power of their wishes and psychic acts – the 'omnipotence of thoughts'; a belief in the magical power[7] of words; a technique for dealing with the external world, namely 'magic', which appears as the logical application of these megalomaniac premisses.[8] We expect to encounter an entirely analogous attitude to the external world in the child of our own day and age, whose development is far less clear to us.[9] We thus find the notion taking shape in our mind that it was the *ego* that originally underwent libido-cathexis;[10] some of this libido is later transferred to objects, but essentially it stays put, and relates to the object-cathexes rather as the body of an amoeba relates to the pseudopodia that it sends forth. This aspect of libido lodgement inevitably remained hidden from us to begin with, given the symptom-based nature of our researches. The only things apparent to us were the emanations of this libido, namely object-cathexes, which can be sent forth and then retracted again. We can also discern what in broad terms we can call an antagonism between the ego-libido and the object-libido – the more replete the one becomes, the more the other is depleted. The highest phase of development achievable by the latter appears to us to be the state of being in love, which presents itself to us as an abandonment by the individual of his own personality in favour of an object-cathexis, and which has its antithesis in the paranoiac's fantasy (or self-perception) regarding the 'end of the world'.[11] What we ultimately conclude regarding the differentiation of psychic energies is that initially, in the state of narcissism, they remain clustered together, and hence undifferentiable in terms of our crude analysis, and that only the supervention of object-cathexis makes it possible to differentiate sexual energy, the libido, from the energy of the ego drives.

❉

Before I go any further, I must touch on two questions that take us to the heart of the difficulties entailed by this topic. First: how does narcissism as we are here proposing it relate to autoeroticism, which we have elsewhere described as an early form of libido? Second: if we attribute a primary libido-cathexis to the ego, why is there any need to differentiate sexual libido from non-sexual energy in the ego drives? Wouldn't the supposition of a single, unified psychic energy spare us all the difficulties associated with trying to distinguish between ego-drive energy and ego-libido, between ego-libido and object-libido?

As to the first question, I say this: it is a necessary hypothesis that there is no entity present in the individual from the very beginning that is equatable with the ego; the ego has to be developed. Auto-erotic drives, however, are primal; therefore something else must supervene in addition to autoeroticism, a new psychic process, in order to produce narcissism.

Any psychoanalyst called upon to give a definitive answer to the second question is bound to feel distinctly uncomfortable. One balks at the idea of abandoning empirical observation for the sake of sterile theoretical disputes, but nonetheless we cannot shirk the obligation to try to resolve the issue. Notions such as that of an ego-libido or an ego-drive energy etc. are undoubtedly neither particularly easy to grasp nor sufficiently weighty in content; a speculative theory of the relevant relationships would want above all to establish a sharply defined concept as a basis for everything else. But in my view that is precisely the difference between a speculative theory and a science founded on the interpretation of empirical facts. The latter will not envy speculation its privilege of resting upon neat and tidy foundations of unassailable logic, but will gladly make do with nebulously evanescent, scarcely conceivable basic ideas, hoping to grasp them more clearly as they develop, and willing if need be to exchange them for others. For these ideas are not the foundation upon which the entire science rests; instead, it rests solely upon observation. They are not the substructure but the superstructure of the whole edifice, and can be replaced or discarded without harm. We are currently seeing the same sort of thing happen in physics, moreover, whose fundamental ideas about matter, centres of force, attraction and such like are scarcely less precarious than their counterparts in psychoanalysis.

The value of the concepts 'ego-libido' and 'object-libido' resides in the fact that they derive from thorough study of the intimate characteristics of neurotic and psychotic processes. The separation of the libido into one that pertains to the ego, and one that becomes attached to objects, is a necessary corollary of a primary hypothesis that differentiated between sexual drives and ego drives. This, at any rate, was the conclusion that I was driven to by analysis of both of the pure forms of transference neurosis (hysteria and obsessional neurosis), and I know only that all attempts to account for these phenomena by other means have utterly failed.

Given the complete lack of any guiding theory of drives, it is legitimate, not to say imperative, first to take a hypothesis of some kind and test it thoroughly and rigorously until it either fails, or proves valid. Now, quite a number of things tend to support the hypothesis of a primal separation of sexual drives and other kinds of drives, i.e. ego drives, not least its efficacy in the analysis of transference neuroses. I admit that this factor on its own would not be unambiguous, for it might well be a question here of indifferent psychic energy that turns into libido only through the process of object-cathexis. For one thing, however, this conceptual distinction corresponds to the distinction so commonly encountered in ordinary life between hunger and love. For another thing, *biological* considerations lend support to the hypothesis. The individual really does lead a double existence both as an end in himself, and as a link in a chain that he serves against his will, or at any rate regardless of his will. He even supposes sexuality to be one of his own designs – whereas on an alternative view he appears as a mere appendage of his germ-plasm,[12] to whose purposes he devotes all his energies in return for the reward of a mere sensation of pleasure. On this view, he is but the mortal vehicle of a – perhaps – immortal essence; like the lord of an entailed estate, he is but the temporary occupant of an institution that will outlast him. The separation of the sexual drives from the ego drives would simply mirror this dual function of the individual. Thirdly, one has to bear in mind that all our tentative psychological theories will need to be grounded at some point in organic systems. It will then very likely transpire that it is particular substances and chemical processes that are responsible for the workings of sexuality, and which make it possible for the life of the individual to carry over into the life of the species. We take full account of this likelihood by substituting particular psychological forces for particular chemical substances.

Precisely because I am normally at pains to keep psychology separate from all that is alien to it, including the mode of thinking characteristic of biology, I wish to concede quite explicitly at this point that the hypothesis of separate ego drives and sexual drives, i.e. the libido theory, is essentially biologically based, and is grounded scarcely at all in psychology. I shall therefore also be consistent enough to drop this hypothesis if a better and more serviceable theory of drives were to emerge from psychoanalytical work itself – though this has not so far proved to be the case. It might then turn out that – at the deepest possible level and at the remotest possible distance – sexual energy, the libido, originated as a part of the energy inherently active in the psyche that then separated off through differentiation. But such a proposition is of little relevance. It concerns things that are so far removed from the problems raised by our clinical observations, and so limited in their contribution to our knowledge, that it is no more worth contesting than it is worth applying in practice. Any such primal oneness is perhaps just as irrelevant to our analytical interests as the primal kinship of all the races of man is to the Probate Officer seeking proof of kinship between an heir and a testator. All these speculations get us nowhere. And as we cannot wait until the definitive theory of drives is handed to us on a plate by some other science, it is far more expedient to try to see what light can be thrown on these fundamental biological puzzles by a synthesis of *psychological* phenomena. By all means let us acquaint ourselves with the possibility of error, but let us not be deterred from rigorously following up the first hypothesis we mentioned,[13] viz. that of an antagonism between ego drives and sexual drives thrust upon us by our analysis of the transference neuroses, and thereby discovering whether it can be developed in a fruitful and consistent way, and whether it can be applied to other disorders as well, e.g. schizophrenia.

Things would be different, of course, if it were proven that the libido theory had already come to grief in failing to explain this latter disorder. C. G. Jung has made precisely this claim (1912) and has thereby forced me to set out the considerations above, which I would much rather have been spared. I should have preferred to follow through to its conclusion the path already taken in my analysis of the Schreber case, without going into its underlying assumptions. Jung's claim, however, is premature at the very least. His reasoning is scant. He bases his argument in the first place on my own supposed admission that in the face of the difficulties of the Schreber analysis I felt driven to modify the libido concept, that is to say, to abandon the notion of its having a sexual content and to regard the libido as being part and parcel of psychic interest[14] in general. As to rectifying this misconception, Ferenczi (1913) has already said all that needs to be said in his thorough critique of Jung's book.[15] I can only agree with Ferenczi, and repeat that I have never voiced any such renunciation of the libido theory. A further argument of Jung's, asserting that there was no reason to think that the loss of the normal reality-function[16] could be caused solely by withdrawal of the libido, is not an argument at all, but an assertion of dogma; it 'begs the question'[17] and pre-empts debate, whereas the question whether and how such a thing might be possible really does need to be explored. In his next major work (1913), Jung touches briefly on the solution that I pointed to quite some time ago: 'Now in all this we admittedly also need to take account of the fact – something incidentally that Freud refers to in his account of the Schreber case – that introversion of the *Libido sexualis* leads to a cathexis of the "ego", which is conceivably what causes this reality-loss effect to appear. The possibility that the psychology of reality-loss might be explained in this way is indeed an enticing one.' Unfortunately, however, Jung does not explore this possibility very far. Only a few lines later he dismisses it with the comment that on such a basis 'the psychology of an ascetic anchorite would emerge successfully, but

9

not a dementia praecox'. To show how little this inapt analogy can contribute to a resolution of the issue, we need only remark that such an anchorite in his 'eagerness to eradicate every trace of sexual interest' (though only in the popular sense of the word 'sexual') does not even need to exhibit any pathogenic libido lodgement. Though he may have completely averted his sexual interest from human beings, he can easily have sublimated it into a heightened interest in the divine or natural or animal realm without falling victim to an introversion of his libido onto his fantasies, or a reversion of his libido to his ego. This analogy appears to disregard from the very outset any possibility of differentiating between interest arising from erotic sources, and that arising from others. If we also bear in mind that the researches of the Swiss school, however commendable, have elucidated only two features of dementia praecox – the existence of complexes familiar to the healthy as well as to neurotics, and the similarity between patients' fantasies and folk myths – whilst for the rest proving unable to throw any light on the actual mechanism of the disorder, then we can readily reject Jung's claim that the libido theory has been proved a 'failure' by its inability to solve the problem of dementia praecox, and is therefore finished in respect of other neuroses too.

II

Any *direct* study of narcissism seems to me to be prevented by a number of special difficulties. The principal means of approaching the matter is likely to remain the analysis of paraphrenias. Just as the transference neuroses have enabled us to trace the libidinal drive-impulses, so, too, dementia praecox and paranoia will afford us insight into the psychology of the ego. Once again, our understanding of the normal in all its seeming simplicity has to be derived from the pathological with all its warped and coarsened features. All the same, a few other paths to a better understanding of narcissism do remain open to us: the study of organic illness, of hypochondria, and of the love-life of the sexes; and I shall now discuss each of these in turn.

In considering the influence of organic illness on the distribution of the libido, I am following a suggestion made to me in conversation by Sándor Ferenczi. It is universally known, indeed it seems self-evident to us, that anyone tormented by organic pain and dire discomfort abandons all interest in the things of the external world, except in so far as they bear on his suffering. Closer observation shows us that he also withdraws all libidinal interest from his love-objects; that so long as he suffers, he ceases loving. The banality of this fact need not prevent us from translating it into the language of the libido theory. We would then say: the patient retracts his libido-cathexes into his ego, and redeploys them once he is well. 'The sole abode of his soul forsooth', says Wilhelm Busch of a toothache-stricken poet, 'is the small black hole in his molar tooth.' Libido and ego-interest share the same fate in this regard, and are once again indistinguishable from each other. The notorious egoism of the ill covers both. We find this egoism so self-evident because we know for certain that in similar circumstances we would behave in exactly the same way. In its own way, comedy, too, exploits this phenomenon whereby physical ailments sweep away even the most passionate inclinations, and replace them with utter indifference.

Like illness, the sleep state, too, involves a narcissistic process whereby the libido is withdrawn from its various positions[18] and focused on the self or, to be more precise, on the sole desire for sleep. The egoism of dreams probably fits in very well in this context. If nothing else, we see examples in both cases of alterations in libido distribution as a result of ego-alteration.[19]

Hypochondria, like organic illness, expresses itself in painful and distressing physical sensations, and matches it, too, in the effect it has on libido distribution. The hypochondriac withdraws both his interest and – particularly markedly – his libido from the objects of the external world, and concentrates both of them on the organ that concerns him. But a disparity between hypochondria and organic illness forces itself on our attention here: in the latter case the painful sensations are grounded in demonstrable physical changes, whereas in the former they seem not to be. However, it would be fully in accord with our conception of neurotic processes as a whole if we were to venture the view that the message given out by hypochondria must indeed be quite right, and that it, too, must surely involve organic changes. But what would these changes consist in?

We are going to let ourselves be guided here by our knowledge that physical sensations of an unpleasant kind, comparable to those encountered in hypochondria, are also present in the other neuroses. I have already on an earlier occasion mentioned my inclination to regard hypochondria as the third 'actual' neurosis[20] alongside neurasthenia and anxiety neurosis.[21] It is probably not going too far to suppose that an element of hypochondria may also routinely be present in the other neuroses; the finest example of this is probably to be seen in anxiety neurosis and its overlying hysteria. It is of course the genital organ in its various states of excitation that constitutes the most familiar exemplar of an organ at once painfully sensitive and physically changed in some way, yet not in any ordinary sense of the word morbid. In such circumstances it becomes engorged with blood, swollen, moist, and the locus of manifold sensations. Let us use the term *erogeneity* to describe the process whereby a part of the body transmits sexual stimuli to the psyche; let us also bring to mind that our reflections on the theory of sexuality have long since accustomed us to the view that certain other parts of the body – the *erogenous* zones – might be able to substitute for the genitals and behave in a similar way to them: there is then just one further step that we must dare to take at this point. We can venture to regard erogeneity as a general property of *all* the organs, and we can then speak of it as increasing or diminishing in intensity in any particular part of the body. Any such variation in the erogeneity of the organs might be paralleled by a change in libido-cathexis within the ego. It is in such factors perhaps that we need to search for whatever it is that we might consider the basis of hypochondria, and that is capable of having the same effect on libido distribution as when the organs are affected by physical illness.

We note that if we continue thinking along these lines we shall come face to face with the problem not only of hypochondria, but also of the other 'actual' neuroses, neurasthenia and anxiety neurosis. Let us therefore call a halt at this juncture: the purposes of a purely psychological study are not served by straying so far into the realm of physiological research. We might simply mention that on the available evidence it seems reasonable to suppose that hypochondria stands in a similar relationship to paraphrenia as the other 'actual' neuroses do to hysteria and obsessional neurosis, that is to say that it depends on ego-libido just as the others depend on object-libido; on this supposition, hypochondriac fear is the counterpart on the ego-libido side to neurotic fear. Furthermore, given that in the case of the transference neuroses we are already familiar with the idea that the mechanism of the onset of illness and of symptom-formation – the progression from introversion to regression – can be linked to a heavy build-up of object-libido,[22] then we may also feel more inclined to embrace the idea of a heavy build-up of ego-libido, and relate it to the phenomena of hypochondria and paraphrenia.

Naturally enough, our thirst for knowledge prompts us at this point to ask why such a build-up of libido in the ego has to be experienced as unpleasurable. I should like to make do here with the reply that unpleasure is routinely the form in which increased tension expresses itself, and that therefore what happens here, as elsewhere, is that a certain quantity of the physical process transmutes into the psychic quality of unpleasure; though it may then well be the case that what determines the degree of unpleasure is not the absolute magnitude of that physical process, but rather some particular function of it. From this vantage point one may even dare to approach the question as to *where* the compulsion comes from in the first place that makes the psyche transcend the boundaries of narcissism and invest the libido in objects. Again, the logical answer in terms of our overall train of thought would be that the compulsion arises when the libidinal cathexis of the ego has exceeded a certain level. A strong ego affords some protection against falling ill; but in the end we must necessarily start loving if we are not to fall ill, and we must necessarily fall ill if refusal[23] makes us incapable of loving – rather along the lines of the model offered by Heinrich Heine when he envisions the psychogenesis of Creation:

> Krankheit ist wohl der letzte Grund
> Des ganzen Schöpferdrangs gewesen;
> Erschaffend konnte ich genesen,
> Erschaffend wurde ich gesund.
>
> (Sickness no doubt was the ultimate cause
> of my urge to become the Creator;
> by dint of creation I was able to recover,
> by dint of creation I regained my health.[24])

We have identified our psychic apparatus as being above all an instrument charged with asserting control over excitations that would otherwise prove distressingly uncomfortable or pathogenic. This psychic processing activity achieves extraordinary things with regard to the inner discharge of excitations that are incapable of direct external release,[25] or for which such release would be undesirable at that particular moment. With inner processing of this kind, however, it is initially irrelevant whether it operates with real objects or imaginary ones. The difference only becomes apparent later on, if there is a heavy build-up of libido as a result of the latter turning to non-real objects (introversion). In the case of the paraphrenias, megalomania permits a similar inner processing of the libido once it has retreated into the ego; it is perhaps only when the megalomania has failed that the build-up of libido within the ego becomes pathogenic and triggers the healing process that strikes us so forcibly as illness.

Trying as I am at this point to penetrate just a little way into the mechanism of paraphrenia, I shall rehearse those concepts that seem to me at the present time to be worthy of attention. In my view, what makes these disorders different from the transference neuroses is the fact that when libido is freed up as a result of refusal, it does not resort with objects in the imagination, but withdraws to the ego; that being so, megalomania corresponds to the process in the transference neuroses whereby the psyche asserts control over this quantum of libido, i.e. introverts it onto products of the imagination; any failure of this psychic control-process gives rise to the hypochondria characteristic of paraphrenia, which is homologous to the fear characteristic of transference neuroses. We know that this latter fear can be dislodged by other forms of psychic processing too, namely conversion,[26] reaction-formation, and the formation of protection mechanisms (phobias). In the case of the paraphrenias, this role is played by the phase of attempted restitution, to which we owe the conspicuous symptoms of morbidity. Given that paraphrenia in many – if not most – cases involves only a partial dislodgement of the libido from objects, the clinical picture may be divided into three distinct groups of symptoms: 1) those reflecting what the subject retains of his normal state or neurosis (residual symptoms); 2) those reflecting the illness process itself (dislodgement of the libido from objects, and also megalomania, hypochondria, affective disorder, regression in all its various forms); 3) those reflecting the restitution process which, after the manner of hysteria (in the case of dementia praecox and paraphrenia proper) or obsessional neurosis (in the case of paranoia), re-attaches the libido to objects. This new libido-cathexis takes place on a different level and under different conditions from the primary one. The difference between the transference neuroses created by this secondary cathexis, and their counterparts as formed by the normal ego, would surely afford us the deepest possible insight into the structure of our psychic apparatus.

A third point of access to the study of narcissism is provided by the love-life of human beings, given the different forms that it takes in men and women. Just as the object-libido initially hid the ego-libido from our inquiring eye, so too in the case of object-choice on the part of the child (and developing individual) we initially focused our attention on the fact that they derive their sexual objects from their gratification experiences. A child's first experiences of autoerotic sexual gratification occur in the context of vital functions conducing to self-preservation. Sexual drives initially develop by imitating the ego drives and their gratification, and only subsequently make themselves independent of them – though the imitative process remains evident in the fact that it is the people concerned with the child's feeding, care and protection who become its first sexual objects, hence primarily the mother or mother-surrogate. But alongside this type and its associated source of object-choice, which we can term the *imitative* type,[27] a second and quite unexpected one has been revealed to us by our psychoanalytical researches. We have found – and this has been particularly clear in the case of people whose libidinal development has been disturbed in some way, such as perverts and homosexuals – that they model their subsequent love-object not on their mother, but on their own person. They quite clearly seek *themselves* as love-object, thereby exhibiting what we can call the *narcissistic* type of object-choice. It is this observation above all that has driven us to our narcissism hypothesis.

Now we have not concluded from all this that human beings fall into two sharply differentiated groups, one predisposed to the imitative type of object-choice and the other to the narcissistic, but instead prefer the hypothesis that both paths are open to each and every individual, and that either is equally capable of being preferred. We are arguing that every human being originally has two sexual objects: himself, and the woman who cares for him; and concomitantly we postulate a primary narcissism in all human beings, which in certain circumstances can prove dominant in their object-choice.

A comparison of males and females then shows that there are fundamental – though not of course universal – differences between them in their relationship to the two types of object-choice. Full object-love as per the imitative type really does seem to be characteristic of males. It displays conspicuous sexual over-valuation, which probably derives from the original narcissism present in childhood, and accordingly represents its transference onto the sexual object. This sexual over-valuation gives rise to the curious condition of being in love, reminiscent of neurotic obsession, and amounting as such to a transfer of libido that depletes the ego for the benefit of the object. Things develop in a quite different way in the commonest, probably purest and most authentic type of female. Here, the onset of puberty manifest in the development of the previously latent female sexual organs appears to be accompanied by an intensification of her original narcissism unfavourable to the forming of any proper object-love with its due complement of sexual over-valuation. Particularly where she develops the attributes of beauty, a woman comes to feel sufficient unto herself, which compensates her for the greatly reduced freedom of object-choice imposed on her by society. Strictly speaking, such women love only themselves, and with the same intensity as men display in loving them. Their need, furthermore, is not to love, but to *be* loved, and they deign to tolerate any man who fulfils this condition. The importance of this type of woman for the love-life of human beings is very great. Such women hold the greatest possible fascination for men, not only for aesthetic reasons, since they are usually the most beautiful, but also because of an interesting combination of psychological factors. For it seems clearly apparent that narcissism in an individual becomes magnetically attractive to those who have altogether relinquished their own narcissism,[28] and who are casting around for object-love. The fascination of the child rests to a great extent on its narcissism, on the fact that it is sufficient to itself and impervious to others; so too does the fascination of certain animals that appear to show no interest in us, such as cats and the great beasts of prey; indeed, even dire criminals and comic heroes captivate us within the context of the arts by dint of the narcissistic rigour with which they keep at bay anything tending to diminish their ego. It is as though we envied them their retention of a blissful psychic state, of an unassailable libido position, that we ourselves have since relinquished. However, the powerful fascination of the narcissistic woman is not without its darker side; the lovelorn male's frustration, his doubts about the woman's love, his lamentations on her enigmatic nature, are largely rooted in this incongruence of the two types of object-choice involved.

It is perhaps not entirely superfluous for me to emphasize that in describing women's love-life in these terms I am not remotely animated by any bias inclining me to disparage women. Quite apart from the fact that bias of any kind is alien to me, I am also well aware that these different patterns of development reflect the differentiation of functions within an extremely complex biological nexus; furthermore, I am quite ready to concede that there are innumerable women who love on the male pattern and also develop the sexual over-valuation characteristic of it.

Even for those women who remain narcissistic, and cool in their response to men, there is a path that can lead them to full object-love. In the child that they bear, they encounter a part of their own body as a distinct and separate object upon which, on the basis of their narcissism, they can now bestow full object-love. Then there are other women who do not need to wait for a child in order to progress from (secondary) narcissism to object-love. These are women who, prior to puberty, feel themselves to be male and manage up to a certain point to develop in a male way; their efforts in this direction are abandoned once female sexual maturity comes upon them – but they thereafter remain capable of yearning for a male ideal, which really amounts to a perpetuation of the boy-like being that they themselves once were.

A brief summary of the various paths to object-choice may serve to bring these adumbrations to a close.

We love one or other of the following:

1) *Narcissistic type:*
   a) what we ourselves are,
   b) what we ourselves were,
   c) what we would like to become,
   d) a person who was once part of our own self.
2) *Imitative type:*
   a) the woman who feeds us,
   b) the man who protects us,
   and the many surrogates who take their place.

Category c) of the first type can only be substantiated at a later stage in the argument.

The significance of narcissistic object-choice in the case of male homosexuality remains to be discussed in a separate context.

The primary narcissism of the child that we have postulated, and that constitutes one of the premises of our libido theories, can be more easily inferred from other factors than captured by direct observation. When one looks at the attitude of affectionate parents towards their children, one cannot but recognize it as a resurgence and repetition of their own long-abandoned narcissism. The trusty characteristic of 'over-valuation', which we have already discussed as a distinctive marker of narcissism in the context of object-choice, predominates in this affective relationship, as is universally known. There is accordingly a compulsion to ascribe to the child all conceivable perfections, something for which dispassionate observation would find no cause, and to conceal and forget all its faults – indeed it is in this context that denial of child sexuality has its place. However, there is also a tendency when faced by the child to suspend all the cultural accretions that we ourselves came to accept only in the teeth of opposition from our narcissism, and to reassert through the child our long-abandoned claims to rights and privileges. Things are to be better for the child than they were for its parents; it is to be saved from subjection to those imperatives that we have accepted as paramount in life. Disease, death, the forgoing of sensual pleasure, the curbing of one's own will – none of this is to apply to the child; the laws of nature and of society are to stop at its door; it really is to become the very core and centre of creation once again: *His Majesty the Baby*,[29] as we once thought ourselves to be. The child is to fulfil all the wishful dreams that its parents dreamed but never realized; it is to become a great man and great hero as proxy for the father, or get a prince for a husband as belated compensation for the mother. That most precarious aspiration of the narcissist scheme of things – immortality of the ego, so gravely threatened by sheer reality – is rendered secure by finding refuge in the child. Parental love, so touching yet essentially so childlike, is nothing other than the resurgent narcissism of the parents, which in its transformation into object-love unmistakably reveals its original nature.

III

There are certain questions that I should like to leave to one side for the time being since they represent an important area of study that has still not been fully dealt with: questions as to what disruptions the primal narcissism in children is prey to, what reactions it displays in resisting them, and what paths it is forced along in the process. The most significant part of all this can be identified as 'castration complex' (penis-fear in the boy, penis-envy in the girl), and can be dealt with in conjunction with the effects of sexual intimidation during infancy. Psychoanalytical research, which normally serves as the means for us to track the various fates of the libidinal drives when they have become isolated from the ego drives and then find themselves in conflict with them, allows us in this present context to draw inferences as to the nature of an earlier stage and psychic situation in which both sets of drives manifest themselves in harmonious interaction and indissoluble combination with each other as narcissistic interests. It was on the basis of this nexus that Alfred Adler arrived at his 'masculine protest', which he elevates to the status of being almost the sole driving force behind the formation of personality and neuroses alike, whilst grounding it not in a narcissistic, i.e. still libidinal impulse, but in a social value-judgement. The standpoint of psychoanalytical research has been to acknowledge from the outset both the existence and the importance of the 'masculine protest', but to argue, in opposition to Adler, that it is narcissistic in nature, and has its origins in the castration complex. It pertains to character-formation, to the genesis of which it contributes along with many other factors, and as such is wholly irrelevant to the elucidation of problems concerning neuroses, the only noteworthy aspect of which for Adler is the way they serve the ego-interest. I find it quite impossible to suppose that the genesis of neurosis rests solely on the slender basis of the castration complex, no matter how powerfully the latter may manifest itself amongst the resistances displayed by men to treatment of their neuroses. I might add, too, that cases of neurosis are known to me in which the 'masculine protest' or, in our terms, the castration complex, plays no pathogenic role, or indeed is entirely absent.

Observation of the normal adult shows his erstwhile megalomania to be much reduced, whilst the psychic characteristics from which we inferred his infantile narcissism are scarcely distinguishable. What then has become of his ego-libido? Are we to suppose that it was entirely absorbed by object-cathexes? Such a possibility clearly contradicts the entire thrust of our argument. But we can find pointers to a quite different answer to this question in the psychology of repression.

We have learned that libidinal drive-impulses are subject to the fate of pathogenic repression when they come into conflict with the individual's cultural and ethical notions. What we understand by this is *not* that the individual has a merely intellectual awareness that these notions exist, but rather that he fully accepts them as his own yardstick and fully submits to the demands that they entail. As we have said, repression emanates from the ego; or, to put it more precisely, from the self-respect of the ego. The same impressions, experiences, impulses, desires that one human being will readily entertain, or at least consciously process, will be rejected by another with utter indignation, or be stifled before they even enter consciousness. However, the difference between the two, which reflects the conditions in which repression takes place, can easily be expressed in terms enabling us to resolve the issue by means of the libido theory. We can postulate that the one individual has set up an *ideal* within himself against which he measures his actual ego,[30] whereas the other has formed no such ideal. On this view, the formation of an ideal[31] constitutes the necessary condition on the part of the ego for repression to take place.

It is this ideal ego that is now the recipient of the self-love enjoyed during childhood by the real ego. The individual's narcissism appears to be transferred onto this new ideal ego which, like the infantile one, finds itself possessed of every estimable perfection. Here too, as is ever the case in matters of the libido, human beings have proved incapable of forgoing gratification once they have enjoyed it. They are unwilling to forsake the narcissistic perfection of their childhood, and when – discomfited by the admonitions raining down on them while they are developing, and with their powers of judgement duly awakened – they fail to retain that perfection, they seek to retrieve it in the new guise of the ego-ideal. What they project as their ideal for the future is a surrogate for the lost narcissism of their childhood, during which they were their own ideal.

It is appropriate at this point to explore the ways in which this forming of an ideal relates to sublimation. *Sublimation* is a process involving object-libido, and consists in a drive latching on to a different goal far removed from sexual gratification, the main aim here being to divert attention away from the sexual. *Idealization* is a process involving the object itself, whereby the object is magnified and exalted in the individual's mind without itself changing in nature. This idealization can occur within the domains of both ego-libido and object-libido. Thus, for instance, sexual over-valuation of an object constitutes an idealization of that object. To the extent, therefore, that sublimation has to do with drives whereas idealization has to do with objects, the two concepts need to be clearly distinguished from each other.

The formation of ego-ideals is frequently confused with the sublimation of drives, to the considerable detriment of our understanding. Just because someone has traded his narcissism for veneration of an exalted ego-ideal does not necessarily mean that he has managed to sublimate his libidinal drives. The ego-ideal certainly demands such sublimation, but cannot force it to happen; sublimation remains a separate process that may be triggered by the ideal, but then runs its course entirely independently of any such trigger. It is precisely in the case of neurotics that one finds the most electric disparities between the sophistication of their ego-ideal and the degree of sublimation of their primitive libidinal drives; and it is generally much harder to convince an idealist that his libido is inappropriately located than it is to convince the uncomplicated sort who has remained modest in his expectations. Sublimation and the formation of ideals also play completely different roles in the causation of neurosis. As we have seen, the formation of ideals intensifies the demands of the ego, and is the strongest single factor favouring repression; sublimation represents the let-out whereby such demands can be met *without* recourse to repression.

It would not be surprising were we to come across a special entity[32] in the psyche charged with ensuring that narcissistic gratification is indeed achieved in accordance with the ego-ideal, and to this end incessantly scrutinizes the actual ego and measures it against the ideal. If indeed such an entity exists, there can be no question of our discovering it as such; all we can do is to assume that it exists, and we may reasonably suppose that the thing we call our *conscience* matches the description. By acknowledging this entity we are better able to understand the so-called object-of-attention delusion or, more correctly, object-of-*scrutiny* delusion, that crops up so conspicuously in the symptomatology of paranoid illnesses, and which may perhaps also occur as a separate illness or as a random element in a transference neurosis. Patients then complain that all their thoughts are known, their actions watched and monitored. They are informed of the workings of this entity by voices, which characteristically speak to them in the third person ('Now she's thinking about that again', 'Now he's going away'). The complaint is justified, it depicts the true situation: such a power really does exist, and it exists in all of us in normal life, registering, scrutinizing, criticizing our every intention. Object-of-scrutiny delusions reflect it in a regressive form, thereby revealing both its genesis and the reason why the patient rebels against it. For what first triggered the formation of the ego-ideal – the duly appointed keeper of which is the conscience – was the critical influence of the individual's parents, communicated by voice, who were joined in the course of time by others involved in his upbringing, by his teachers, by the vast and indeterminate mass of all the other people in his milieu (people in general, public opinion).

Large quantities of essentially homosexual libido are drawn on for the purposes of forming the narcissistic ego-ideal, and achieve discharge and gratification through keeping it going thereafter. Conscience is instituted basically as an embodiment first of parental criticism, and subsequently of criticism by society at large, a process that more or less repeats itself in the emergence of repressive tendencies stemming from prohibitions and obstacles initially encountered in the external world. Neurosis then brings to light both the inner voices and the indeterminate mass, and the whole developmental history of the person's conscience is thereby regressively reproduced. However, his recalcitrance against this *censorial entity* derives from the fact that – in full accord with the fundamental nature of his illness – he wants to free himself from all these influences, starting with that of his parents, and withdraws his homosexual libido from them. He then sees his conscience in regressive refraction as a hostile force bearing down on him from outside.

The bitter complaining characteristic of paranoia also demonstrates that the self-criticism expressed via the conscience is essentially all of a piece with the self-scrutiny upon which it is based. The same mental process that has taken on the function of conscience has thus also lent itself to the exploration of the inner self, which is what provides philosophy with the material for its cerebrations. This may well have considerable bearing on the urge to construct speculative systems that is characteristic of paranoia.[33]

It will doubtless be a significant step for us when we are able to find evidence in other realms, too, of the activity of this entity dedicated to critical scrutiny – duly elevated to its role as both conscience and agent of philosophical introspection. I would like to draw here on what Herbert Silberer has termed the 'functional phenomenon', one of the few incontestably valuable additions to the theory of dreams. As is well known, Silberer has demonstrated that in states between sleeping and waking one can directly observe the conversion of thoughts into visual images, but that often in such circumstances what is actually represented is not the thought content but the *state* (of willingness, tiredness etc.) that the person fighting sleep finds himself in. He has also shown that dream closures and breaks within dreams in some cases signify nothing but the dreamer's own perception of sleeping and waking. He has thus proved that self-scrutiny – in the sense of paranoid object-of-scrutiny delusion – plays a role in dream-formation. This role is not a constant one; I probably overlooked it because it plays no great part in my own dreams; it may well become very marked in the case of people who are philosophically gifted and accustomed to introspection.

We might remind ourselves at this point that we have argued elsewhere that the formation of dreams takes place under the sway of a censorial process that forces dream-thoughts to become distorted. In positing this censorship, however, we did not envisage any special power at work, but chose the term to describe that portion of the repressive tendencies governing the ego that is directed at dream-thoughts. If we go more deeply into the structure of the ego, then we may reasonably see in the ego-ideal and the dynamic utterances of the conscience the *dream censor*[34] as well. Supposing that this censor also remains alert to some extent during sleep, then we can readily comprehend that the prerequisite of its activity, namely self-scrutiny and self-criticism, helps to shape the content of dreams with contributions like 'now he's too sleepy to think', 'now he's waking up'.[35]

We can now attempt a discussion of self-feeling[36] in normal individuals and in neurotics.

Self-feeling seems to us in the first place to be an expression of the ego in its totality, without further regard being paid to its essentially composite nature. Everything one possesses or has achieved, every remnant of one's primitive sense of omnipotence that has been borne out by experience, helps to enhance this self-feeling.

If we are going to introduce our distinction between sexual drives and ego drives, then we must also acknowledge that self-feeling is particularly intimately dependent on narcissistic libido. We base this contention on the two fundamental facts that in the paraphrenias self-feeling is enhanced whereas in the transference neuroses it is diminished; and that in love-relationships an individual's self-feeling is increased by his being loved, and decreased by his *not* being loved. We have already argued that, in the case of narcissistic object-choice, being loved constitutes both the goal and the means of gratification.

It is easy to see, moreover, that the libidinal cathexis of objects does not enhance self-feeling. Dependence on the love-object has a belittling effect; to be in love is to be humble. Loving someone means, so to speak, forfeiting part of our narcissism, and we can make good the deficit only by being loved. In all these respects self-feeling appears to remain directly proportional to the degree of narcissism involved in the subject's love-life.

The realization of impotence, of one's own inability to love, as a result of some psychological or physical disorder, has an extremely debilitating effect on self-feeling. Here, so it seems to me, may lie one of the sources of the feelings of inferiority so readily avouched by those suffering from transference neuroses. The main source of these feelings, however, is the depletion of the ego that occurs when extraordinarily large cathexes of libido are withdrawn from it; in other words, impairment of the ego by sexual urges that are no longer subject to control.

A[lfred] Adler has rightly argued that when people recognize deficiencies in their own organs, this acts as a spur to their psyche (assuming the latter to be functioning adequately), and by means of over-compensation serves to lift their level of achievement. But it would be a gross exaggeration if we were to follow Adler's procedure and regard organ deficiency as the origin and necessary condition of every instance of high achievement. Not all painters are afflicted by eye defects, not all orators were originally stutterers. There are abundant examples, too, of excellent things achieved by people blessed with exceptional organs. When it comes to the aetiology of neurosis, organic deficiency and wasting play a minor role, perhaps much the same as that played by the perceptual material of the moment in the formation of dreams. The neurosis uses it as a pretext just as it uses every other expedient factor. One has no sooner given credence to a neurotic patient's notion that she was bound to become ill because – as she saw it – she was ugly, misshapen and devoid of charm, so that no one could ever conceivably love her, than one is taught a lesson by the very next female neurotic to come along, who doggedly cleaves to her neurosis and rejection of sexuality despite seeming more than averagely desirable, and indeed being actively desired. The majority of hysterical women may be numbered among the attractive and even beautiful representatives of their sex; and inversely, the heavy incidence of ugliness, infirmity and wasted organs in the lower classes of our society has no effect whatever on the frequency of neurotic disorders occurring amongst them.

The relationship of self-feeling to the erotic (i.e. to libidinal object-cathexes) may be summed up in the following terms. We need to determine which of two alternatives applies: whether the love-cathexes are *ego-accordant*,[37] or whether on the contrary they have undergone repression. In the former case (i.e. where libido deployment is ego-accordant), the same value attaches to loving as to any other activity of the ego. The process of loving in itself, inasmuch as it entails yearning and going without, diminishes self-feeling; the process of being loved, of finding one's love returned, of gaining possession of the loved object, restores it to its previous level. In the case of repressed libido, the love-cathexis is experienced as a severe depletion of the ego; no gratification of the love is possible; replenishment of the ego can be achieved only by withdrawal of the libido from its objects. The return of object-libido to the ego, and its transformation into narcissism, creates as it were a semblance of love happily achieved, whilst a love happily achieved in actual reality corresponds in turn to the primal state in which object-libido and ego-libido cannot be differentiated from one another.

The importance and complexity of this subject is perhaps sufficient justification for appending a few extra paragraphs here in more or less random order:

The development of the ego consists in an ever-increasing separation from one's primary narcissism, and gives rise to an intense struggle to retrieve it. This separation occurs through the displacement of libido onto an ego-ideal imposed from without; gratification occurs through fulfilment of that ideal.

At the same time, the ego sends forth libidinal object-cathexes. It becomes depleted for the sake of these cathexes and for the sake of the ego-ideal, but replenishes itself through object-gratifications[38] and through fulfilment of the ideal.

One part of self-feeling is primary, the residue of childhood narcissism; another derives from our sense of omnipotence as borne out by experience (fulfilment of the ego-ideal); a third arises out of the gratification of our object-libido.

The ego-ideal puts considerable difficulties in the way of libido gratification through objects by causing some of them to be rejected by its censor[39] as unsuitable. Where no such ideal has developed, the relevant sexual urge enters the individual's personality in unmodified form as a perversion. Becoming our own ideal again in respect of our sexual urges as well as everything else, just as in our childhood: therein lies the happiness that human beings aspire to.

Being in love consists in the ego-libido overflowing abundantly onto the object. It has the power to undo repressions and remedy perversions.[40] It exalts the sexual object into the status of sexual ideal. Given that in the case of the 'object' or 'imitative' type it has its basis in the fulfilment of infantile conditions of love, we may venture the dictum: 'Whatever fulfils this condition of love is consequently idealized.'

The sexual ideal can enter into an interesting support role in relation to the ego-ideal. Where narcissistic gratification encounters real obstacles, the sexual ideal can be used for surrogate gratification. The person then enacts the narcissistic type of object-choice by loving what he once was but has meanwhile forfeited, or by loving whatever possesses the qualities that he himself doesn't have at all (cf. above under *c*) [page 19]). The formula parallel to the one cited above runs as follows: 'Whatever possesses the qualities that the ego lacks *qua* ideal, is consequently loved'. This particular resort holds special significance for the neurotic, whose ego becomes depleted because of his excessive object-cathexes, and who is hence incapable of achieving his ego-ideal. Having squandered his libido on objects, he then seeks a way back to narcissism by adopting the narcissistic type of object-choice and choosing a sexual ideal possessed of the qualities he himself cannot attain. This is healing through love, which as a rule he prefers to the psychoanalytical variety. Indeed, he has no faith in any other healing mechanism; he generally embarks on his therapy in expectation of it, and duly focuses this expectation on the person of the physician treating him. What stands in the way of this curative scheme, of course, is the patient's incapacity for love as a result of his panoply of repressions. If the treatment manages to remedy this to some degree, we often meet with a successful if unintended outcome in that the patient withdraws from treatment in order to make a love-choice, and to entrust his further recovery to his shared life with the loved person. We might be content with this outcome if it did not bring with it all the dangers of a crushing dependence on his helper in adversity.

The ego-ideal opens up a significant new avenue for our understanding of mass psychology.[41] This ideal has a social element as well as an individual one, for it is also the shared ideal of family, class, nation. Besides narcissistic libido, it also harnesses a large quantum of a person's homosexual libido, which thereby reverts to the ego. Non-gratification resulting from non-fulfilment of this ideal releases homosexual libido, which converts into guilty conscience (social fear).[42] Guilty conscience originates as fear of parental punishment, or rather – to put it more accurately – fear of losing the parents' love; later, the indeterminate mass of fellow human beings takes the parents' place. We can thus more readily understand the fact that paranoia is frequently caused by the ego being wounded, by gratification being refused within the domain of the ego-ideal. Also, in the case of the paraphrenic illnesses, we can better understand the concomitance within the ego-ideal of ideal-formation and sublimation, the retrogression of sublimations, and the re-formation[43] of ideals that occurs in certain circumstances.

(1914)

Remembering, Repeating, and Working Through

It seems to me by no means superfluous to remind the student of psychoanalysis again and again of the profound changes that psychoanalytical technique has undergone since its first beginnings. First of all, in the phase of catharsis as practised by Breuer, the technique was to focus directly on the factor of symptom-formation, and make a rigorously sustained attempt to reproduce the psychic processes of that situation in order to resolve them through conscious activity. Remembering and abreacting[1] were the goals at that stage, to be achieved with the help of hypnosis. Once hypnosis had been discarded, the task that then demanded our attention was to use the free associations of the patient to work out what he himself was failing to remember. The process of interpretation and the communication of its results to the patient were seen as the means to overcome the resistance within him; there was still the same focus on the situations in which the symptoms first arose, and any others that proved to underlie the onset of the illness, whilst abreaction diminished in importance and appeared to be replaced by the considerable effort that the patient had to expend when forced to overcome his hostility towards his free associations (in accordance with the basic rule of psychoanalysis). Then finally the rigorous technique of the present time evolved whereby the physician no longer focuses on a specific factor or problem, but is quite content to study the prevailing surface-level of the patient's mind, and uses his interpretative skills chiefly for the purpose of identifying the resistances manifest there, and making the patient conscious of them. A new kind of division of labour then comes into being: the physician reveals the resistances that were hitherto unknown to the patient; and once these have been overcome, the patient often recounts without any difficulty the situations and contexts that he had forgotten. The goal of these various techniques has of course remained the same throughout; in descriptive terms, to fill the gaps in the patient's memory; in dynamic terms, to overcome the resistances brought about by repression.

The old technique of hypnosis still deserves our gratitude for having shown us in discrete and schematized form a number of psychic processes that occur in analysis. It was thanks to this alone that we were able to develop the boldness, within psychoanalytic practice itself, to create complex situations and keep them transparent.

'Remembering' took a very simple form in these hypnotic treatments. The patient reverted to an earlier situation, which he appeared never to confuse with his present one, conveyed the psychic processes of that earlier situation in so far as they had remained normal, and in addition conveyed whatever resulted from translating the unconscious processes of that time into conscious ones.

I shall add a few remarks at this point that every analyst has seen confirmed by his own experience.[2] The forgetting of impressions, scenes, experiences comes down in most cases to a process of 'shutting out' such things. When the patient speaks of these 'forgotten' things, he rarely fails to add 'I've always known that really, I've just never thought about it.' He not uncommonly expresses disappointment that so few things seem to want to come to mind that he can acknowledge as 'forgotten', things that he has never thought about again since the time they happened. Even this yearning, however, is capable of being gratified, particularly in the case of conversion hysterias.[3] The term 'forgetting' becomes even less relevant once there is due appreciation of the extremely widespread phenomenon of screen-memories.[4] In quite a number of cases of childhood amnesia,[5] that familiar condition so important to us in theoretical terms, I have gained the impression that the amnesia is exactly counterbalanced by the patient's screen-memories. These memories contain not merely *some* essential elements of the patient's childhood, but *all* such elements. One simply has to know how to use analysis to retrieve these elements from the memories. The latter represent the forgotten childhood years as completely as the manifest content of dreams represents the dream-thoughts.

The other group of psychic processes which, as purely internal acts, can be contrasted to impressions and experiences – fantasies, relationary processes,[6] emotional impulses, thought-connections[7] – need to be considered separately as regards their relationship to forgetting and remembering. Something that occurs particularly frequently here is that something is 'remembered' that can never have been 'forgotten', since it was never at any point noticed, never conscious; moreover it appears to make no difference whatsoever to the psychic outcome whether such a 'connection' was a conscious one that was then forgotten, or whether it never reached the status of consciousness in the first place. The conviction that the patient arrives at in the course of analysis is entirely independent of this kind of memory.

Particularly in the case of the many forms of obsessional neurosis, forgetting is limited in the main to losing track of connections, misremembering the sequence of events, recalling memories in isolation.

A memory usually cannot be retrieved at all in the case of one particular group of extremely important experiences, namely those occurring at a very early stage of childhood that are experienced at the time without understanding, but are then *subsequently* understood and interpreted. We become aware of them via the patient's dreams, and are compelled to credit their existence by overwhelming evidence within the overall pattern of the neurosis; we are also persuaded by the fact that, once the patient has overcome his resistances, he does not see the absence of a memory or sensation of familiarity as grounds for not accepting that they took place. This topic needs to be approached with so much care, however, and introduces so much that is new and disturbing, that I shall deal with it quite separately with reference to appropriate material.[8]

✿

Now the introduction of the new technique has meant that very little, and in many instances nothing whatever, has remained of this splendidly smooth progression of events. Here, too, there are cases that initially develop just as they would under the hypnotic technique, only to diverge at a later stage; other cases behave differently right from the outset. If for the purposes of defining the difference we stick to the latter type, then we may say that the patient does not *remember* anything at all of what he has forgotten and repressed, but rather *acts it out*. He reproduces it not as a memory, but as an action; he *repeats* it, without of course being aware of the fact that he is repeating it.

For example, instead of the patient recounting that he remembers having been defiant and refractory *vis-à-vis* his parents' authority, he behaves in just such a manner towards the physician. Instead of remembering that he became hopelessly stuck in his infantile sexual explorations, he presents a mass of confused dreams and associations, wails that he is no good at anything, and sees it as his fate never to bring any undertaking to a successful conclusion. Instead of remembering that he was intensely ashamed of certain sexual activities and fearful of discovery, he exhibits shame regarding the treatment that he has embarked upon, and tries to keep it secret from all and sundry – and so on.

More particularly, he *begins* the treatment with just such a repetition. Often when one has explained the basic rule of psychoanalysis to a patient with an eventful life story and a long history of illness, and asks him to say whatever comes into his mind, and then expects a stream of utterances to come bursting forth, the first thing one discovers is that he has no idea what to say. He remains silent, and maintains that nothing at all has come into his mind. This is of course nothing other than the repetition of a homosexual stance, which manifests itself as a resistance to remembrance of any kind. He remains in the grip of this compulsion to repeat for as long as he remains under treatment; and in the end we realize that this is his way of remembering.

What is chiefly going to interest us, of course, is the relationship that this repetitional compulsion bears to the transference and the resistance exhibited by the patient. We soon realize that the transference is itself merely an instance of repetition, and that this repetition involves transference of the forgotten past not only onto the physician, but onto all other areas of the patient's current situation. We must therefore expect that the patient will yield to the compulsion to repeat – which now takes the place of the impulse to remember – not only in his personal relationship to the physician, but in all other activities and relationships taking place in his life at the same time; for example, if during the course of the treatment he chooses a love-object, takes some task upon himself, involves himself in a project of any sort. The role played by resistance is also easy to recognize. The greater the resistance, the more thoroughly remembering will be replaced by acting out (repetition). After all, in hypnosis the ideal form of remembering corresponds to a condition in which resistance is completely pushed aside. If the treatment begins under the aegis of a mild and tacit regime of positive transference, this initially encourages submersion in the domain of memory (just as happens in hypnosis), during the course of which even the symptoms of the patient's illness are mute; however, if this transference subsequently becomes hostile or unduly intense, and therefore needs to be repressed, then remembering immediately gives way to acting out. From that point onwards it is the resistances that determine the sequence of what is repeated. The patient uses the arsenal of the past to arm himself with weapons to fight against the continuation of the treatment – weapons that we have to wrest from him one by one.

Now having seen that the patient repeats rather than remembers, and does so under conditions of resistance, we may now ask what it really is that he repeats or acts out. The answer is that he repeats everything deriving from the repressed element within himself[9] that has already established itself in his manifest personality – his inhibitions and unproductive attitudes, his pathological characteristics. Indeed, he also repeats all his symptoms during the course of the treatment. And we can now see that in emphasizing the compulsion to repeat we have not discovered a new fact, but merely arrived at a more coherent view. It is now quite plain to us that the start of a patient's analysis does not mean the end of his illness, and that we need to treat the illness not as a matter belonging to the past, but as a force operating in the present. Piece by piece the entire illness is brought within the scope and ambit of the treatment, and while the patient experiences it as something intensely real and immediate, it is our job to do the therapeutic work, which consists to a very great extent in leading the patient back to the past.

Getting the patient to remember, as practised in hypnosis, inevitably had the air of a laboratory experiment. Getting the patient to repeat, as practised under the more modern technique of analysis, means summoning up a chunk of real life, and cannot therefore always be harmless and free of risk. The whole problem arises here of 'deterioration during treatment', a phenomenon that often proves unavoidable.

Most importantly, the very inception of the treatment itself necessarily induces a change in the patient's conscious attitude to his illness. As a rule he has been content up to then to bemoan his illness, to despise it as so much nonsense and to underestimate its significance, whilst for the rest applying the same repressive behaviour, the same head-in-the-sand strategy, to the manifestations of his illness that he applied to its origins. Thus it can happen that he does not properly appreciate the conditions under which his phobia functions, does not listen carefully enough to what his obsessional ideas are saying to him, or does not grasp the real intention of his obsessional impulse. This of course is the last thing his treatment needs. He has to find the courage to focus his attention on the manifestations of his illness. He must no longer regard the illness as something contemptible, but rather as a worthy opponent, a part of his very being that exists for good reasons, and from which he must extract something of real value for his subsequent life. The way is thus prepared from the outset for him to be reconciled with the repressed element within himself, which expresses itself in his symptoms, whilst at the same time allowing for a certain tolerance towards his illness. And if as a result of this new relationship to his illness the patient's conflicts are exacerbated, or if symptoms are forced into the open that had previously remained in the shadows, then one can easily reassure him on this score by pointing out that these merely constitute a necessary but transitory deterioration in his condition, and that one cannot destroy an enemy if he is absent or out of range. However, the resistance can exploit the situation for its own ends and seek to abuse the licence to be ill. It then seems to exclaim: 'Look what happens when I really do let myself become involved in these things! Wasn't I quite right to consign them all to repression?' Juvenile and child patients are particularly prone to use the focus on their illness necessitated by their treatment as an excuse to wallow in their symptoms.

Further dangers arise as treatment progresses, in that new, more deep-seated drive-impulses – still nascent rather than fully established – can emerge as repetition. Lastly, the patient's actions outside the transference process can cause temporary harm in his everyday life, indeed can be so chosen as to permanently undermine that very condition of health that the treatment is meant to achieve.

The tactic that the physician has to adopt in this situation is easily justified. The goal that he holds fast to, even though he knows it to be unattainable under the new technique, remains the old form of remembering, that is, reproducing things within the psychic domain. He prepares himself for a constant battle with the patient, in order to keep within the psychic domain all those impulses that the patient would prefer to divert into the motor domain, and regards it as a therapeutic triumph when he successfully uses the remembering process to resolve an issue that the patient would rather get rid of in the form of an action. If the bond formed through transference is at all effective, then the treatment will successfully prevent any really significant acts of remembering on the part of the patient, and will use the nascent stage of any attempts at such acts as material contributing to the therapeutic process. One can best protect the patient from being damaged through giving rein to his impulses if one puts him under an explicit obligation not to make any decisions during the course of his treatment that vitally affect his life, such as choosing a career or a definitive love-object, but instead to wait until he is fully recovered.

In doing this, however, it is sensible to give scope to such aspects of the patient's personal freedom as are consistent with these pre-cautions, and not to stop him from carrying out intentions which, though foolish, are without consequence, whilst also bearing in mind that people can really only achieve insight through their own hurt and their own experience. There are indeed also cases in which the patient cannot be prevented from entering upon some wholly inappropriate undertaking, and which only later become ripe for psychoanalytical treatment, and responsive to it. Occasionally there are also bound to be cases where one does not have the time to put the bridle of transference on a patient's rampant drives, or where the patient in the course of an act of repetition destroys the bond that ties him to the treatment. As an extreme example of this I might mention the case of an elderly lady who, when afflicted by twilight states,[10] had repeatedly left home and husband and fled somewhere or other without ever becoming conscious of the force impelling her to 'run away' in this manner. On starting her treatment with me she displayed a well-developed form of affectionate transference, this intensified with uncanny rapidity over the first few days, and by the end of the week she had 'run away' from me too, without my having had the time to say anything to her that might have prevented this repetition.

However, the chief means for controlling the patient's compulsion to repeat, and turning it into a means of activating memory,[11] lies in the way that the transference is handled. We render the compulsion harmless, indeed beneficial, by allowing it some sovereignty, by giving it its head within a specific domain. We offer it transference as a playground in which it has licence to express itself with almost total freedom, coupled with an obligation to reveal to us everything in the way of pathogenic drives that have hidden themselves away in the patient's psyche. The patient's co-operation need extend only as far as respect for the conditions of existence of the analysis, and, provided this is the case, we can routinely succeed in giving all the symptoms of his illness a new meaning in terms of transference; in replacing his ordinary neurosis with a transference neurosis, of which he can be cured through the therapeutic process. Transference thus creates an intermediate realm between sickness and a healthy life by means of which the transition from one to the other is accomplished. The new condition has assumed all the characteristics of the illness, but it constitutes an artificial illness that is in all respects amenable to treatment. At the same time it is a real, lived experience, but one made possible by particularly favourable conditions, and purely temporary in nature. The repetition reactions exhibited in transference then lead along familiar paths to the reawakening of memories, which surface without any apparent difficulty once the patient's resistances have been overcome.

I could close here if it were not for the fact that the title of this essay obliges me to demonstrate one further element of psychoanalytical technique. As is well known, what opens the way to the overcoming of resistances is that the physician identifies the resistance that the patient himself had never recognized, and reveals it to him. Now it seems that beginners in the practice of analysis are inclined to think that this purely preliminary phase constitutes the entire task. I have often been asked for advice in cases where the physician complained that he had shown the patient his resistance, yet nothing had changed, indeed the resistance had merely intensified and the entire situation had become even more impenetrable than before. The treatment seemed to be going nowhere. But this gloomy assessment invariably proved to be wrong. In most cases the treatment could not have been going better, the physician had simply forgotten that identifying the resistance can never result in its immediate cessation. One has to give the patient time to familiarize himself with the resistance now that he is aware of it, to *work his way through it*, to overcome it by defying it and carrying on with the therapy in accordance with the basic rule of analysis. Only when the resistance is at its most intense can one manage in co-operation with the patient to detect the repressed drive-impulses that sustain the resistance; and it is only by directly experiencing it in this way that the patient becomes truly convinced of its existence and power. The physician need do nothing other than wait, and allow things to take their course – a process that cannot be prevented, and cannot always be accelerated. If he bears this steadfastly in mind, he will often save himself from the delusion that he has failed, when in fact he is conducting the treatment along entirely the right lines.

This process of working through the resistances may in practice become an arduous task for the patient and a considerable test of the physician's patience. But it is the phase of treatment that effects the biggest change in the patient, and which distinguishes psycho-analytical treatment from any form of suggestion-based therapy. Theoretically speaking, one can equate it to the 'abreacting'[12] of the emotional quanta pent up through repression that hypnotic treatment entirely depended on for its success.

(1914)

Beyond the Pleasure Principle

I

In psychoanalytic theory we assume without further ado that the evolution of psychic processes is automatically regulated by the pleasure principle; that is to say, we believe that these processes are invariably triggered by an unpleasurable tension, and then follow a path such that their ultimate outcome represents a diminution of this tension, and hence a propensity to avoid unpleasure or to generate pleasure. When, in our study of psychic processes, we look at them with specific reference to this manner in which they evolve, we introduce the 'economic' perspective into our work. An account that pays due attention to this economic factor, as well as to the topical and dynamic aspects, seems to us to be the most complete kind that is presently conceivable, and to merit special distinction by use of the term *metapsychological*.[1]

It is of no interest to us in any of this to investigate the extent to which, in postulating the pleasure principle, we have echoed or embraced any particular, historically established philosophical system. We have arrived at such speculative assumptions simply as a result of our efforts to give a description and account of the facts that we observe on a daily basis in our field of study. Being original or getting there first do not figure among the aims laid down for psychoanalytic inquiry, and the impressions on which the postulation of this principle is based are so obvious that it is scarcely possible to overlook them. On the other hand, we would gladly acknowledge our gratitude to any philosophical or psychological theory capable of revealing to us the *meaning* of these sensations of pleasure and unpleasure that are so imperative for us. In this respect, unfortunately, nothing of any use is available to us. This is the darkest and most impenetrable area of the psyche, and whilst we cannot possibly avoid touching upon it, it seems to me that we do best to offer only the most tentative of suppositions on the subject. After much consideration we are minded to posit a connection between pleasure/unpleasure and the quantity of excitation present – yet not annexed[2] in any way – within the psyche; a connection whereby unpleasure corresponds to an *increase* in that quantity, and pleasure to a *decrease*. We are not thinking here in terms of a simple relationship between the strength of the sensations and the quantitative changes that we are linking them to; least of all – in view of everything that psycho-physiology has taught us – are we thinking in terms of a directly proportional relationship. The key determining factor so far as the sensation is concerned is probably the intensity of the decrease or increase over a particular period of time. Experimentation may well have a part to play here: we analysts would certainly be well advised not to venture any more deeply into these problems until such time as we can be guided by very specific observations.

However, we cannot help but feel a certain excitement when we discover that such a penetrating scientist as G. T. Fechner advocated an interpretation of pleasure and unpleasure that accords in all essential respects with the one so forcefully suggested to us by our psychoanalytic work. Fechner's statement on the matter is contained in his brief study *Einige Ideen zur Schöpfungs- und Entwicklungsgeschichte der Organismen* [*Some Ideas on the Origin and Evolution of Organisms*] of 1873 (Section XI, supplementary note, p. 94), and reads as follows: 'Inasmuch as conscious impulses are always associated with pleasure or unpleasure, we may suppose that pleasure and unpleasure, too, are linked psycho-physically to conditions of stability and instability; and this gives grounds for a hypothesis that I shall develop in more detail elsewhere, namely that every psycho-physical motion that passes the threshold of consciousness involves pleasure to the degree that it moves beyond a certain point *towards* complete stability, and unpleasure to the degree that it moves beyond a certain point *away from* that stability; whilst *between* these two points – which may be defined as the qualitative thresholds of pleasure and unpleasure – there is a certain margin of aesthetic indifference . . .'

The facts that have caused us to believe in the dominion of the pleasure principle within the psyche also inform our assumption that one aspiration of the psychic apparatus is to keep the quantity of excitation present within it at the lowest possible level, or at least to keep it constant. The latter postulate is the same as the former, albeit expressed in different terms, for if the psychic apparatus is geared to minimizing the quantity of excitation, then anything tending to *increase* that quantity is bound to be experienced as counterfunctional, and hence unpleasurable. The pleasure principle arose out of the constancy principle; in reality, however, the constancy principle was inferred from the same facts that compelled us to postulate the pleasure principle. We shall also discover on deeper consideration that the particular aspiration we attribute to the psychic apparatus is subsumable as a special case under Fechner's principle of 'the tendency to stability', to which he linked the sensations of pleasure and unpleasure.

That being so, however, we have to acknowledge that it is strictly speaking incorrect to say that the pleasure principle has dominion over the way in which psychic processes evolve. If this were the case, then the vast majority of our psychic processes would need to be accompanied by pleasure or lead to pleasure, whereas all common experience contradicts such a conclusion. The true situation, therefore, can only be that the pleasure principle exists as a strong *tendency* within the psyche, but is opposed by certain other forces or circumstances, so that the final outcome cannot possibly always accord with the said tendency in favour of pleasure. Compare Fechner's remark in a similar context (op. cit., p. 90) that 'the tendency to achieve a particular goal does not imply the actual achievement of that goal, and the goal may not be achievable at all except in approximate terms'. If we now turn to the question as to which circumstances are capable of preventing the pleasure principle from being carried into effect, we find ourselves back on safe and familiar ground, and in seeking an answer we are able to draw on a rich profusion of psychoanalytical experience.

The primary example of the pleasure principle being thus inhibited is already familiar to us as a spontaneous and automatic process. We know that the pleasure principle belongs to a *primary* operational level of the psychic apparatus, and that so far as self-preservation is concerned it is never anything but useless, indeed highly dangerous, given the challenges posed by the external world. Thanks to the influence of the ego's self-preservation drive it is displaced by the *reality principle*,[3] which, without abandoning the aim of ultimately achieving pleasure, none the less demands and procures the postponement of gratification, the rejection of sundry opportunities for such gratification, and the temporary toleration of unpleasure on the long and circuitous road to pleasure. This notwithstanding, the pleasure principle remains for a long period of time the vehicle of the much less 'educable' sexual drives, and there are countless occasions – be it on the basis of these latter drives, be it within the ego itself – where the pleasure principle overwhelms the reality principle, to the detriment of the entire organism.

There is no doubt, however, that displacement of the pleasure principle by the reality principle can be held responsible for only a very few experiences of unpleasure, and for none whatever of the most intense ones. Another source of unpleasure, no less spontaneous and automatic, arises from the conflicts and divisions that occur within the psychic apparatus during the course of the ego's development to more highly composite forms of organization.[4] Almost all the energy that fills the psychic apparatus stems from its innate drive-impulses, but not all of these are granted access to the same phases of development. As things evolve, so there are numerous occasions where individual drives, or elements of individual drives, prove to be incompatible in their aims and demands with all those others that are capable of joining together to yield the all-embracing unity of the ego. They are therefore separated off from this unified whole through the process of repression; they are restricted to lower levels of psychic development and, for the time being at least, cut off from any possibility of gratification. If they subsequently manage by circuitous means to fight their way to some form of direct or surrogate gratification – as so easily happens in the case of repressed sexual drives – this success, which otherwise would have offered an opportunity for pleasure, is experienced by the ego as unpleasure. Because of the earlier conflict with its outcome in repression, the pleasure principle is once again confuted, right at the very time when various other drives are busy giving effect to it by occasioning new pleasure. The details of the process whereby repression converts an opportunity for pleasure into a source of unpleasure are not yet clearly understood, and cannot be described with any precision, but it is doubtless the case that *all* neurotic unpleasure is of this kind, that is to say, pleasure that cannot be experienced as such.[5]

The two sources of unpleasure identified here by no means account for the majority of our experiences of unpleasure, but of the remainder one can say with some semblance of justification that their existence does not contradict the dominion of the pleasure principle. After all, most of the unpleasure that we feel is *perceptual* unpleasure, involving perception of the turbid pressure of ungratified inner drives, or perception of *external* things; this latter perception may be unpleasant in itself, or it may provoke unpleasurable expectations within the psychic apparatus, and hence be recognized by the latter as a 'danger'. The reaction to these demands of the drives within and dangers posed from without – a reaction that manifests the proper activity of the psychic apparatus – may thus quite correctly be regarded as deriving from the pleasure principle or from its modifier,[6] the reality principle. This being so, it might seem otiose to grant the existence of any further constraints upon the pleasure principle; yet it is precisely an investigation of the psyche's response to external dangers that affords new material and raises new questions concerning the problem at issue here.

II

A condition consequent upon severe mechanical shock, train crashes, and other life-threatening accidents has long since been identified and described – a condition that has come to be known as 'traumatic neurosis'. The terrible war that has only just ended[7] gave rise to a great many such disorders, and did at least put an end to the temptation to attribute them to organic impairment of the nervous system brought about by mechanical force.[8] The clinical picture presented by traumatic neurosis is not unlike that of hysteria in its plethora of similar motor symptoms, but generally goes well beyond it in the very marked signs of subjective suffering that it displays – not unlike those in hypochondria or melancholia – and in the clear evidence it affords of a far more comprehensive and generalized enfeeblement and attrition of the individual's psychic capabilities. As yet, no one has managed to attain to a full understanding of either the neuroses of war or the traumatic neuroses of peacetime. In the case of the war neuroses, it seemed on the one hand illuminating, yet simultaneously baffling, that the selfsame clinical picture occasionally arose *without* the involvement of any raw mechanical force. In the case of ordinary traumatic neurosis, two features stand out very clearly, and have proved a useful starting point for further thought: first, the fact that the key causative element appeared to lie in the surprise factor, the *fright* experienced by the victim; and second, the fact that if any physical wound or injury was suffered at the same time, this generally inhibited the development of the neurosis. The words 'fright', 'dread' and 'fear' are wrongly used as interchangeable synonyms, for they can be easily differentiated from each other in their relationship to danger.[9] 'Fear' represents a certain kind of inner state amounting to expectation of, and preparation for, danger of some kind, even though the nature of the danger may well be unknown. 'Dread' requires a specific object of which we are afraid. 'Fright', however, emphasizes the element of surprise; it describes the state that possesses us when we find ourselves plunged into danger without being prepared for it. I do not believe that fear can engender a traumatic neurosis; there is an element within fear that protects us against fright, and hence also against fright-induced neurosis. We shall return to this proposition later on.

The study of dreams may be regarded as the most reliable approach route for those seeking to understand the deep-level processes of the psyche. Now it is a distinctive feature of the dream-life of patients with traumatic neurosis that it repeatedly takes them back to the situation of their original misadventure, from which they awake with a renewed sense of fright. People have shown far too little surprise at this phenomenon. The fact that the traumatic experience repeatedly forces itself on the patient even during sleep is assumed to be proof indeed of just how deep an impression it made. The patient is assumed to be, so to speak, psychically fixated[10] on the trauma. Such fixations on the experience that first triggered the illness have long been familiar to us in the context of hysteria. Breuer and Freud expressed the view in 1893 that hysterics suffer mainly from reminiscences. In the case of war neuroses, too, observers such as Ferenczi and Simmel have been able to explain various motor symptoms as arising from a fixation on the moment of trauma.

On the other hand, however, I am not aware that those suffering from traumatic neurosis are very much preoccupied in their *waking* life with memories of their misadventure. Perhaps, rather, they are at pains *not* to think of it. To take it for granted that night-time dreams automatically thrust them back into the situation that pro-voked their illness would be to misunderstand the nature of dreams. It would be rather more in the nature of dreams to conjure up pictures from the time when the patient was healthy, or else pictures of the return to health that is hoped for in the future. If the dreams of those with accident-induced neurosis are not to make us start doubting the wish-fulfilling tendency of dreams in general, then we might have recourse to the explanation that in this disorder the dream-function, like so much else, is thrown into disarray and distracted from its proper purposes; or we might have to turn our minds to the mysterious *masochistic* tendencies of the ego.[11]

I should now like to suggest that we leave the dark and dismal topic of traumatic neurosis and study the workings of the psychic apparatus by reference to one of its earliest forms of *normal* activity. I mean the play of children.

The various theories of children's play have only recently been collated and psychoanalytically evaluated by S[igmund] Pfeifer in *Imago* (vol. V, no. 4), and I would refer readers to this paper. These theories seek to divine the motive forces behind children's play, but they do so without paying sufficient attention to the *economic* perspective: the concern of the individual to gain pleasure. Without wishing to embrace the whole gamut of these phenomena, I took advantage of an opportunity that happened to present itself to me in order to elucidate a game played by a one-and-a-half-year-old boy, the first that he had ever invented for himself. It was more than a fleeting observation, as I lived under the same roof as the child and his parents for several weeks, and it was quite some time before the puzzling and constantly repeated behaviour of the child yielded up its meaning to me.

The child was by no means precocious in his intellectual development; at one and a half he spoke only a few intelligible words, and in addition had a small repertoire of expressive sounds comprehensible to those around him. But he had a good rapport with his parents and the family's one maid, and was praised for being a 'good boy'. He didn't disturb his parents during the night; he conscientiously heeded injunctions not to touch certain things and not to enter certain rooms; above all, he never cried when his mother left him for hours at a time, even though he was fondly attached to her, she having not only fed him herself, but also cared for him and looked after him without any outside help. However, this good little boy had the sometimes irritating habit of flinging all the small objects he could get hold of far away from himself into a remote corner of the room, under a bed, etc., so that gathering up his toys was often no easy task. While doing this he beamed with an expression of interest and gratification, and uttered a loud, long-drawn-out 'o-o-o-o' sound, which in the unanimous opinion of both his mother and myself as observer was not simply an exclamation but stood for *fort* ('gone'). I eventually realized that this was probably a game, and that the child was using all his toys for the sole purpose of playing 'gone' with them. Then one day I made an observation that confirmed my interpretation. The child had a wooden reel with some string tied around it. It never crossed his mind to drag it along the floor behind him, for instance, in other words to play toy cars with it; instead, keeping hold of the string, he very skilfully threw the reel over the edge of his curtained cot so that it disappeared inside, all the while making his expressive 'o-o-o-o' sound, then used the string to pull the reel out of the cot again, but this time greeting its reappearance with a joyful *Da!* ('Here!'). That, then, was the entire game – disappearing and coming back – only the first act of which one normally got to see; and this first act was tirelessly repeated on its own, even though the greater pleasure undoubtedly attached to the second.[12]

The interpretation of the game readily presented itself. It was associated with the child's immense cultural achievement in successfully abnegating his drives (that is, abnegating the gratification thereof) by allowing his mother to go away without his making a great fuss. He compensated for it, so to speak, by *himself* re-enacting this same disappearance–reappearance scenario with whatever objects fell to hand. So far as the affective evaluation of this game is concerned, it is of course immaterial whether the child invented it himself or adopted it in response to a cue from someone else. What interests us is a different point altogether. The going away of the mother cannot possibly have been pleasant for the child, nor even a matter of indifference. How then does his repetition of this painful experience in his play fit in with the pleasure principle? One might wish to reply that the mother's departure would need to be re-enacted in the game as the precondition of her happy return, and that this latter event was its real purpose. Such a view would be contradicted by the evident fact that Act One, the departure, was played as a game all on its own, indeed vastly more often than the full performance with its happy conclusion.

The analysis of a single case such as this cannot resolve the issue with any certainty; but the impression gained by an unprejudiced observer is that the child had a different motive in turning the experience into a game. The experience affected him, but his own role in it was passive, and he therefore gave himself an active one by repeating it as a game, even though it had been unpleasurable. This endeavour could be attributed to an instinctive urge to assert control that operates quite independently of whether or not the memory as such was pleasurable. But we can also try another interpretation. The act of flinging away the object to make it 'gone' may be the gratification of an impulse on the child's part – which in the ordinary way of things remains suppressed – to take revenge on his mother for having gone away from him; and it may thus be a defiant statement meaning 'Alright, go away! I don't need you; I'm sending you away myself!' This same child whose game I had observed when he was one and a half had the habit a year later of flinging down any toy that had made him cross and saying 'Go in war!' At the time he had been told that his absent father was away in the war, and he didn't miss his father in the least, instead giving out the clearest indications that he did not want his exclusive possession of his mother to be disrupted.[13] We know from other children, too, that they are capable of expressing similar hostile impulses by flinging away objects in place of people.[14] One accordingly begins to have one's doubts as to whether the urge to psychically process powerful experiences, to achieve full control over them, is capable of manifesting itself on a primary level, independently of the pleasure principle. After all, in the case discussed here the child may well only have been able to repeat an unpleasant experience in his play because the repetition was associated with a different but direct gain in pleasure.

Even if we proceed further with our examination of children's play, this does not resolve our uncertainty as to which of the two postulates to adopt. It is plainly the case that children repeat everything in their play that has made a powerful impression on them, and that in so doing they abreact the intensity of the experience and make themselves so to speak master of the situation. On the other hand, however, it is equally clear that all their play is influenced by the one wish that is dominant at that particular age: the wish to be grown up, and to be able to do the things that grown-ups do. It is also an observable fact that the unpleasurable nature of an experience does not always render it unusable for play purposes. If a doctor examines a child's throat or performs some minor operation on him, we can be quite sure that this frightening experience will become the content of his next game – but the gain in pleasure from a different source is plain to see. Exchanging his passive role in the actual experience for an active role within the game, he inflicts on his playmate whatever nasty things were inflicted on him, and thus takes his revenge by proxy.

One thing that *does* emerge from this discussion is that there is no need to posit a specific imitative drive as the motive force behind children's play. We might also bear in mind that the form of play and imitation practised by adults, which in contradistinction to that of children is directed at an audience, does not spare its spectators the most painful of experiences, for instance in the performance of tragedies, and yet may none the less be regarded by them as something supremely enjoyable. This encourages us in the conviction that even under the dominion of the pleasure principle there are ways and means enough for turning what is essentially unpleasurable into something to be remembered and to be processed in the psyche. Some economically oriented aesthetic theory may wish to concern itself with these cases and situations where unpleasure leads ultimately to a gain in pleasure; for our particular purposes, however, they are of no value at all, for they presuppose both the existence and the dominion of the pleasure principle, and offer no evidence for the prevalence of tendencies *beyond* the pleasure principle; tendencies, that is, that are arguably more primal than the pleasure principle, and quite independent of it.

III

Twenty-five years of intensive work have meant that the immediate aims of psychoanalytic practice are completely different today from what they were at the beginning. At first, the analysing physician could hope to do no more than construe the unconscious of which the patient himself was quite unaware, put the various elements together into a coherent picture, and communicate this to the patient at the appropriate time. Psychoanalysis was above all an art of interpretation. As the therapeutic need was not met by this process, the next task that immediately arose was to compel the patient to confirm the analyst's interpretation on the basis of his own memory. In this enterprise the emphasis lay chiefly on the patient's resistances. The art at this juncture was to uncover these resistances as rapidly as possible, make them clear to the patient, and then induce him to relinquish them by bringing one's influence to bear on a directly human level (this being the point where suggestion[15] plays its part, operating in the form of 'transference').

It then became increasingly clear, however, that the intended aim of making the patient conscious of his unconscious could not be fully achieved even by this means. The patient is unable to remember all that is repressed within him, especially perhaps its most essential elements, and thus fails to be convinced that the interpretation presented to him is the correct one. Instead he is driven to *repeat* the repressed matter as an experience in the present, instead of *remembering* it as something belonging to the past, which is what the physician would much rather see happen.[16] The content of these all-too-accurate reproductions of the past is always a particular element of infantile sexual life, namely the Oedipus complex and its offshoots, and they always take place within the ambit of the transference process, that is to say of the relationship with the physician. Once the treatment has reached this point, one may reasonably say that the original neurosis has been replaced by a brand-new transference neurosis – the physician having done his best to limit the scope of this transference neurosis as much as possible, to force as much as possible into the realm of memory, to allow as little as possible to come out in the form of repetition. The ratio as between remembrance and repetition varies from case to case. As a rule the physician cannot spare the patient this phase of the treatment; he must necessarily make him re-experience a certain portion of his past life, and must see to it that he remains to some degree above it all so that he remains cognizant at every turn that what appears to be reality is in truth the refracted image of a forgotten past. If the physician manages to achieve this, then the battle is won: the patient accepts the validity of the interpretation, and the therapy – which wholly depends on this acceptance – can be successfully concluded.

If we are to stand a better chance of understanding this 'compulsion to repeat' that manifests itself during the psychoanalytic treatment of neurotics, we must above all free ourselves of the mistaken idea that in combating the resistances within a patient we are dealing with resistance on the part of the 'unconscious'. The unconscious, that is, the 'repressed',[17] offers no resistance whatever to the endeavours of the therapy; indeed it has but a single aim itself, and that is to escape the oppressive forces bearing down on it, and either break through to consciousness, or else find release in some form of real action. The resistance that manifests itself in the course of treatment derives from the same higher levels and systems of the psyche that effected the repression in the first place. However, since experience tells us that patients undergoing treatment are initially not conscious of the motive forces behind the resistances, or indeed of the resistances themselves, we would do well to amend our inappropriate terminology. We make things much clearer if we posit an antithesis not between the conscious and the unconscious, but between the coherent *ego* and the *repressed*. Much of the ego is itself no doubt unconscious – especially the part we may term its nucleus[18] – and only a small portion of that is covered by the term 'pre-conscious'. Once we have thus substituted a systematic or dynamic definition for what was merely a descriptive one, we can say that the patient's resistance stems from his *ego*,[19] and we then immediately realize that the compulsion to repeat is attributable to the unconscious *repressed* within him. It seems likely that this compulsion to repeat can only manifest itself once the patient's treatment has had the necessary benign effect of loosening the grip of the repression.[20]

There can be no doubt that the resistance of the conscious and pre-conscious ego serves the interests of the pleasure principle; it seeks after all to forestall the unpleasure that would be caused if the repressed part of the psyche were to break free – whereas our own efforts are all directed at opening the way to just such unpleasure by calling upon the reality principle. But what of the compulsion to repeat, the show of strength put on by the repressed part of the psyche: how does *that* stand in relation to the pleasure principle? It is plain that most of what the compulsion to repeat makes the patient relive necessarily causes the ego unpleasure, since it brings out into the open the workings of repressed drive-impulses; but, as we have already seen, this is unpleasure of a kind that does not conflict with the pleasure principle, for though it constitutes unpleasure for the one system, it simultaneously constitutes gratification for the other. The new and remarkable fact that we now have to report, however, is that the compulsion to repeat *also* brings back experiences from the past that contain no potential for pleasure whatever, and which even at the time cannot have constituted gratification, not even in respect of drive-impulses that were only subsequently repressed.

The early florescence of infantile sexuality is doomed to come to nothing because a child's desires are incompatible with reality, and its physical development insufficiently advanced. Its demise is brought about in the most harrowing circumstances, and accompanied by intensely painful emotions. The loss of love and the failure that this represents leave an enduring legacy of diminished self-feeling amounting to a narcissistic scar; in my experience, as also corroborated by the findings of Marcinowski (1918), this contributes more than any other factor to the 'feeling of inferiority' so common in neurotics. Sexual exploration, necessarily circumscribed by the child's state of physical development, cannot be brought to any gratifying conclusion; hence the lament later on that 'I can't accomplish anything, I can't succeed in anything'. The child's bond of intimacy, usually with the parent of the opposite sex, is killed off by disappointment, by the vain wait for gratification, by jealousy at the birth of a sibling – an event that unambiguously demonstrates the infidelity of the loved one. The child's attempt – undertaken with tragic solemnity – to produce such a baby himself is a humiliating failure. The ever-diminishing affection shown to the child, the ever-increasing demands of his upbringing, the reprimands, the occasional punishments – all ultimately reveal to him the full measure of the rejection that it has fallen to him to suffer. There is a fairly small and regularly recurring range of ways in which the love so typical of this phase of childhood is brought to an end.

All these unwelcome circumstances and painful layers of emotion are accordingly repeated by neurotic patients in the transference process, and are brought back to life with immense ingenuity. They seek to break off the treatment in mid-stream; they contrive to rekindle their vivid sense of rejection, and to goad the physician to harsh words and a cold demeanour; they find suitable objects for their jealousy; in place of the passionately desired child of yore they offer the prospect or promise of some grandiose gift, the latter mostly just as unreal as the former had been. None of this was capable of bringing pleasure in the past – and one might reasonably suppose that it would bring less unpleasure in the present if it were to emerge in memories or dreams, rather than reconstituting itself as a lived experience. It is a question, of course, of the action of drives that were supposed to lead to gratification. However, the patient's experience of the fact that then, too, they brought unpleasure instead of gratification makes not a scrap of difference: the action is repeated regardless. The patient is driven to this by a compulsion.

The same thing that psychoanalysis makes manifest in the transference phenomena exhibited by neurotic patients can also be found in the lives of people who are *not* neurotic. In their case it takes the guise of an ineluctable fate dogging their every step, a daemonic current running through their whole existence, and from its earliest beginnings psychoanalysis has regarded such semblances of fate as being largely self-engendered, and determined by experiences in early infancy. The compulsion that reveals itself in these cases is no different from the neurotic's compulsion to repeat, even though such people have never shown the telltale signs of a neurotic conflict resolved as a result of symptom-formation. Thus we all know people whose human relationships invariably end in the same manner: benefactors who are angrily abandoned after a certain period by each of their protégés in turn, no matter how much these may otherwise differ from one another, and who thus seem destined to drink the cup of ingratitude to its bitter dregs; men whose every friendship ends in betrayal; others who in the course of their lives repeatedly elevate some individual to the status of Great Authority for themselves or even for society at large, and then in due course bring them crashing down in order to replace them by someone else; lovers whose every intimate relationship with a woman goes through the selfsame phases and leads to the selfsame outcome. We are never particularly surprised at this 'eternal recurrence of the same' when it involves *active* behaviour on the part of the individual concerned, and when we recognize the unchanging character trait that defines his being, and that necessarily finds expression in the repetition of similar experiences. We are much more strongly affected by cases where people appear to be the *passive* victim of something which they are powerless to influence, and yet which they suffer again and again in an endless repetition of the same fate. One need only think, for instance, of the story of the woman who married three men in succession, each one of whom soon fell ill and had to be nursed until finally he died.[21] The most moving poetical depiction of such a predisposition to fate is given by Tasso in his romantic epic *Gerusalemme liberata*. The hero Tancred unwittingly kills his beloved Clorinda, she having done battle with him in the armour of an enemy knight. After her burial he penetrates the strange charmed forest that so frightens the army of crusaders. There he smites a tall tree with his sword, but blood gushes from the wound, and the voice of Clorinda, whose spirit has magically entered into that very tree, accuses him of yet again doing harm to his beloved.

Taking due account of such observations of the way patients behave in the transference process and of the kinds of fate that befall people in ordinary life, we shall dare to postulate that within the psyche there really is a compulsion to repeat that pays no heed to the pleasure principle. We shall accordingly also be disposed to relate both the dreams of patients with accident-induced neurosis and the play-urge of children to this same compulsion. At the same time, though, we do need to bear in mind that only on rare occasions will we be able to catch the compulsion to repeat operating purely on its own, without the interaction of other motive forces. In the case of children's play we have already emphasized that its emergence lends itself to a variety of different interpretations. The compulsion to repeat, and the direct and pleasurable gratification of drives, seem here to interconnect with each other in an intimate mutuality. The phenomena of transference clearly serve the interests of the resistance offered by the ego, which remains bent on repression; the compulsion to repeat, which the therapy sought to divert to its own ends, is so to speak enlisted by the ego in its determination to hold fast to the pleasure principle. As for what one might term the 'fate compulsion', much of it seems on rational consideration to be comprehensible, so that we see no need to posit some new and mystical motive force behind it. The case that least arouses our suspicions is perhaps that of dreams recalling accidents; but on closer reflection one really does have to admit that in the other examples, too, the facts of the matter are not fully accounted for by the effect of the motive forces currently known to us.[22] Sufficient evidence remains to justify the hypothesis of a compulsion to repeat; and this compulsion appears to us to be more primal, more elemental, more deeply instinctual than the pleasure principle, which it simply thrusts aside. But if there is indeed such a compulsion to repeat in the psyche, then we should like to know something about it. We should like to know what function it corresponds to, what circumstances it can arise in, and what relationship it bears to the pleasure principle – to which, after all, we have hitherto attributed sole dominion over the manner in which excitational processes develop within the psyche.

IV

What now follows is speculation, often quite extravagant speculation, which readers will regard or disregard according to their own particular standpoint. For the rest, it is an attempt to follow an idea right through to its logical conclusion, undertaken out of sheer curiosity as to where this will lead.

Psychoanalytic speculation takes its impetus from the strong impression conveyed by the study of unconscious processes, that consciousness surely cannot constitute the universal character of psychic processes, but can only be one particular function of them. To express it in metapsychological terms: such speculation asserts that consciousness is the product of a particular system that it terms *Cs*. Since consciousness chiefly delivers perceptions of excitations emanating from the external world, and feelings of pleasure and unpleasure that can come only from within the psychic apparatus, a specific locus can be attributed to the *Pcpt-Cs* system:[23] it must lie at the border between the external and the internal; it must face out towards the external world, and simultaneously embrace the other psychic systems. We might note at this point that in making these suppositions we are not taking some bold new step, but are aligning ourselves with the locational hypotheses of cerebral anatomy, which places the 'seat' of consciousness in the cerebral cortex, the outermost, enveloping layer of the central organ. Cerebral anatomy has no need to devote any thought to the question of why – anatomically speaking – consciousness is located on the surface of the brain, instead of being safely lodged somewhere in its innermost recesses. Perhaps we shall help to clarify the issue by explaining this location in terms of our *Pcpt-Cs* system.

Consciousness is not the only distinctive characteristic that we are disposed to ascribe to the processes in this system. We are basing ourselves on the evidence garnered in our psychoanalytic experience when we postulate that all excitation processes occurring in the *other* systems leave lasting traces within them which form the basis of memory – residual memories, in other words, that have nothing to do with consciousness. These traces are often strongest and most enduring when the process that brought them into being never entered consciousness at all. We find it difficult to believe, however, that such lasting traces of excitation also arise in the *Pcpt-Cs* system. Were they to remain conscious, they would very soon limit the ability of the system to absorb new excitations;[24] if on the other hand they were *un*conscious, they would land us with the problem of explaining the presence of unconscious processes in a system the operation of which is otherwise characterized by the phenomenon of consciousness. We would, so to speak, have changed nothing and gained nothing by putting forward our hypothesis that consciousness belongs within a specific system. While this may not be an absolutely binding consideration, it may none the less lead us to the supposition that it is not possible within a given system for something both to enter consciousness and also to leave a memory trace. We would accordingly be able to argue that excitation processes do indeed enter consciousness within the *Cs* system, but leave no lasting trace there; and that all the traces of these processes that memory depends upon arise in the proximate inner systems to which the excitations migrate. It is in precisely these terms that I conceived the diagram included in the speculative section of my *Interpretation of Dreams* in 1900.[25] When one considers how little we know from other sources about the origins of consciousness, one is bound to give at least *some* credence to the proposition that 'consciousness arises *instead of* a memory trace'.

One might thus say that the *Cs* system has the particular distinguishing feature that excitation processes do not leave a mark in the form of an enduring alteration of its elements, as they do in all the other psychic systems, but simply evaporate, as it were, in the process of entering consciousness. Such a departure from the general rule can only be explained by some factor relevant solely to this one system, and this exclusive factor, not found in any of the other systems, could easily be the exposed location of the *Cs* system, its direct contiguity with the external world.

Let us imagine living organisms in their simplest possible form as an undifferentiated vesicle of irritable matter; its *surface*, inasmuch as it faces out towards the external world, is thus differentiated by its very position, and serves as the vesicle's receptor organ. Embryology *qua* recapitulation of evolution really does show, moreover, that the central nervous system develops from the ectoderm; and the grey cerebral cortex remains a derivative of the primordial outer surface, and may well have inherited some of its essential attributes. It is therefore easily conceivable that by dint of constant bombardment of the vesicle's outer surface by external stimuli, the substance of the cell becomes permanently altered down to a certain depth, with the result that excitation occurs differently in this surface layer from the way it occurs in the deeper layers. A cortex would thus form that ultimately becomes so tempered by the effect of the stimuli that it becomes perfectly adapted to their reception and becomes incapable of further modification. Applying this analogy to the *Cs* system, it would mean that the latter's elements cannot undergo any enduring change as a result of the excitation passing through it, since they are already modified to the fullest possible extent in terms of this particular process. But they *do* now have the capability to allow consciousness to come into being. What exactly constitutes this modification of both the matter itself and the excitation process taking place within it, is open to a variety of conjectures, none of which is currently susceptible of being properly tested. We can suppose that in passing from one element to the other the excitation has to overcome a resistance, and that it is precisely in dissipating this resistance that the excitation lays down an enduring trace ('path-making'[26]); and we can further suppose that in the *Cs* system there no longer exists any such resistance to the transition from one element to another. We can link this notion to Breuer's distinction between *quiescent* (i.e. already annexed[27]) and *free-moving* cathectic energy within the elements of psychic systems;[28]

on this basis, the elements of the *Cs* system would not carry any energy that is already annexed, but only such as is readily available for release. But I rather think that for the time being it is better to speak of these things only in the most general terms. In speculating thus we have at least perhaps established some kind of connection between the origins of consciousness and both the location of the *Cs* system, and the particular characteristics of the excitation process that are attributable to that system.

There are other matters that we still need to discuss with regard to the above-mentioned living vesicle with its stimulus-receiving cortical layer. This tiny piece of living matter floats around in an external world charged with energies of the most powerful kind, and would be destroyed by their stimulative effect if it were not equipped with some form of *protection* against stimulation. It acquires this protection by virtue of the fact that its outermost surface abandons the structure proper to living things, becomes to all intents and purposes inorganic, and in consequence operates as a special covering or membrane impeding the stimuli; that is to say, it allows only a fraction of the external energies' intensity to pass through it to the layers immediately beyond, which remain fully organic. These latter, safe behind their protective screen, can now devote themselves to receiving the reduced levels of stimuli that are thus allowed through. The outer layer becomes necrotic – but by doing so it protects all the deeper-lying ones from suffering a similar fate, at any rate so long as the stimuli do not bombard it with such force that they break through the protective barrier. For the living organism, the process *protecting* it against stimuli is almost more important than the process whereby it *receives* stimuli; the protective barrier is equipped with its own store of energy, and must above all seek to defend the particular transformations of energy at work within it against the assimilative and hence destructive influence of the enormously powerful energies at work outside it. The process of receiving stimuli chiefly serves the purpose of determining the direction and nature of the external stimuli, and for that it must clearly be sufficient to take small specimens from the external world, to sample it in tiny quantities. In highly developed organisms the stimulus-receiving cortical layer of the erstwhile vesicle has long since retreated into the inner depths of the body, but parts of it have remained on the surface immediately beneath the general protective barrier. These are the sense organs, which essentially are equipped to register the effects of specific stimuli, but also include special devices to provide additional protection against excessively high levels of stimulation, and to exclude unsuitable types of stimulus. It is characteristic of them that they process only very small quantities of the external stimulus; they merely take samples of the external world. One can perhaps compare them to feelers that reach out tentatively towards the external world and then repeatedly draw back.

At this point I shall venture to touch very briefly on a topic that would merit the most thorough consideration. As a result of certain insights afforded to us by psychoanalysis, Kant's dictum that time and space are necessary forms of human thought is today very much open to debate. We have come to appreciate that unconscious psychic processes are in themselves 'timeless'. This primarily means that they are not temporally ordered; that time does not alter them in any way; and that the notion of time cannot be applied to them. These are negative attributes that we can only clearly discern by means of a comparison with *conscious* psychic processes. Indeed, our abstract notion of time seems to be altogether derived from the *modus operandi* of the *Pcpt-Cs* system, and to be equivalent to its perception of itself. Given that the system functions in this way, the protection process may well follow a quite different path. I realize that the ensuing propositions sound very obscure, but I must confine myself here to mere suggestions of this sort.

We argued just now that the living vesicle is equipped with a barrier protecting it against stimuli in the external world. Prior to that we established that the cortical layer immediately beneath this barrier must be differentiated in such a way as to receive stimuli from the outside. However, this sensitive cortical layer, which later becomes the *Cs* system, also receives excitation from within. The location of this system between the outside and the inside, and the difference between the conditions determining the penetration achieved by the one side and those determining the penetration achieved by the other, become decisive for the performance of the system and indeed of the entire psychic apparatus. There is a protective barrier *vis-à-vis* the *outside*, so that any quanta of excitation arriving from that quarter can exert their effect only on a much reduced scale. But no such protection is possible *vis-à-vis* the *inside*: the excitations that come from the deeper layers carry over into the system directly and without diminution, whereby certain features of their mode of progression generate successive sensations of pleasure and/or unpleasure. It is true that, given their type of intensity and other qualitative characteristics (possibly also their amplitude), the excitations coming from within are going to be better suited to the *modus operandi* of the system than the barrage of stimuli coming from the external world. But two things are decisively determined by these circumstances; first, the fact that the sensations of pleasure and unpleasure – which are an index of processes going on *within* the psychic apparatus – take precedence over all *external* stimuli; second, a response-pattern tending to counter those inner excitations that bring about an excessive increase in unpleasure. A tendency inevitably emerges to treat them as if they came from without rather than from within, in order to be able to deploy the protective barrier's defensive capabilities against them. This is the origin of *projection*, which plays such a major role in the causation of pathological processes.

I have the sense that while these latter reflections may have given us a clearer understanding of the dominant role of the pleasure principle, we have not managed to cast any light on those cases that defy it. Let us therefore go a step further. We may use the term *traumatic* to describe those excitations from outside that are strong enough to break through the protective barrier; in my view the notion of 'trauma' cries out to be applied to such a case given that the resistance to stimuli is normally so effective. An event such as external trauma will doubtless provoke a massive disturbance in the organism's energy system, and mobilize all available defence mechanisms. In the process, however, the pleasure principle is put into abeyance. It is no longer possible to prevent the psychic apparatus from being flooded by large quanta of stimulation; instead a quite different challenge presents itself: to assert control over the stimuli; to psychically annex the quanta of stimulation that have burst in, and then proceed to dispose of them.

The *specific* unpleasure of the physical pain experienced probably results from the fact that the protective barrier has been penetrated over a very small area. From this one point on the periphery a continuous stream of excitations floods into the central apparatus of the psyche, such as can normally come only from *within* the apparatus itself.[29] And how can we expect the psyche to react to this invasion? Cathectic energy is summoned up from all sides in order to create appropriately large cathexes in the area where the breach occurred. A massive 'counter-cathexis' is brought into being, for the sake of which all the other psychic systems are deprived of their energy, with the result that general psychic activity is extensively paralysed or diminished. We aim to learn from such examples, we aim to use them as models on which to base our metapsychological suppositions. We therefore conclude from this particular response-pattern that a system that is itself highly cathected is capable of taking in a whole stream of new energy and converting it into quiescent cathexis, thus psychically 'annexing' it. The more powerful the system's own quiescent cathexis, the greater its annexative power would seem to be; and conversely, the less powerful the cathexis, the less the system is going to be capable of taking in a stream of energy from outside, and the more violent the consequences of such a breach of the protective barrier must necessarily be. It would not be a valid objection to this hypothesis to argue that the increase in cathexis around the point of entry could far more easily be explained in terms of a direct dispersal of the incoming quanta of excitation. If that were the case, then of course the psychic apparatus would simply experience an increase in its energy-cathexes, and both the paralysing nature of the pain and the depletion of all the other systems would remain unexplained. The very powerful release effects of pain do not detract from our explanation either, for they occur reflexively, that is to say, they happen without any prompting from the psychic apparatus.

Needless to say, the haziness of all these deliberations of ours, which we term metapsychological, derives from the fact that we know absolutely nothing about the nature of the excitation process within the elements of the various psychic systems, and do not feel justified in forming any hypothesis on the matter; we thus constantly operate with a massive unknown quantity 'x', which we carry with us into every new formula that we propose. It is reasonable to assume that this process takes place with energies that differ *quantitatively* from each other, and it seems probable that there are also *qualitative* differences (for instance in the *type* of a given amplitude). A new possibility that we have taken into consideration is Breuer's prop-osition that *two* kinds of energy charge are involved, such that a distinction may be drawn between two different forms of cathexis of the psychic systems (or their elements): a quiescent form, and one that is free-flowing and constantly pressing for release. We might reasonably suspect that the 'annexing' of the energy flooding into the psychic apparatus consists in its being transferred from the free-flowing to the quiescent state.

I believe we can reasonably venture to regard ordinary traumatic neurosis as resulting from an extensive breach of the protective barrier. This would appear to reinstate the old, naïve 'shock' theory, seemingly at the expense of a later and psychologically more sophisti-cated one that sees the key aetiological factor not in the direct impact of the mechanical violence itself, but in the element of fright and in the threat to life. These contrasting perspectives are not irreconcil-able, however, and the psychoanalytic view of traumatic neurosis is not identical to the shock theory in its crudest form. Whereas for the latter the essential thing about the shock is that it directly damages the molecular or even the histological structure of the nerve elements, we for our part seek to understand its effects in terms of the breaching of the protective barrier around the psyche, and the new challenges that this gives rise to. For us, too, fright remains an important factor. Fright can occur only in the absence of a state of apprehensiveness,[30] a state that would bring with it a hypercathexis of the systems that initially receive the extra stimu-lation. Because of the lower level of cathexis that this absence entails, the systems are not adequately primed to annex the quanta of excitation that now supervene, and so the consequences of the breaching of the protective barrier make themselves felt that much more easily. We thus find that apprehensiveness, together with the attendant hypercathexis of the receiving systems, constitutes the last line of defence of the protective barrier. Across quite a broad range of traumas, the outcome may well depend on whether the relevant systems are primed (by virtue of hypercathexis) or unprimed; though this factor is probably no longer of any importance once the trauma has reached a certain level of intensity. Under the dominion of the pleasure principle, it is the function of dreams to make a reality of wish-fulfilment, albeit on a hallucinatory basis; but the purposes of wish-fulfilment are certainly not being served by the dreams of patients with accident-induced neurosis when they thrust them back – as they so regularly do – into the original trauma situation. We may reasonably assume, however, that such dreams are thereby contributing to a quite different task that has to be completed before the pleasure principle can begin to prevail. These dreams seek to assert control over the stimuli *retrospectively* by generating fear – the absence of which was the cause of the traumatic neurosis in the first place. They thus afford us a clear view of a function of the psyche which, without contradicting the pleasure principle, is none the less independent of it, and appears to be more primal than the objective of gaining pleasure and avoiding unpleasure.

This might be an appropriate point, therefore, to acknowledge for the first time that there is an exception to the proposition that dreams are a form of wish-fulfilment. Fear-based dreams[31] do *not* constitute such an exception, as I have repeatedly and exhaustively demonstrated, and nor do 'punishment dreams', for these simply replace the forbidden wish-fulfilment with the punishment appropriate to it, and thus represent the wish-fulfilment of the individual's guilty conscience in its reaction to the drive that has been rejected. But the above-mentioned dreams of patients with accident-induced neurosis can no longer be viewed in terms of wish-fulfilment, and nor can those dreams, familiar to us from psychoanalysis, that bring back memories of the psychic traumas of childhood. Instead they obey the compulsion to repeat, though of course this is reinforced in analysis by the wish – itself strongly encouraged by 'suggestion' – to summon up all that has been forgotten and repressed. We might therefore also suppose that it was not the *original* function of dreams to dispel the forces tending to interrupt sleep by fulfilling the wishes of the impulses causing the disruption; dreams were able to acquire this function only *after* the entire psyche had accepted the dominion of the pleasure principle. If there is indeed a prior realm 'beyond the pleasure principle', then it is only logical to allow that there must likewise have been a prior era before dreams developed their predisposition to wish-fulfilment. This is not to gainsay their subsequent function. But as soon as we accept that this predisposition is capable of being breached, a further question arises: dreams such as these that enact the compulsion to repeat in furtherance of the psychic annexing of traumatic experiences – can they not also occur *outside* analysis? The answer to this question is emphatically 'yes'.

With regard to 'war neuroses', in so far as this term signifies more than simply a reference to the circumstances in which the condition arose, I have already argued elsewhere that they could very well be traumatic neuroses facilitated by an ego conflict.[32] The aforementioned fact that the chances of a neurosis arising are less when the trauma simultaneously causes a gross physical injury (see above, p. 50) no longer seems incomprehensible when we bear in mind two circumstances highlighted by psychoanalytic research: first, the fact that mechanical jolts and vibrations have to be acknowledged as one of the sources of sexual excitation (cf. the remarks on the effects of swings and of railway travel in *Three Essays on Sexual Theory*, 1905); and second, the fact that throughout their duration, painful and feverish illnesses exert a powerful effect on the distribution of the libido. Thus it may well be the case that while the mechanical violence of the trauma unleashes a quantum of sexual excitation which in the absence of a state of apprehensiveness is potentially traumatic in its effect, the simultaneous physical injury annexes the excessive excitation by making use of a narcissistic hypercathexis of the affected organ (see *On the Introduction of Narcissism*, p. 11). It is also a well-known fact – though one insufficiently taken into account in the development of the libido theory – that even such severe disruption of libido distribution as occurs in melancholia is put into abeyance by intercurrent organic illness; indeed, under the same conditions even a fully developed dementia praecox is capable of temporary regression.

V

The fact that the stimulus-receiving cortical layer lacks any shield protecting it against excitations from within must presumably mean that these stimuli acquire greater economic importance, and often give rise to economic dysfunctions, which are equatable with traumatic neuroses. The most abundant sources of such excitation from within are the organism's so-called drives, which represent all those manifestations of energy that originate in the inner depths of the body and are transmitted to the psychic apparatus – and which are themselves the most important and the most inscrutable element of psychological research.

We shall perhaps not think it too bold to suppose that the impulses deriving from the drives adhere not to the 'annexed' type of nervous process, but rather to the type that is free-flowing and constantly pressing for release. The best information we possess concerning these processes comes from our study of dream-work. We found that the processes in the unconscious systems are fundamentally different from those in the (pre-)conscious ones; that within the unconscious, cathexes can easily be completely transferred, displaced, compressed – something that could only produce flawed results if applied to pre-conscious material, and indeed for that very reason produces the familiar peculiarities of manifest dreams, the pre-conscious residua of the preceding day having been processed according to the laws of the unconscious. I termed this kind of process in the unconscious the 'primary' psychic process, in contradistinction to the 'secondary' process that obtains in our normal waking life. As the drive-impulses all act on our *unconscious* systems, it is scarcely a new departure to assert that they follow the primary process, and it is also no very great step to identify the primary psychic process with Breuer's 'free-flowing' cathexis, and the secondary one with his 'annexed' or 'tonic' cathexis.[33] This would then mean that it was the task of the higher echelons of the psychic apparatus to annex excitations originating from the drives and reaching it via the primary process. Any failure of this annexion process would bring about a dysfunction analogous to traumatic neurosis. Only when the annexion has taken place would the pleasure principle (or, once the latter has been duly modified, the reality principle)[34] be able to assert its dominion unhindered. In the meantime, however, the psychic apparatus's other task of controlling or annexing the excitation would be very much to the fore – not, it is true, in opposition to the pleasure principle, but independently of it, and to some extent quite heedless of it.

The manifestations of a compulsion to repeat that we have described with respect to the early activities of the infant psyche, and also with respect to our experiences in the course of psychoanalytic practice, plainly bear the stamp of drives, and wherever they are in opposition to the pleasure principle they equally plainly exhibit their daemonic character.[35] In the case of children's play it seems readily comprehensible to us that the child also repeats *un*pleasurable experiences, because by thus being active he gains far more thorough-going control of the relevant powerful experience than was possible when he was merely its passive recipient. Each new repetition seems to add to the sense of command that the child strives for; and in the case of pleasurable experiences, too, the child never tires of repeating them, and will be implacable in insisting that every experience is identical to the first. This trait is destined to disappear later on: a joke will fall flat at the second time of hearing; a play will never again make the same impression that it did on first viewing; indeed it would be difficult to get an adult to re-read a much-enjoyed book until considerable time had elapsed. Novelty will always be the precondition of enjoyment. The child, however, will never tire of requiring adults to repeat a game that they showed him or played with him, until they refuse out of sheer exhaustion. And once anyone has told him a nice story, he wants to hear the same story again and again rather than a new one; he implacably insists that every repetition be exactly the same; and he corrects every least change that the story-teller misguidedly incorporates, perhaps fondly imagining it will gain him extra kudos. In this, the pleasure principle is not being contradicted; it is evident that the repetition, the replication of the original experience in identical terms, itself represents a source of pleasure. In the case of analysis, on the other hand, it becomes clear that the compulsion to repeat the events of infancy in the transference process flouts the pleasure principle in *every* way. The patient behaves in a completely infantile manner, and thus shows us that the repressed memory traces of his primal experiences are not in an annexed state, indeed are to all intents and purposes incapable of secondary processing. It is this non-annexed state, moreover, that accounts for their ability to form a wish-fantasy[36] by latching on to the residua of the day, a fantasy that finds expression in dreams. The same compulsion to repeat very often confronts us as an obstacle to therapy when at the end of a patient's course of treatment we seek to bring about his complete disattachment from the physician; and we may reasonably suppose that the turbid fear of patients unfamiliar with analysis, who shrink from reawakening something that in their view is best left dormant, essentially reflects their dread of seeing this daemonic compulsion make its appearance.[37]

But what is the nature of the connection between the realm of the drives and the compulsion to repeat? At this point we cannot help thinking that we have managed to identify a universal attribute of drives – and perhaps of *all* organic life – that has not hitherto been clearly recognized, or at any rate not explicitly emphasized. A drive might accordingly be seen as *a powerful tendency inherent in every living organism to restore a prior state*, which prior state the organism was compelled to relinquish due to the disruptive influence of external forces; we can see it as a kind of organic elasticity, or, if we prefer, as a manifestation of inertia in organic life.[38]

This conception of drives sounds strange, for we have become accustomed to seeing drives as the key factor pressing for change and development, and now we are supposed to see them as the direct opposite: as the expression of the *conservative* nature of organic life. On the other hand it doesn't take us very long to think of examples in the animal world that seem to confirm that drives are indeed historically determined. When certain kinds of fish undertake arduous journeys at spawning time in order to lay their eggs in particular waters, far from their normal habitat, then in the view of numerous biologists they are simply returning to the previous domain of their species, which, in the course of time, they have exchanged for others. The same is said to apply to the migration of birds; but we have no need to search around for further examples once we remember that the phenomena of heritability and the facts of embryology offer us the most spectacular proofs of the existence of an organic compulsion to repeat. We see how in the course of its development the embryo of any existing animal is compelled to repeat – albeit in the most fleeting and abbreviated way – the structures of all the forms from which the animal is descended, instead of hurrying by the shortest route to its definitive shape; and given that we can explain this behaviour scarcely at all in *mechanical* terms, we have no call to disregard the *historical* explanation. And we similarly find a reproductive faculty extending far into the higher echelons of the animal kingdom whereby a lost organ is replaced through the creation of a new one altogether identical to it.

Some consideration must doubtless be given to the evident objection that as well as the conservative drives that compel repetition, there may also be others that press for new forms and for progress; indeed, we shall take account of this objection later in our discussions. But in the meantime we may find it enticing to pursue the hypothesis that 'all drives seek to restore a prior state' right through to its logical conclusion. While the outcome of this might seem airy-fairy or reminiscent of the mystical, we are none the less confident in the knowledge that no one can accuse us of *intending* such an outcome. We seek the sober results of research or of reflections founded on research, and we seek to impart to these results no other quality but that of reliability.[39]

If, then, all organic drives are conservative, historically acquired, and predisposed to regression and the restoration of prior states, we must accordingly ascribe the achievements of organic development to external influences and their disruptive and distracting effects. On this view, the elementary organism did not start out with any desire to change, and given the continuance of the same circumstances would have constantly repeated the selfsame life-cycle; but in the final analysis, so the argument goes, it must be the developmental history of our planet and its relationship to the sun that has left its imprint for us to behold in the development of organisms. The conservative organic drives have assimilated every one of these externally imposed modifications of the organism's life-cycle and duly preserved them in order to repeat them, and therefore inevitably give the misleading impression of being forces bent on change and progress, whereas they merely seek to achieve an old goal by new means as well as old. And this ultimate goal of all organic striving may be equally susceptible of definition. It would contradict the conservative nature of drives if it were the goal of life to achieve a state never previously attained to. Rather, it must aspire to an *old* state, a primordial state from which it once departed, and to which via all the circuitous byways of development it strives to return. If we may reasonably suppose, on the basis of all our experience without exception, that every living thing dies – reverts to the inorganic – for *intrinsic* reasons, then we can only say that *the goal of all life is death*, or to express it retrospectively: *the inanimate existed before the animate*.

At some point or other, the attributes of life were aroused in non-living matter by the operation upon it of a force that we are still quite incapable of imagining. Perhaps it was a process similar in essence to the one that later, at a certain level of living matter, gave rise to consciousness. The tension generated at that point in previously inanimate matter sought to achieve equilibrium; thus the first drive came into existence: the drive to return to the inanimate. At that stage death was still easy for living matter; the course of life that had to be gone through was probably short, its direction determined by the newly created organism's chemical structure. In this way living matter may have experienced a long period of continual re-creation and easy death, until decisive external factors changed in such a way that they compelled still-surviving matter to take ever greater diversions from its original course of life and ever more complex detours in achieving its death-goal. These detours on the path to death, all faithfully preserved by the conservative drives, may well be what gives us our present picture of the phenomena of life. If one holds fast to the notion that the drives are exclusively conservative in nature, one cannot arrive at any other logical postulates concerning the origin and goal of life.

These conclusions may seem disturbing, but so too is the picture that emerges in respect of the great groups of drives that we posit behind the vital phenomena of organisms. The theory that there are drives directed at self-preservation, drives that we ascribe to all living beings, stands in striking opposition to the hypothesis that the entire life of the drives serves to procure death. Considered in this light, the theoretical significance of the drives concerned with self-preservation, self-assertion and dominance diminishes greatly. They are indeed 'partial' drives,[40] charged with the task of safeguarding the organism's own particular path to death and barring all possible means of return to the inorganic other than those already immanent; but the baffling notion of the organism striving to endure in defiance of the entire world – a notion incapable of being fitted into any sensible nexus – simply evaporates. The fact that remains is that the organism wants only to die in its own particular way; and so these guardians of life, too, were originally myrmidons of death.[41] Thus arises the paradox that the living organism resists in the most energetic way external influences ('dangers') that could help it to take a short cut to its life's goal (to short-circuit the system, as it were); but it is precisely this sort of behaviour that characterizes purely drive-engendered strivings as against those of intelligence.

But if we really think about it, this cannot be true! Things take on a quite different aspect in the light of the sexual drives, to which neurosis theory has attached particular importance. Not *all* organisms have yielded to the external pressure impelling them to ever greater development. Many have succeeded in remaining at their own lowly level right into the present time; indeed, there are many living things still in existence today that must resemble, if not all, then at least many of the early stages in the development of the higher animals and plants. And by the same token, not *all* the individual organic elements that make up the complex body of a higher organism stay with it throughout the entire course of its development to the point of natural death. Some of them, the germ-cells, probably retain the original structure of living matter, and after a certain period they separate off from the organism, carrying with them the full gamut of inherited and newly acquired drives. It is perhaps precisely these two characteristics that enable these cells to have an independent life. Given favourable circumstances, they begin to develop, i.e. they repeat the game to which they owe their own existence, and the outcome of this is that one portion of their matter continues its development right through to the end, while another reverts once more to the beginnings of the development process as a new germ particle. These germ-cells thus work in opposition to the death of living matter, and succeed in giving it what in our eyes must seem like potential immortality, while in reality perhaps signifying merely an extension of the dying process. We attach the greatest possible significance to the fact that the germ-cell acquires the strength, not to say the actual ability to achieve this feat only by merging with another germ-cell similar to it and yet different.

The drives that take charge of the destiny of these organic elements that outlive the larger entity, keep them safe while they are vulnerable to the stimuli of the external world, and bring about their encounter with the other germ-cells – these constitute the group termed sexual drives. They are conservative in the same sense that the others are in that they reincorporate previous states of the relevant living matter, only to a more marked degree inasmuch as they show themselves to be particularly resistant to external influences; and they are also conservative in a further sense, since they preserve life itself for longer periods.[42] They constitute the true life-drives; and the fact that they act *against* the intent of the other drives, an intent that by its very nature conduces to death, points to a conflict between them and the rest, the importance of which was recognized very early on by neurosis theory. It amounts to a kind of fluctuating rhythm within the life of organisms: one group of drives goes storming ahead in order to attain the ultimate goal of life at the earliest possible moment, another goes rushing back at a certain point along the way in order to do part of it all over again and thus prolong the journey. But even though sexuality and gender differentiation were assuredly not present when life began, it none the less remains possible that the drives that subsequently merited the term 'sexual' were active from the very beginning, and that it was *not* only at some later stage that they began to counter the antics of the 'ego drives'.[43]

Let us go back for a moment ourselves and ask whether all these speculations are not perhaps entirely baseless. Are there really no other drives *apart from the sexual drives* that seek to restore a prior state, nor others again that strive for a state never previously attained to? I know of no reliable example in the organic world that contradicts the picture that we have suggested. There seems to be no clear evidence of a universal drive favouring higher development within the animal and plant worlds, even though it remains an undisputed fact that developments do in fact proceed in that direction. But for one thing, it is in many cases merely a matter of subjective judgement when we declare one level of development to be 'higher' than some other; and for another thing, biology shows us that higher development in one particular respect is very often paid for or balanced out by regression in another. Moreover, there are plenty of animal forms whose early stages clearly reveal that they have developed regressively rather than progressively. Higher development and regression might both be the result of the pressure to adapt exerted by external forces, and the role of the drives might be limited in both cases to the task of assimilating the imposed change as an inner source of pleasure.[44]

Many of us, too, may find it difficult to abandon the belief that there is in mankind itself an inherent drive towards perfection that has brought human beings to their present high level of intellectual attainment and ethical sublimation, and that can be relied on to ensure their further development to the status of *Übermensch*. For my own part, however, I do not believe in any such inner drive, and can see no way of salvaging this agreeable illusion. The development of mankind thus far appears to me to call for no other explanation than that applicable to animals; and the restless urge for ever greater perfection that we observe in a minority of individual human beings can readily be understood as resulting from the repression of drives – the foundation on which all that is most precious in human civilization is built. The repressed drive never abandons its struggle to achieve full gratification, which would consist in the repetition of a primary gratification experience. All the sublimations and reaction-formations and surrogate-formations in the world are never enough to resolve the abiding tension; and the gulf between the level of gratificatory pleasure *demanded* and the level actually *achieved* produces that driving force that prevents the individual from resting content with any situation he ever contrives, and instead – as the poet says – he 'presses ever onward unbridled, untamed' (Mephisto in *Faust* I, 'Faust's Study'). The way back, the way to full gratification, is usually blocked by the resistances that keep the repressions fully active, and there is accordingly no alternative but to proceed in the one direction still available, namely that of development – though without any prospect of bringing the process to a conclusion and attaining the desired goal. The pattern of events during the formation of a neurotic phobia (which is nothing other than an attempt to evade the gratification of a drive) offers us a model exemplifying the genesis of this seeming 'drive for perfection', which, however, we cannot possibly attribute to *all* individual human beings. The dynamic conditions for the phenomenon are indeed universally present, but the economic circumstances appear to favour it only in rare cases.

However, we would draw attention here, albeit very briefly, to the fact that, having rejected the 'perfection drive', we can probably find a replacement in the striving of Eros to concentrate organic matter in ever larger units.[45] Taken in conjunction with the effects of repression, it could well account for the phenomena attributed to the 'perfection drive'.

VI

There are no doubt many respects in which we ourselves are going to feel dissatisfied with our conclusions thus far, which posit a sharp contrast between the 'ego drives' and the sexual drives, and argue that the former are bent on death, the latter on the continuation of life. Furthermore, it was really only the *former* that we could claim showed the conservative character of drives or – better – their regressive character, corresponding to the compulsion to repeat. For according to our hypothesis, the ego drives arise when inanimate matter becomes animate, and set out to restore the inanimate state. In the case of the sexual drives, on the other hand, they clearly *do* reproduce the primitive states of the organism – but the goal they strive for with all the means at their disposal is the merging of two germ-cells that are differentiated in a particular way. If this union does not come about, then the germ-cell dies, just like all the other elements of multicellular organisms. Only in this one circumstance can the sexual function extend life and confer upon it a semblance of immortality. But what important event in the developmental history of living matter is being repeated by sexual reproduction or by its precursor, the conjugation of two individual organisms amongst the protista? We do not know the answer to this question, and would therefore find it a considerable relief if our entire theory were to prove wrong. The antithesis of ego drives (death drives) and sexual drives (life drives) would then lose all validity, and at the same time the compulsion to repeat would lose the significance that we have attached to it.

Let us therefore go back to one of the postulates woven into our argument, in the confident expectation that it will lend itself to complete rebuttal. We based a whole variety of conclusions on the presupposition that all living matter dies for reasons that are *intrinsic* to it. We made this assumption so blithely because it does not appear to us to *be* an assumption. It is our habit of mind to think in these terms, and the habit is reinforced by our poets and playwrights. Perhaps we have decided to embrace this belief because it brings us comfort. If we are to die ourselves, having first lost to death all those most dear to us, then we prefer to succumb to an implacable law of nature, the majestic Ἀνάγχη ['necessity'], rather than to a chance event that might well have proved avoidable. But perhaps this belief that death has its own intrinsic logic is simply one of the illusions we have created for ourselves in order to be able to 'bear the heavy burden of existence'.[46] It is certainly not primal: the idea of 'natural death' is alien to primitive peoples, who attribute every death that occurs amongst them to the influence of an enemy or an evil spirit. To investigate this belief, therefore, let us turn without further ado to biological science.

Once we do so, however, we are entitled to feel astonished at how little agreement there is amongst biologists on the question of 'natural death', indeed at the way the whole concept of death loses all substance the moment they touch it. The fact that, in the case of the higher animals at least, there is a distinct average lifespan does, of course, tend to support the notion that death occurs for intrinsic reasons; but this impression is cancelled out again by the circumstance that individual large animals and giant trees reach a very great age that we are as yet unable to calculate. According to Wilhelm Fliess's grand conception, all the vital phenomena of an organism – and doubtless its death as well – are tied to the fulfilling of a specific timescale that expresses the dependence of two living substances, one male, one female, on the solar year. But when we look at how easily and how extensively external factors can influence the timing of physiological events in plants in particular, accelerating or delaying them, we see a picture that is sharply at variance with the rigidity of Fliess's formulae, and at the very least raises doubts as to whether the laws he postulates do indeed reign supreme.

In our view, the most interesting treatment of the topic of the lifespan and death of organisms is to be found in the publications of August Weismann (1882, 1884, 1892 etc.). It was Weismann who proposed the differentiation of living matter into two parts: the mortal and the immortal. The mortal part is the body in the narrower sense of the word, the 'soma'; it alone is subject to natural death. The germ-cells, however, are potentially immortal inasmuch as they are capable under certain favourable conditions of developing into a new individual, or – to put it another way – of enveloping themselves with a new soma.[47]

What is truly fascinating here is the unexpected similarity of this to the view that we ourselves arrived at by such a very different route. Weismann, who looks at living matter in morphological terms, discerns in it one part that is doomed to die – the soma, the entire body *except* the element concerned with sexuality and heredity – and another that is immortal, precisely this latter element, the germ-plasm, that serves to preserve the species by reproducing it. We for our part focused not on living matter itself but on the forces at work within it, and this led us to identify two different kinds of drives: those that seek to guide life towards death; and others, the sexual drives, that continually seek and achieve the *renewal* of life. This sounds very much like a dynamic corollary to Weismann's morphological theory.

However, all sense of a basic concurrence of views immediately evaporates once we take note of Weismann's position on the problem of death. For in Weismann's view the distinction between mortal soma and immortal germ-plasm is applicable only to multicellular organisms, while in unicellular organisms the specific individual and the reproductive cell remain one and the same.[48] He therefore declares unicellular organisms to be potentially immortal, death only entering the picture with the metazoa, i.e. multicellular organisms. While the death of these higher organisms is indeed a natural one in his view, that is to say a death arising from inherent factors, it does not rest upon a primal attribute of living matter,[49] and therefore cannot be regarded as an absolute necessity grounded in the very essence of organic life.[50] He sees it instead as a purely functional device, a phenomenon reflecting adaptation to the external conditions of life:

once the body-cells separated into soma and germ-cells, it would have been a functionally quite inappropriate luxury if the individual had carried on having an unlimited lifespan. As soon as this differentiation took place in multicellular organisms, death became possible and functionally appropriate. Ever since then the soma of higher organisms has died after a certain span of time due to inherent factors, whereas the protista have remained immortal. Reproduction, on the other hand, did not appear only when death did, but instead is for Weismann a primal attribute of living matter, just like growth, out of which indeed it arose, and life has accordingly been continuous right from its very beginnings on earth.[51]

It will be readily appreciated that our own argument gains very little from the fact that Weismann grants that the higher organisms die a natural death. If death is a late acquisition on the part of living beings, then there can no longer be any question of death drives that date from the very beginning of organic life. In this scenario, multicellular organisms may well still die due to inherent factors, be it shortcomings in their differentiation or imperfections in their metabolism – but this is wholly irrelevant to the question that concerns us. It is surely the case, too, that this sort of view, and this sort of explanation of the origins of death, are much closer to people's customary way of seeing things than the discomfiting theory of 'death drives'.

The debate prompted by Weismann's propositions did not in my judgement decide the issue either one way or the other.[52] Some authors reverted to the position taken by Goette (1883), who regarded death as the direct consequence of reproduction. Hartmann does not characterize death in terms of the supervention of a 'corpse', of a portion of living matter that has become dead, but instead defines death as the 'conclusion of individual development'. In this sense, the protozoa are mortal too; in their case death is always coincident with reproduction, but is masked as it were by the latter, in that the entire substance of the parent organism can be transferred directly into the individual offspring.[53]

Researchers soon turned their attention to testing the alleged immortality of living matter by means of experiments on unicellular organisms. An American, Woodruff, started to breed a ciliate infusorium, a 'slipper animalcule', which reproduces by dividing into two new individual organisms, and followed it right through to the 3,029th generation before breaking off the experiment, each time isolating one of the two products of the division process and putting it into fresh fluid. The remote descendant of the first animalcule was just as vigorous as its ancestor, without any signs of ageing or degeneration; the hypothesis of the immortality of the protista thus appeared to be susceptible of experimental proof, assuming that figures of this order can be deemed conclusive.[54]

Other researchers came to other conclusions. In contradistinction to Woodruff, it was found by Maupas, Calkins and others that after a certain number of divisions these infusoria, too, become weaker, diminish in size, lose part of their organic structure, and ultimately die, unless they are revitalized by certain influences acting upon them. According to this view, the protozoa die after a period of senile decay just as the higher animals do – which directly contradicts the assertions of Weismann, who sees death as an attribute acquired by living organisms only relatively late in their evolution.

From this whole body of research we would single out for special emphasis two particular facts which appear to support our argument.

First: if, at a point before they exhibit signs of senescence, two animalcules are able to coalesce with each other, to 'conjugate' – after which in due course they separate again – then they remain unaffected by age; they have become 'rejuvenated'. This conjugation is surely the precursor of sexual reproduction in the higher animals; at this stage, however, it has nothing to do with propagation, but is limited simply to the merging of the respective individuals' living matter (Weismann's 'amphimixis'). But the rejuvenating effect of conjugation can also be achieved by other means: use of certain stimulative agents, changes in the composition of the nutrient fluid, increase in temperature, or shaking. One is reminded of the famous experiment undertaken by J[acques] Loeb, who by the use of certain chemical stimuli induced segmentation in the eggs of sea-urchins – a process that normally occurs only after fertilization.

Second: it *does* seem altogether probable that the infusoria proceed via their own life-processes to a natural death, for the contradiction between Woodruff's results and those of others derives from the fact that Woodruff put each new generation in fresh nutrient fluid. When he tried *not* doing so, he observed the same senescence across the generations as the other researchers did. He concluded that the animalcules must be damaged by the metabolic products given off into the surrounding fluid, and was then able to demonstrate convincingly that it is only the products of their *own* metabolism that have this lethal effect. For when placed in a solution supersaturated with the waste products of a less closely related species, these same animalcules that would surely have perished if massed in their own nutrient fluid flourished in a quite remarkable way. Left to itself, therefore, an infusorium dies a natural death because it does not satisfactorily dispose of the products of its own metabolism; but perhaps all the higher animals also die essentially because of the same deficiency.

We might begin to doubt at this point whether it was at all helpful to try to resolve the question of 'natural death' by reference to the study of protozoa. The primitive structure of these organisms may conceal from us certain features which, though present in them too, are actually *observable* only in the higher animals, where they have found morphological expression. If we shift from a morphological to a dynamic standpoint, then we can regard it as a matter of complete indifference whether or not the protozoa can be said to die a natural death. In their case the matter identified as being immortal at some later point has not yet separated off in any way whatever from the part that is mortal. The drives that seek to convert life into death could easily be at work from the very beginning in them too, and yet their effect could be so well masked by the effect of the life-preserving forces that it becomes extremely difficult to demonstrate their presence. As we have discovered, the biologists' observations *do* allow us to suppose that such inner processes conducing to death may be present in the protista as well. Even if the protista prove to be immortal in Weismann's sense, however, his assertion that death is an attribute acquired at a relatively late stage applies only to the physical *manifestations* of death, and does not rule out hypotheses about *processes* doing all they can to bring about death.

Our expectation that biology would simply scupper the notion of death drives thus turns out to be unfounded. We can continue to entertain the possibility of such drives, assuming we have other grounds for doing so. Furthermore, the striking similarity between Weismann's soma/germ-plasm distinction and our own differentiation of death drives and life drives not only still exists, but has regained all its relevance.

Let us dwell for a moment on this exquisitely dualistic conception of the life of the drives. According to Ewald Hering's theory of what happens in living matter, two processes are ceaselessly at work within it that run in opposite directions to each other: one that is anabolic or 'assimilative', and another that is catabolic or 'dissimilative'. We are surely not presuming too much if we see in these two contrary directions taken by the vital processes the workings of our two sets of drive-impulses, the life drives and the death drives. One thing we cannot close our eyes to, however, is the fact that we have unwittingly fetched up in the philosophical domain of Schopenhauer, for whom, of course, death is the 'proper result' of life and hence its purpose,[55] whereas the sexual drive is the embodiment of the will to life.

Let us boldly attempt to take the argument a step further. It is generally accepted that the coming together of numerous cells to form a single animate unit – the multicellularity of organisms – became a means of extending their lifespan. Each cell helps to preserve the life of the others, and the community of cells can survive even if individual cells have to die off. We have already heard that even conjugation, the temporary coalescence of two unicellular organisms, has a life-preserving and rejuvenating effect on both of them. All of this being so, we might try to take the libido theory evolved through psychoanalysis and apply it to the cells' relationship to each other. We might then try to imagine that it is the life drives or sexual drives active within each cell that make the other cells their object, partially neutralizing their death drives (or rather the processes that the latter instigate) and thereby keeping them alive, while other drives do exactly the same for them, and others again sacrifice their whole existence by performing this libidinal function. The germ-cells themselves could be said to behave in a totally 'narcissistic' fashion – to apply the term we are accustomed to use in neurosis theory when an individual retains his libido entirely within his own ego and expends none of it on object-cathexes. The germ-cells need their libido, the activity of their life drives, entirely for themselves by way of reserves for their later, magnificently anabolic activity. (Perhaps we may also use the term 'narcissistic' in the same sense to describe the cells of malignant neoplasms that destroy the organism. After all, pathologists are prepared to accept that the seeds of these growths are present at birth, and to concede that they display features characteristic of embryos.)[56] All of this being so, it would appear that the libido of our sexual drives is one and the same thing as the Eros evoked by poets and philosophers, the binding force within each and every living thing.

This seems an opportune moment for us to review the slow evolution of the libido theory. The psychoanalysis of transference neuroses initially compelled us to postulate an antithesis between 'sexual drives' directed outwards at an object, and other drives that we only very imperfectly understood, and that we provisionally termed 'ego drives'. Amongst the latter, the drives that were inevitably recognized first were those that contribute to the individual's self-preservation; for the rest, no one was in a position to know what other drives might be identified. In order to establish psychology on a sound footing, nothing could have been more important than some kind of insight, however approximate, into the general nature of drives and the particular characteristics they might prove to have; but there was no other field of psychology in which people were groping so completely in the dark. Everyone posited as many drives or 'basic drives' as they liked, and played around with them rather as the ancient Greek philosophers did with their four elements: earth, air, fire and water. Psychoanalysis, which couldn't escape having *some* kind of theory on the subject, stuck initially to the distinction popularly made between drives, exemplified in the phrase 'hunger and love'. At least this was no new arbitrary act. And it enabled us to progress quite a long way in the analysis of neuroses.

The concept of 'sexuality' – and with it the concept of a sexual drive – did of course have to be considerably extended, to the point where it included much that could not be classed as having a reproductive function, and this caused quite a stir in the world of the puritanical, the posh and the purely hypocritical.

The next step came about when psychoanalysis was able to feel its way a bit closer to the psychological ego, which initially it had known only as an entity given to repression and censorship, and adept at reaction-formation and the construction of protective mechanisms.[57] It is true that critical spirits and others of a far-sighted disposition had long since objected to the libido concept being restricted solely to the energy manifested by *object-oriented* sexual drives; but they neglected to tell us the source of this superior knowledge, and they had no idea how to turn it to advantage in the actual practice of psychoanalysis. Things then began to progress in a more considered way when practitioners of psychoanalysis observed how regular an occurrence it was for libido to be withdrawn from the object and directed onto the ego (introversion); and in the process of studying the earliest phases of libido development in children, they came to the conclusion that the ego is the true and original reservoir of the libido, and that it is from *there* that the libido is first extended to objects.[58] The ego thus took its place amongst the sexual objects, and was immediately recognized as the most sophisticated of them all. When the libido resided in the ego in this way, it was termed 'narcissistic'.[59] This narcissistic libido was of course also in psychoanalytical terms a manifestation of energy on the part of *sexual* drives, which one had no choice but to identify with the 'self-preservation drives' that had been acknowledged from the outset. This meant that the original antithesis of ego drives and sexual drives was no longer adequate. A part of the ego drives was now recognized as being libidinal; within the ego there were – in addition to others no doubt – sexual drives at work as well. None the less, it can justifiably be said that the old principle that psychoneurosis[60] rests upon a conflict between the ego drives and the sexual drives contains nothing that we would nowadays reject. The distinction between the two kinds of drives, which was originally thought of as being *qualitative* in some way, now simply has to be differently defined, namely as being *topical* in nature.[61] The transference neuroses in particular – the real object of study in psychoanalysis – are still the result of a conflict between the ego and a libidinal object-cathexis.

It is all the more necessary that we stress the libidinal character of the self-preservation drives at this point since we want to take the argument a step further by venturing to see in the sexual drive the all-preserving force that is Eros, and to suggest that the ego's narcissistic libido derives from the quotas of libido that enable the soma cells to adhere to each other. But we now find ourselves suddenly confronted by a challenging question: if the self-preservation drives are *also* libidinal in nature, then perhaps we have no drives whatever *except* libidinal ones? There are certainly no others in evidence. But if this is so, then we are going to have to concede the point after all to those critics who suspected from the outset that psychoanalysis would explain *everything* in terms of sexuality, or to those innovators like Jung who opted without further ado to use 'libido' for 'drive-energy' in general. Is this not the case?

This would certainly not be the outcome we intended. On the contrary, the starting point of our whole argument was the sharp distinction that we drew between ego drives – death drives – on the one hand, and sexual drives – life drives – on the other. (We were of course prepared at one stage to include amongst the death drives the self-preservation drives attributed to the ego, but we have since decided that this view was incorrect and withdrawn it.[62]) Our conception has been a *dualistic* one right from the outset, and remains so today more emphatically than ever, particularly since we started classifying the two opposites as 'life drives and death drives' rather than 'ego drives and sexual drives'. Jung's theory, on the other hand, is *monistic*; the fact that he used the term 'libido' for what he saw as a single drive-energy was bound to cause confusion, but need not concern us any further.[63] We strongly suspect that other drives are active within the ego besides the libidinal self-preservation drives; we just need to be able to produce evidence of them. It is regrettable that analysis of the ego has made so little progress that we find it exceedingly difficult to provide this proof. The libidinal ego drives may of course be tied in some very particular way to the other ego drives that are as yet unknown to us. Even before we had fully recognized the phenomenon of narcissism, it was suspected within psychoanalysis that the 'ego drives' had acquired libidinal components. But these are distinctly shaky notions that will hardly do much to convince our opponents. It really is most unfortunate that analysis has thus far only ever enabled us to demonstrate the presence of *libidinal* drives.[64] None the less, the conclusion that there simply aren't any others is not one that we are minded to share.

Given that so much is obscure at present in the theory of drives, it would surely not be sensible of us to reject any idea that promises to cast light on the matter. Our departure point was the great antithesis of life drives and death drives. Object-love itself shows us a second such polarity – that of love (affection) and hate (aggression). What if we succeeded in connecting these two polarities, what if we succeeded in tracing one back to the other! We have always acknowledged a sadistic component in the sexual drive;[65] as we know, this component can develop a life of its own and turn into a perversion that dominates a person's entire sexual life. It also occurs as a dominant partial drive in one of those forms of organization of sexual life that I have termed 'pre-genital'. But how could we possibly suppose that the sadistic drive, which aims to harm its object, derives from Eros, the preserver of life? Isn't it altogether plausible to suppose that this sadism is actually a death drive that has been ousted from the ego at the instance of the narcissistic libido, and as a result only becomes apparent in conjunction with the object? It then becomes an ancillary of the sexual function. In the oral stage of the organization of the libido, 'taking possession of the love object' and 'destroying the object' are still coterminous; later, the sadistic drive separates off, and ultimately, in the phase of genital primacy, it serves the purposes of reproduction by taking on the role of subjugating the sexual object to the extent necessary for the fulfil-ment of the sexual act. Indeed, one could say that, following its expulsion from the ego, the sadistic element shows the libidinal components of the sexual drive which direction to take; in due course they follow its example and strive to reach the object. Where the primal sadism element does not undergo any mitigation or dilution, the outcome is an erotic life marked by the familiar ambivalence of love and hate.[66]

If such a supposition is indeed permissible, then we might be said to have met the requirement that we produce an example of a death drive, albeit a displaced one. The only problem is that this conception is altogether impalpable, and indeed has a positively mystical air. We will be suspected of having resorted to desperate measures in an effort to escape from a gravely embarrassing situation. In that case we may reasonably point to the fact that such a supposition is by no means new, that we have indeed already put it forward at an earlier stage, before there was ever any mention of an 'embarrassing' situation. At that particular time, clinical observations compelled us to form the view that masochism, the partial drive complementary to sadism, has to be understood as the sadism within an individual turning back upon his own ego. But a drive turning from object to ego is in principle no different from a drive turning from ego to object – the latter phenomenon being the new contention at issue here. That being so, then masochism – an individual's drive turning back upon his own ego – is in reality a return to an earlier stage of the drive, a regression. The account of masochism given at that time may need correcting in one particular, on the grounds that it was altogether too restrictive: masochism could also very possibly be a primary phenomenon – a notion I then sought to dispute.[67]

But let us return to the life-preserving sexual drives. As we have already learnt from the research carried out on protista, the coalescence of two individuals *without* subsequent [cell-]division (i.e. conjugation) has a strengthening and rejuvenating effect on both individuals, assuming that they separate from each other soon afterwards (see above, p. 87; cf. also Lipschütz). In later generations they display no symptoms of degeneration, and appear to be capable of withstanding the injurious effects of their own metabolism for a longer period. I believe that this particular observation may *also* be regarded as exemplifying the effect of sexual union. But in what way does the coalescence of two cells that differ very little from one another bring about such a revitalization? The experiment in which the action of chemical and even of mechanical stimuli[68] is substituted for conjugation in protozoa surely allows us to answer this question with complete confidence: it happens because of the supply of new quanta of stimulation. This in turn accords well with the hypothesis that the life process of the individual leads for intrinsic reasons to the equilibration of chemical tensions, that is to death, whereas union with the living matter of a different individual *increases* these tensions, introduces new *vital differentiae* as it were, which must then be 'lived out'. Needless to say, this differentness must be subject to one or more optima. One of our strongest motives for believing in the existence of death drives is indeed the fact that we have perceived the dominant tendency of the psyche, and perhaps of nervous life in general, to be the constant endeavour – as manifested in the pleasure principle – to reduce inner stimulative tension, to maintain it at a steady level, to resolve it completely (the *Nirvana principle*, as Barbara Low has called it).[69]

However, we still see it as a major drawback in our argument that in the case of the sexual drive, of all things, we remain unable to demonstrate a compulsion to repeat, the very attribute that put us on the trail of the death drives in the first place. It is true that the realm of embryonal development processes exhibits a plethora of such repetition phenomena; indeed the two germ-cells involved in sexual reproduction, together with their whole life-history, are themselves but repetitions of the very beginnings of organic life. But the fact remains that the essence of the processes that fall within the purview of the sexual drive is the coalescence of two cell bodies. In the case of the higher organisms, it is this coalescence alone that ensures the living matter's immortality.

In other words, we would really need to attain to a full understanding of the genesis of sexual reproduction and the origins of the sexual drives in general – a task that non-specialists are bound to shrink from, and one that the specialists themselves have so far been unable to accomplish. Let us therefore focus – in the most compressed and concentrated manner possible – on those elements amidst the mass of conflicting assertions and opinions that will permit us to pick up the thread of our argument.

One particular interpretation takes the teasing mystery out of the problem of reproduction by treating it as a manifestation of just one aspect of growth (fissiparation, gemmation, blastogenesis). Taking a sober Darwinian view of how reproduction through sexually differentiated germ-cells came about, we might envisage a scenario in which the advantage of amphimixis[70] that arose from the chance conjugation of two protista at some point in the past was retained and exploited in the subsequent development process.[71] On this premiss, therefore, 'sex' is not all that old, and the extraordinarily fierce drives that seek to bring about sexual union are thereby merely repeating something that happened by chance at a random moment in time and subsequently became firmly established because of the advantages it brought.

The same question arises here as arose earlier in respect of death, namely whether we should rely solely on the characteristics that the protista actually exhibit, and whether we should assume that forces and processes that only become *manifest* in the higher organisms also only began to *exist* in those organisms. For our particular purposes, the above-mentioned interpretation of sexuality has very little to offer. One can reasonably object that it presupposes the existence of life drives that were already active in the simplest organisms, for otherwise conjugation – which runs counter to the course of life and makes it more difficult to live life out and then die – would obviously have been avoided, not seized on and elaborated. Therefore if we do not want to abandon the hypothesis of death drives, we have to see them as having been accompanied from the very beginning by life drives. But we then have to admit that we are working on an equation with two unknowns.

When we look to see what else science can tell us about the origins of sexuality, we find so very little that we can liken the problem to a Stygian darkness that remains unrelieved by even the faintest glimmer of a hypothesis. We *do* come upon such a hypothesis in a very different sort of place, but one that is so fantastic – unquestionably more myth than scientific explanation – that I would not dare to mention it here but for the fact that it meets precisely that particular condition that we are so keen to see met. For it traces a drive back to *the need to restore a prior state*.

Needless to say, I mean the theory that Plato has Aristophanes expound in the *Symposium*, and which deals with the origins not only of the sexual drive, but also of its most important variation in relation to the object: 'Long ago, our nature was not the same as it is now but quite different. For one thing, there were three human genders, not just the present two, male and female. There was also a third one, a combination of these two . . . [the] "androgynous".' In these human beings, however, everything was double; they therefore had four hands and four feet, two faces, two sets of genitalia, etc. Zeus then decided to 'cut humans into two, as people cut sorb-apples in half before they preserve them . . . Since their original nature had been cut in two, each one longed for its own other half and stayed with it. They threw their arms round each other, weaving themselves together, *wanting to form a single living thing*.'[72]

Shall we follow the poet-philosopher's hint and venture the hypothesis that when living matter *became* living matter it was sundered into tiny particles that ever since have endeavoured by means of the sexual drives to become reunited? That in the course of the protistan era these drives, in which the chemical affinity of inanimate matter still subsists, gradually overcame the difficulties put in the way of such an endeavour by an environment charged with life-threatening stimuli, and developed a cortical layer as a necessary protection against that environment? That in this way the scattered fragments of living matter achieved multicellularity and ultimately transferred the reunificatory drive to the germ-cells in the most intensely concentrated form? – But this, I think, is the appropriate point at which to stop.

Not, however, before adding a few words of critical reflection. People might ask me whether and to what extent I myself am convinced by the hypotheses set out here. My answer would be that I am not convinced myself, nor am I trying to persuade others to believe in them. Or to put it more accurately: I do not know how far I believe in them. It seems to me that the emotional factor of 'conviction' need not enter into it at all. One can certainly give oneself over completely to a particular line of thought, and follow it through to wherever it leads, out of sheer scientific curiosity, or out of a desire to act as devil's advocate – without signing oneself over to the devil. I am well aware that this third step in the theory of drives that I have undertaken here cannot lay claim to the same degree of certainty as the previous two, namely the broadening of the concept of sexuality, and the postulate of narcissism. These latter innovations were a direct translation of actual observations into theory, and were susceptible to sources of error no greater than those that inevitably pertain in all such cases. To be sure, the assertion that drives are *regressive* in nature is also based on the observation of facts, namely those manifest in the compulsion to repeat – but I have perhaps overestimated their importance. In any event, it is only possible to carry this idea through by repeatedly combining the factual with the purely notional, and thereby moving far away from empirical observation. One knows very well that the more often one does this in elaborating a theory, the more unreliable the end result becomes, but the degree of uncertainty cannot be calculated. One might have made a lucky guess, or one might have gone horribly wrong. In work of this kind I put little trust in so-called intuition, which, whenever I have encountered it, has always seemed to me more the fruit of a certain impartiality of mind – except that people are unfortunately seldom impartial when it comes to the ultimate questions, the great problems of science and of life. Here, I think, we are all ruled by proclivities that go to the very root of our being, and in our speculations we unwittingly play into their hands. Given such good grounds for mistrust, the only way for us to approach the results of our own intellectual endeavours is probably to regard them with cool benevolence. I hasten to add, however, that a self-critical stance of this kind entails absolutely no obligation to show particular tolerance to discrepant opinions. One can pitilessly reject theories that even the briefest analysis of empirical evidence serves to refute, while at the same time recognizing that the validity of one's own theory is merely provisional.

In judging our speculations about life drives and death drives we would be little bothered by the fact that so many strange and impalpable processes figure within them, such as one drive being ousted by others, or a drive turning from the ego to the object, and so on. All of this simply arises from the fact that we must necessarily operate with the given scientific terminology, i.e. the *figurative* language specific to psychology (or, more precisely, depth psychology). Otherwise we couldn't describe the relevant processes at all, indeed we wouldn't even have realized that they were there. The shortcomings in our account of things would probably disappear if, instead of using psychological terminology, we were already in a position to use that of physiology or chemistry. It is true that this terminology, too, belongs to a merely figurative language – but a perhaps simpler one, and one that we have known for a longer period of time.

On the other hand we need to be fully aware that the uncertainty of our speculations has been greatly increased by the need to borrow repeatedly from the science of biology. Biology is truly a realm of infinite possibilities; we can expect it to yield the most astonishing insights, and we cannot begin to guess what answers it might give to our questions in a few decades' time. Perhaps such as will sweep our carefully contrived edifice of hypotheses entirely away. 'If that is the case', someone might ask, 'then what is the point of writing papers like this, and why on earth bother to make them public?' Well, I just have to admit that some of the analogies, correlations and connections contained therein have seemed to me to be worthy of attention.[73]

VII

If it really is such a universal characteristic of drives to seek to restore a prior state, we should not be surprised that so many processes in the psyche take place quite independently of the pleasure principle. This characteristic would automatically be transmitted to each and every partial drive, and in the case of such drives would involve the retrieval of a particular stage of the development process. But while the pleasure principle may not as yet have gained command of these things, this does not necessarily mean that they are in conflict with it; in fact the problem of determining the relationship of the drives' repetition processes to the dominion of the pleasure principle still remains unsolved.

We have found it to be one of the earliest and most important functions of the psychic apparatus to 'annex' newly arriving drive-impulses, replace the primary process prevailing within them by a secondary process, and change their free-moving cathectic energy into a largely quiescent (tonic) cathexis. While this transformation is taking place no attention can be paid to any unpleasure that may arise – but that does not mean that the pleasure principle is thereby nullified. On the contrary, the transformation occurs on *behalf* of the pleasure principle: the annexion is a preparative act that both heralds and ensures the dominion of the pleasure principle.

Let us distinguish more sharply than we have done hitherto between 'function' and 'tendency'.[74] The pleasure principle can then be seen as a tendency serving the interests of a specific function whose responsibility it is *either* to render the psychic apparatus completely free of excitation, *or* to keep the quantum of excitation within it constant, *or* to keep it at the lowest possible level. We cannot yet decide for certain which of these alternatives is the correct one, but we note that this function as here defined would partake in that most universal endeavour in all living matter to revert to the quiescence of the inorganic world. We have all experienced how the greatest pleasure we can ever achieve, namely that of the sexual act, is accompanied by the momentary vanishment of a supremely intense excitation. The annexing of the drive-impulse, however, might be seen as a preparative function intended to make the excitation ready for its final dissolution in the pleasure of release.

This same context gives rise to the question whether sensations of pleasure and unpleasure can be produced equally by both annexed and non-annexed excitation processes. Now it does appear to be clear beyond all doubt that the non-annexed, primary processes result in far more intensive sensations in both directions (pleasure and unpleasure) than do the annexed, secondary ones. The primary processes are also the ones that occur first; they are the only ones operative at the start of the psyche's life; and we can reasonably infer that if the pleasure principle were not already active within these earlier processes, it would not be able to materialize at all for the later ones. We thus arrive at the basically rather convoluted conclusion that at the beginning of the psyche's life the striving for pleasure manifests itself far more intensively than it does later on, but enjoys less of a free run, in that it has to put up with frequent irruptions. Once the psyche is more developed the dominion of the pleasure principle is very much more secure, but the pleasure principle itself has no more escaped the taming process than any of the other drives have. In any event, the element within the excitation process that gives rise to the sensations of pleasure and unpleasure must be present in the secondary process just as much as in the primary one.

This would be the appropriate starting-point for further research. Our consciousness transmits to us from within ourselves sensations not only of pleasure and unpleasure, but also of a peculiar tension that again can be either pleasurable or unpleasurable. Are we then, on the basis of these sensations, to differentiate annexed and non-annexed energy processes from one another? Or does the sensation of tension relate to the *absolute* quantum, or perhaps level, of cathexis, whilst the incidence of pleasure/unpleasure reflects *changes* in the quantum of cathexis within a particular period of time? We also cannot fail to be struck by the fact that the life drives have so much more to do with our inner perception, since they behave as troublemakers and constantly bring tensions, the resolving of which is perceived as pleasurable, whereas the death drives appear to do their work unobtrusively. The pleasure principle seems to be positively subservient to the death drives; but it *does* also watch for any stimuli from without that are adjudged by both kinds of drives to be dangerous, and more particularly for any increases in stimulation emanating from within that make the task of living more difficult.

This all leads on to countless other questions to which at present we have no answers. We have to be patient and wait for new means and opportunities for research. And we must also be prepared to abandon any path that appears to be going nowhere, even though we may have followed it for quite some time. Only those fond believers who demand of science that it take the place of the catechism they have forsaken will object to a scientist developing or even changing his ideas. For the rest, let us take consolation for the slow progress of our scientific knowledge from the words of a poet (Rückert in his *Makamen des Hariri*):

Was man nicht erfliegen kann, muss man erhinken.

. . .

Die Schrift sagt, es ist keine Sünde zu hinken.

(Whatever we cannot achieve on the wing, we have to achieve at a patient limp . . . Scripture tells us clear enough: it never was a sin to limp.)

(1920)

The Ego and the Id

The arguments set forth in these pages are an elaboration of ideas first broached in my essay *Beyond the Pleasure Principle* – ideas which, as I mentioned at the time, I myself viewed with a kind of benevolent curiosity.[1] This present essay takes up those ideas, links them with various facts derived from psychoanalytical observation, and seeks to arrive at new conclusions on the basis of this conjunction; it does not make any further borrowings from biology, however, and in consequence is much closer to psychoanalysis than *Beyond the Pleasure Principle* was. It is more in the nature of synthesis than speculation; and while it evidently aspires to an elevated goal, I am well aware that it never really ventures beyond the crudest level, and I fully acknowledge this limitation.

In the process, the essay touches on matters that have never yet been a focus of psychoanalytical interest, and so inevitably makes reference to various theories propounded by non-psychoanalysts, or by ex-psychoanalysts in the course of withdrawing from their previous position. As a rule I have always been quite ready to acknowledge my debt to other researchers, but in this present case I do not feel burdened by any such debt of gratitude. If psychoanalysis has hitherto failed to show due appreciation of certain things, this was never because it had overlooked their contribution or sought to deny their importance, but rather because it had been following a particular path that had not yet progressed that far. And in any case, when it *does* finally reach that point it sees things very differently from the way others see them.

I

The Conscious and the Unconscious

In this introductory section there is nothing new to be said, and there is no avoiding the repetition of things that have often been said before.

The division of the psychic realm into the conscious and the unconscious is the fundamental premiss of psychoanalysis; it alone enables psychoanalysis to understand the pathological processes that are such a common and important feature of psychic life, and to offer a systematic scientific account of them. To put this another way: psychoanalysis cannot regard the psyche as being coterminous with consciousness, but necessarily sees consciousness as just one particular quality of the psychical which may or may not manifest itself in addition to other qualities.

If I were able to imagine every last person with an interest in psychology reading this essay, then I should not be one whit surprised to find a number of those readers calling a halt right now and refusing to read another word – for here at once is the first shibboleth of psychoanalysis. To most people whose education is grounded in philosophy, the idea of a psychic realm that is not also a *conscious* one is so incomprehensible as to seem an absurdity easily refuted by plain, straightforward logic. This is due, I think, to the simple fact that they have never studied the relevant phenomena of hypnosis and dreams which – quite regardless of any pathological element – leave us no option but to take such a view. Furthermore, their consciousness-based psychology is quite incapable of solving the problems presented by dreams and hypnosis.

To say that something 'is conscious' is to use a term that in the first instance is purely descriptive,[2] a term based on perception of the most direct and certain kind. Now experience tells us that as a rule a psychic element – a notion, for instance – is conscious for no great length of time. Indeed, states of conscious awareness are typically very short-lived. A notion tends to be conscious one moment, then no longer conscious the next – though it can become so again in certain circumstances that are easily brought about. What became of it in the meantime, we do not know. We can say that it was *latent*, and what we mean is that it was *capable of becoming conscious*[3] at any moment. And if we say that it was *unconscious*, that too is an accurate description. 'Unconscious' in this context thus amounts to the same thing as 'latent and capable of becoming conscious'. True: the philosophers would object and tell us 'No! The term "unconscious" is *not* applicable here! So long as the notion was in a state of latency, it wasn't in any sense psychical.' But if we started arguing with them at this early stage, we would slither into a polemic that would get us nowhere.

'Unconscious', however, is a term or concept that we have arrived at by a different route, namely by looking at experiences in which the *dynamics* of the psyche play a role. We have found – or rather, we have been compelled to assume – that there exist very powerful psychic processes or notions (a quantitative and hence *economic* factor enters the picture for a moment here), all of which can have a considerable effect on the subject's inner life, just like any other notions, but which themselves remain unconscious even though their *effects* may in turn become conscious as notions.[4] There is no need to repeat at length here what has so often been propounded before. Suffice it to say that psychoanalytical theory comes into play at this point, arguing that the reason such notions cannot be conscious is that a certain force actively opposes such an outcome, and that otherwise they would indeed be able to become conscious, whereupon it would become clear how little they differ from other psychic elements already acknowledged as such. This theory is rendered irrefutable by the fact that psychoanalysis has devised techniques enabling us to neutralize the opposing force and make the relevant notions conscious. We use the term *repression* to describe the status in which these notions existed before they were made conscious, and we argue that the force that brought about the repression and then kept it in place makes itself felt during the psychoanalytic process as *resistance*.

We thus derive our concept of the unconscious from the theory of repression. The repressed[5] is in our view the paradigm for the unconscious. As we can see, however, we have two forms of the unconscious: one that is latent, but capable of becoming conscious, and one, consisting of the repressed, that is not inherently and spontaneously capable of becoming conscious. The insight we have gained into the dynamics of the psyche inevitably influences both our nomenclature and our definitions. For the latent component – which is unconscious only in the descriptive[6] and not the dynamic sense – we use the term *pre-conscious*; we restrict the term *unconscious* to the dynamically unconscious repressed. Thus we now have three terms – 'conscious' (*Cs*), 'pre-conscious' (*Pcs*) and 'unconscious' (*Ucs*), none of which any longer has a purely descriptive meaning. The *Pcs*, so we assume, is much closer to the *Cs* than the *Ucs* is; and having defined the *Ucs* as psychical, we shall do so all the more readily in the case of the latent *Pcs*. But wouldn't it be preferable for us to stay in line with the philosophers, and rigorously separate the *Pcs* as well as the *Ucs* from the conscious psychic element? The philosophers would then suggest that we describe the *Pcs* and the *Ucs* as two forms or levels of the *psychoidal*[7] – and hey presto, harmony would reign between us. But endless expositional difficulties would result from this, and the singularly important fact that these 'psychoids' correspond in almost all other respects to the psychical as it is generally understood, would be pushed into the background for the sake of a prejudice – and a prejudice dating from a period when nothing was yet known of these 'psychoids', or at any rate of their most important aspect.[8]

We can now operate very happily with our three terms *Cs*, *Pcs* and *Ucs*, provided we bear in mind that whereas there are two kinds of unconscious in the *descriptive* sense, there is only one in the *dynamic* sense. For the purposes of our account of things, we can in some cases ignore this distinction, while in others it is of course indispensable to the argument. After all, we have become quite accustomed to this ambiguity regarding the unconscious, and we have coped with it perfectly well. We cannot get rid of it, so far as I can see: whether something is conscious or unconscious is ultimately a question of perception that can only be answered 'yes' or 'no', and the act of perception itself tells us nothing whatever about the reason why something is or is not perceived. We have no right to complain about the fact that when the dynamic element happens to become manifest, it does so only in an ambiguous form.[9]

As our psychoanalytical work proceeds, however, it soon becomes clear that these categories, too, prove to be inadequate, to be quite simply insufficient for practical use. Amongst the various situations that demonstrate this, let us single out one in particular – and the most important of them all. We have evolved the notion of a coherent organization of the psychic processes present within each individual, and we call this organization their *ego*.[10] It is this ego that consciousness attaches to; it controls the pathways leading to motor activity, i.e. to the release of excitations into the external world; it is the arbiter[11] that controls all the psyche's constituent processes and, despite going to sleep at night, still contrives to censor dreams. This ego is also the source of the repressions that are intended to exclude certain psychic tendencies not only from consciousness, but also from all other areas where they might come into their own or be otherwise activated. In psychoanalysis, these tendencies, having been thrust aside by the repression process, present themselves in direct opposition to the ego, and it is the job of the analysis to remove the resistances mounted by the ego against any involvement with what has been repressed. Now in the course of analysis we find that the patient encounters difficulties when we set him certain tasks: his associations fail to work whenever they are meant to get anywhere near the repressed element. We then tell him that he is under the sway of a resistance, but he is wholly unaware of this fact, and even if his feelings of unpleasure cause him perchance to guess that a resistance is at work within him, he is incapable of identifying or defining it. But since this resistance undoubtedly emanates from his ego and entirely belongs to it, we find ourselves confronted with an unexpected situation. We have come upon something within the very ego itself that is *also* unconscious, something that behaves exactly like the repressed element in producing powerful effects without becoming conscious itself, and which we can render conscious only by working on it in a special way. The implication of this discovery for psychoanalytic practice is that we shall incur endless difficulties and ambiguities if we carry on doggedly using our accustomed terminology, and thus for instance seek to attribute neurosis to a conflict between the conscious and the unconscious. On the basis of our insight into the structural conditions that obtain in the life of the psyche we need to replace this antithesis with a different one – namely that between the coherent ego and the repressed element that has been split off from it.[12]

The implications are even more significant, however, with respect to our general conception of the unconscious. We first corrected our position as a result of considering the *dynamic* aspect, and a second correction is necessitated by our insight concerning *structure*. We now realize that the Ucs and the repressed are not conterminous; while it remains correct to say that all of the repressed is Ucs, it is not also the case that all of the Ucs is repressed. Part of the ego – God alone knows how important a part – may also be Ucs, indeed is undoubtedly Ucs. And this Ucs component of the ego is not latent in a Pcs sense, otherwise it could surely not be activated without becoming Cs, and it would surely not be so enormously difficult to render it conscious. If we thus find ourselves compelled to postulate a third kind of Ucs, i.e. a non-repressed one, then we have to admit that 'unconsciousness' as a category loses some of the significance that it otherwise holds for us. It becomes a multivalent quality that allows no scope for the far-reaching and definitive conclusions that we would have liked to draw from it. And yet we must be careful not to disregard it, for in the end the attribute 'conscious/unconscious' is our one and only beacon in the darkness of depth psychology.[13]

II

The Ego and the Id

Pathological[14] research has focused our attention too exclusively on the repressed. We should like to learn more about the ego now that we know that it, too, can be unconscious in the proper sense of the word. The only touchstone available to us throughout our investigations so far has been the designation 'conscious' or 'unconscious' – and we have finally realized how ambiguous this can be.

Now our entire knowledge depends at all times on consciousness. Even the *Ucs* can only become known to us in so far as we make it conscious. But wait a moment: how is that possible? What does 'making something conscious' actually mean? How on earth can such a thing happen?

We already know exactly where to start in order to answer this question. We have said that consciousness constitutes the *outer surface* of the psychic apparatus, which is to say that we have defined it as a function of a system that is spatially the closest to the external world – a spatial proximity, incidentally, that applies not only in terms of function but also, in this particular case, in terms of anatomical location.[15] For the purposes of our present investigations, too, we need to take this 'perceiving surface' as our starting point.

All perceptions that come from without (sense perceptions) and from within – what we call 'sensations' and 'feelings' – are *Cs* from the very first. But what is the position with respect to those inner processes that we might sum up – albeit crudely and imprecisely – as 'thought processes'? These processes that occur somewhere in the depths of the apparatus as displacements of psychic energy on its path to becoming action – do they betake themselves to the outer surface that gives rise to consciousness? Or does consciousness betake itself to them? As we can see, this is one of the difficulties that result once we make any serious attempt to envisage the workings of the psyche in spatial, *topical* terms. Both alternatives are equally inconceivable, and the truth must surely lie in a third.

I have already put forward the hypothesis elsewhere[16] that the real difference between a *Ucs* and a *Pcs* notion resides in the fact that the former runs its course wholly within the context of material of which the subject remains unaware, whereas in the case of the latter the connection with *word-notions* supervenes as well.[17] This represents our first attempt to propose identifiers for the two systems *Pcs* and *Ucs* that rely on something other than their relationship to consciousness. The question 'How does something become conscious?' can thus be more pertinently formulated as follows: 'How does something become pre-conscious?' And the answer would be: 'By being connected to the corresponding word-notions'.

These word-notions are residual memories; they were once perceptions, and like all residual memories they are capable of becoming conscious again. Before we deal with their nature in more detail, however, the following new insight suddenly dawns on us: the only things that can become conscious are things that have already at some point been *Cs* perceptions; and anything – apart from feelings – that wants to become conscious from within has to try to convert itself into an external perception. This is made possible by means of memory traces.

We conceive of residual memories as being contained within systems that are immediately adjacent to the *Pcpt-Cs* system,[18] with the result that the cathexes of these residues can easily extend outwards onto the constituent elements of the *Pcpt-Cs* system. One immediately thinks of hallucinations at this point, and of the fact that even the most vivid memories remain readily distinguishable from hallucinations and from external perceptions – but an answer to this problem presents itself no less quickly, namely that when a memory is revived its cathexis is retained within the memory system, whereas a hallucination that is indistinguishable from a perception may well arise when the cathexis passes completely from the memory trace to the *Pcpt* system instead of making simply a minor incursion.

Verbal residua derive in the main from *auditory* perceptions, and this means that the *Pcs* system may be said to have a specifically sensory origin, as it were. For the time being we can disregard the *visual* components of word-notions, these being secondary elements acquired through reading, and the same applies to the *dynamic* images of words,[19] which play the role of auxiliary signals (except in the case of deaf-mutes[20]). After all, a word is strictly speaking the memorative residuum of a word that has been *heard*.

We should not be tempted – for the sake of simplicity, for instance – to forget the importance of *optical* memorative residua (in respect of physical objects), or to deny that it is possible to make thought processes conscious by reverting to the relevant visual residua, and that for many people this seems to be the preferred method. We can get an idea of the specific nature of this visual thinking from the study of dreams and pre-conscious fantasies written on the basis of his own observations by J[ulian] Varendonck.[21] We discover that in most cases only the concrete matter of the thought becomes conscious, whereas the various relations and connections that give the thought its particular character find no visual expression at all. Thinking in pictures thus only makes for a very imperfect form of consciousness. It is also rather more akin to unconscious processes than is thinking in words, and it is without any doubt both ontogenetically and phylogenetically older than the latter.

To return to our argument: given that this is indeed the way in which something intrinsically unconscious becomes pre-conscious, then the question 'How do we make something that has been repressed (pre)conscious?' may be answered as follows: we do so by generating precisely such *Pcs* intermediary links through our psychoanalytical work. Consciousness thus stays where it is – but so too does the *Ucs*, which does not for instance move up to the level of the *Cs*.

While the relationship of *external* perceptions to the ego is perfectly obvious, the relationship to the ego of *internal* perceptions calls for special consideration. It once again raises doubts as to whether we really are right to associate the whole of consciousness with the one surface system of the *Pcpt-Cs*.

Internal perceptions yield sensations of processes that emanate from extremely diverse layers of the psychic apparatus, probably including the very deepest. These sensations are not at all well known, those forming the pleasure/unpleasure group being perhaps still the best example. They are more primal, more elemental than perceptions that come from outside, and can arise even in an imperfect state of consciousness. I have written elsewhere about their greater economic importance, and about the metapsychological reasons for this.[22] Like external perceptions, these sensations are multilocular: they can come from several different places at the same time, and in consequence can possess different, even contrary qualities.

Sensations of a pleasurable kind generate no pressures at all; unpleasurable sensations, on the other hand, exert pressure to an extreme degree. They press for change, for release, and because of this we believe that unpleasure entails an *increase* in energy-cathexis, and pleasure a *decrease*.[23] Suppose that whatever it is that becomes conscious as pleasure or unpleasure be defined as quantitatively and qualitatively 'other'[24] within the workings of the psyche: the question then arises whether this 'other' is capable of becoming conscious in situ, or first has to be transmitted to the *Pcpt-Cs* system.

Clinical experience clearly points to the latter. It shows that this 'other' behaves like a repressed impulse. It can develop powerful energies without the ego noticing the intense pressure that these exert. It is only the onset of resistance to the pressure, the arresting of the release-reaction, that suddenly makes the 'other' conscious as unpleasure. Just as the tension caused by unmet needs can remain unconscious, so too can pain – this half-and-half thing, somewhere between external and internal perception, that behaves like an internal perception even when it derives from the world without. It is thus still correct to say that sensations and feelings, too, only become conscious if they manage to reach the *Pcpt* system; if the transmission pathway is blocked, then they never actually become sensations, even though the 'other' that corresponds to them in the excitatory process remains just the same as it would otherwise be. We then – using a shorthand and not entirely accurate formulation

113

– speak of 'unconscious sensations', thereby adhering to the not altogether justifiable analogy with unconscious *notions*; the difference being that in the case of *Ucs* notions, connecting links have to be created first before they can be brought into the *Cs*, whereas this is not necessary in the case of sensations, which are directly transmitted. To put this another way: the distinction between *Cs* and *Pcs* is meaningless in the case of sensations;[25] they are either conscious or unconscious, and the *Pcs* doesn't come into it at all. Even when they are attached to word-notions, they by no means depend on them in order to become conscious: they do this directly.

The role of word-notions now becomes fully clear: they are the intermedium that enables inner thought processes to become perceptions. The proposition might thus seem to have been duly proved that 'All knowledge derives from external perception'. When thinking becomes highly cathected, individual thoughts really *are* perceived – just as if they came from outside – and are therefore regarded as true.

Having thus clarified the relationship between external/internal perception and the surface system of the *Pcpt-Cs*, we can now go on to elaborate our notion of the ego. We see it as proceeding from the *Pcpt* system, this being its essential nucleus,[26] and going on next to embrace the *Pcs*, which is chiefly dependent on memorative residua. But, as we have already learned, the ego is also unconscious.

Now I think it will profit us greatly if we take our cue from a writer who for his own particular reasons, and quite in vain, would have us believe that his work has nothing to do with the stern, exalted realm of science. I am referring to Georg Groddeck and his tireless insistence that what we call our ego very largely remains passive throughout our life; that rather than living our lives ourselves, we are 'lived' – to use Groddeck's expression – by unknown and uncontrollable forces.[27] We have all had the same sort of experience, even if it has not overwhelmed us to the exclusion of all others, and we do not shrink from according Groddeck's insight its due place within the edifice of science. I suggest that we take account of it by employing the term *ego* for the entity that proceeds first from the *Pcpt* system and is then *Pcs* – but the term *id*, as used by Groddeck, for the other psychic realm that constitutes the further continuation of that same entity, and behaves in a *Ucs* way.[28]

We shall soon discover whether we can derive any benefit from this approach in terms of understanding and description. We now see the individual as consisting in a psychic id, unrecognized and unconscious, on top of which sits the ego, having duly developed out of its nucleus, the *Pcpt* system.[29] If we are aiming to represent this diagrammatically, then we need to add that the ego does not envelop the id completely, but only to the extent that the *Pcpt* system constitutes its[30] outer surface, rather in the way that the germinal disk sits on the top of the egg. The ego is not sharply separated from the id, but flows on down into it, such that both then merge.

But the repressed merges into the id as well, indeed is merely a part of it. The repressed is cut off from the ego only by the resistances generated by repression, and can communicate with it via the id. We immediately realize that almost all the distinctions that we have drawn on the basis of our pathological[31] work relate solely to the *surface* layers of the psychic apparatus – the only ones that are known to us. This disposition of things may be shown by a diagram

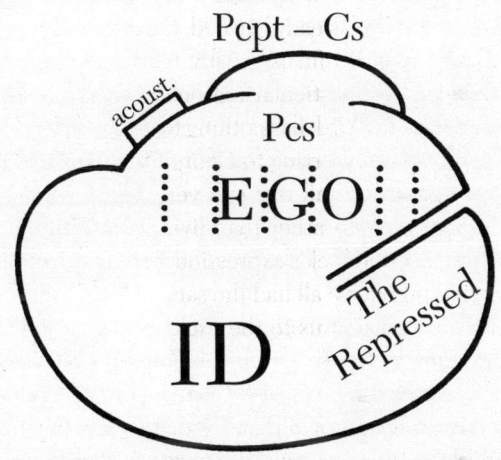

– the contours of which are purely illustrative, however, and are not meant to betoken any particular interpretation. We might perhaps add that the ego sports an 'acoustic cap', but on one side only, in line with the evidence of cerebral anatomy. It sits at a crooked angle, so to speak.

As we can readily see, the ego is that part of the id that has been altered by the direct influence of the external world as mediated by the *Pcpt-Cs*; in a sense it is an extension of the process of surface differentiation.[32] Furthermore, the ego endeavours to bring the influence exerted by the external world fully to bear on the id and its designs, and makes every effort to substitute the reality principle[33] for the pleasure principle that reigns supreme within the id. Perception plays the same role for the ego that the drives are required to play in the id. The ego represents what may be called reason and calm consideration, in contrast to the id, which harbours the passions. While all of this accords with well-known popular conceptions and distinctions, it should none the less be understood as having validity only in a normative or theoretical sense.

The functional importance of the ego is manifest in the fact that it is normally given control of the pathways leading to motor activity. In its relationship to the id it thus resembles the rider charged with bridling the superior power of his horse – with the difference that the rider tries to do this by using his own strength, the ego by using strength it has borrowed from elsewhere. This analogy can be carried a little further. Just as the rider who doesn't wish to be parted from his horse often has no alternative but to lead it where it wants to go, so too the ego habitually enacts the will of the id as though it were its own.

The genesis of the ego and its separation from the id appear to have been influenced not only by the *Pcpt* system but also by another factor. Our own body, and particularly its surface, can be a point of origin for both external and internal perceptions at the same time. We see it as a distinct object – but touching it produces *two* sensations, one of which can be equated to an inner perception. Psychophysiology has dealt in ample detail with the way our body has its own special place within our world of perception. Pain also seems to play a role in this, and the manner in which we gain a new awareness of our organs when we suffer painful illnesses is perhaps paradigmatic for the way in which we arrive at our notion of our own body.

The ego is above all a *corporeal* entity; it is not merely a surface entity, but is itself the *projection* of a surface.[34] If we seek an anatomical analogy for it, then we can identify it most readily with the anatomists' 'cerebral homunculus', which stands on its head in the cortex with its heels sticking upwards, its eyes pointing backwards, and its speech-area located, as we know, on the left-hand side.[35]

There have been numerous detailed appraisals of the relationship between the ego and consciousness, but there are still some important new facts that need to be set out here. Accustomed as we are to viewing things according to a scale of social or ethical values that we take with us wherever we go, we are not at all surprised to learn that the machinations of the baser passions take place in the unconscious, but we rather assume that the higher a psychic function comes in that scale of values, the easier it is for it to gain access to the realm of consciousness. Our expectations in this respect are confounded by our actual experience in psychoanalysis, however. For one thing, we see clear evidence that even subtle and complex intellectual tasks that normally demand sustained and strenuous thought can also be carried out pre-consciously, without entering consciousness at all. There is no doubt whatever that such cases occur; they happen during sleep, for example, and are evidenced by the fact that on waking up, the person concerned immediately knows the answer to a difficult mathematical or other problem that they had vainly struggled to solve the day before.[36]

However, we also encounter another, far more disconcerting phenomenon. We discover in analysis that there are people in whom the faculties of self-criticism and conscience – that is, psychic activities to which we attach an extremely high value – are unconscious, and as such produce effects of the greatest importance; resistance in analysis is thus by no means the only such feature to remain unconscious. But this second new discovery, which compels us despite our better judgement to speak of an *unconscious guilt-feeling*, perplexes us far more, and sets us new puzzles – particularly once we begin to realize that in a large number of neuroses precisely such an unconscious guilt-feeling plays a crucial economic role, and puts extremely powerful obstacles in the way of recovery. If we want to return to the topic of our 'scale of values', then we need to make the point that it is not only the basest appurtenances of the ego that can remain unconscious, but also the most elevated ones. It is as if proof were being thus vouchsafed to us of what we said a moment ago about the conscious ego – that it is above all a *corporeal* ego.[37]

III

The Ego and the Super-Ego (the Ego-Ideal)

The situation confronting us would be straightforward indeed if the ego were simply the portion of the id that is influenced and thus modified[38] by the perceptual system; if it were the representative within the psychic realm of the objective external world. But another factor comes into the picture as well.

We have explained in other contexts the various considerations that led us to postulate a separate level within the ego – a differentiation that has come about inside the ego itself – that may be termed the *ego-ideal* or *super-ego*.[39] These considerations remain entirely valid.[40] What is new here, and very much in need of explanation, is the fact that this part of the ego is less firmly and clearly connected to consciousness.

We need to range a little further afield at this juncture. We managed to throw light on the painful affliction of melancholia with our hypothesis that it involves resurrecting a lost object within the ego, in other words substituting identification for object-cathexis.[41] At that time, however, we did not yet realize the full significance of this process, or how frequent and typical it is. Since then we have come to understand that surrogation of this kind plays a major part in shaping the ego, and contributes signally to forming what may be termed its *character*.

Right at the very beginning, in the primitive oral phase of an individual, object-cathexis and identification probably cannot be distinguished from one another. At a later stage, one can only suppose that object-cathexes emanate from the id, which registers erotic urges as needs. The ego – initially still in a somewhat puny state – becomes aware of the object-cathexes, and either puts up with them, or seeks to fight them off through the process of repression.[42]

Where an individual is required or compelled to give up a sexual object, there is not uncommonly a compensatory process in the form of that particular ego-alteration[43] that we can only describe as 'erecting the object within the ego', just as occurs in melancholia. We do not yet know the precise circumstances in which this surrogation process takes place. Perhaps the ego uses this introjection, which is a form of regression to the mechanism of the oral phase, in order to make it easier to give up the object, or even to make it possible in the first place. Perhaps this identification is the one and only condition under which the id will give up its objects. Be that as it may, the process is a very frequent one, especially in the early phases of development, and gives grounds for the view that the character of the ego is a residual imprint of the object-cathexes that have been given up, and contains the entire history of those object-choices. Needless to say, it must be granted from the outset that there is a considerable range in the capacity for resistance that determines whether a person's character rejects or accepts these influences deriving from his or her cumulative history of erotic object-choices. In the case of women who have had numerous amorous experiences it would appear to be quite easy to demonstrate that vestiges of their various object-cathexes are present in their character traits. We must also consider the possibility that object-cathexis and identification can occur simultaneously, in other words, that there can be a character-alteration[44] *before* the object has been given up. In this event the character-alteration may well last beyond the subject's relationship to the object, and in some sense preserve it.

Looked at from another point of view, this process of converting an erotic object-choice into an ego-alteration can also be seen as a device enabling the ego to gain control of the id and strengthen its links to it, albeit at the cost of showing considerable complaisance with regard to its experiences. When the ego adopts the features of the object, it so to speak presses *itself* on the id as a love-object; it seeks to make good the id's loss by saying 'There, you see, you can love me too – I look just like the object.'

The conversion of object-libido into narcissistic libido that takes place here clearly entails an abandonment of sexual goals, a desexualization – in other words a kind of sublimation. Indeed the question arises – and would merit detailed analysis – whether this is not perhaps the standard path to sublimation; whether *all* sublimation doesn't perhaps take place via the medium of the ego, which first transforms sexual object-libido into narcissistic object-libido, in order perhaps then to set it a different goal.[45] At a later stage we shall consider whether this transformation cannot perhaps affect the destiny of the drives in other ways too, for instance by bringing about a de-mergence[46] of the various drives that are interfused with one another.

Even though it diverts us from our main objective, we really cannot avoid focusing our attention for a moment on the ego's object-identifications. If these get out of hand, if they become excessive in number and intensity and prove incompatible with one another, then a pathological outcome is altogether likely. Frag-menting of the ego may occur as a result of the separate identifica-tions shutting themselves off from one another by means of resistances, and in cases of so-called *multiple personality* the secret may well be that the separate identifications take turns seizing hold of consciousness. Even if things do not reach such a pass, there is certain to be an issue with regard to conflicts between the various identifications that the ego separates out into – conflict that in the end cannot all be described as pathological.

But whatever may be the *subsequent* capacity of a person's charac-ter to resist the influence of object-cathexes that have been given up, the effects of that person's *initial* identifications, those that occur at a very young age, will be pervasive and long-lasting. This leads us back to the origins of the ego-ideal, for behind it lurks the individual's first and most important identification: that with the father during his personal pre-history.[47] This first identification does not itself seem to be the fruit or end-product of an object-cathexis: it occurs on its own, without any mediation, and at an earlier stage than any object-cathexis. But it seems that the object-choices that belong to the first sexual period, and involve the father and mother, culminate in normal circumstances in precisely the same identification, and thereby reinforce the primary one.

However, these relationships are so complicated that we are going to have to analyse them in rather more detail. Two factors are to blame for this complexity: the triangular nature of the Oedipus situation, and the constitutional bisexuality of the individual.

Reduced to its essentials, the picture that presents itself in the case of a male child is as follows: at a very early age he develops an object-cathexis in respect of his mother, the starting-point for which is the mother's breast, and which constitutes a paradigmatic example of the imitative type of object-choice;[48] the boy takes possession of the father through identification. The two relationships continue in tandem for a while, until the intensification of the boy's sexual desire for the mother and his recognition that the father constitutes an obstacle to this desire bring the Oedipus complex into being.[49] The father-identification now takes on a hostile air; it turns into a desire to get rid of the father and take his place *vis-à-vis* the mother. From this point onwards, the relationship to the father is ambivalent; it seems as if the ambivalence inherent in the identification from the beginning has now become manifest. In the case of boys, the ambivalent attitude to the father and the purely affectionate impulse towards the mother as object are the defining features of the simple and positive form of the Oedipus complex.

Once the Oedipus complex is demolished, the object-cathexis in respect of the mother has to be given up. Its place can be taken by one of two things: either an identification with the mother, or an intensification of the already existing identification with the father. We generally regard the latter outcome as the more normal one; it allows the affectionate relationship to the mother to be retained to some degree. The masculine element in the boy may thus be said to have gained in strength as a result of the dissolution of the Oedipus complex. In an altogether analogous way, the outcome of the Oedipus attitude in a little girl may be an intensification of her identification with the mother (or the creation of such an identification), which firmly establishes the feminine character of the child.

These identifications do not accord with our expectations,[50] in that they do not convey the surrendered object into the ego – but this outcome *does* also occur, and is more readily observed in girls than in boys. We very often find in psychoanalysis that a little girl who has had to relinquish the father as love-object proceeds to emphasize her maleness, and instead of identifying with the mother identifies with the father, i.e. with the object that she has lost. What decides the issue here is evidently whether the male elements in her make-up – whatever these may be – are sufficiently strong.

Whether the final outcome of the Oedipus situation is a father-identification or a mother-identification thus seems to depend in both sexes on the relative strength of the male and female elements in the individual's make-up. This is one of the two ways in which bisexuality interferes in the fate of the Oedipus complex. The other is even more significant. For we get the impression that the simple form of the Oedipus complex is by no means the one that actually occurs most commonly, but amounts to a simplification or schematiz-ation – though one that quite often proves justifiable in practical terms.[51] As a rule a more detailed investigation reveals the more *complete* form of the Oedipus complex, which is twofold in nature, comprising both a positive complex and a negative one, due to the child's original bisexuality; i.e. the boy not only exhibits an ambiva-lent attitude towards the father and an affectionate object-choice in respect of the mother, but at the same time also behaves like a girl, displaying an affectionate feminine attitude towards the father and a correspondingly jealous and hostile one towards the mother. This extra complication brought about by bisexuality makes it very diffi-cult to discern the circumstances that obtain in primal object-choices and identifications, and even *more* difficult to describe these in an intelligible way. It may even be the case that the ambivalence that we noted in the child's relationship to its parents is wholly ascribable to bisexuality, and does not – as I argued earlier – derive from the relevant identification as a result of an attitude of rivalry.

It seems to me to be a sensible policy to assume that the complete Oedipus complex will prove to exist in the generality of cases, and most particularly in the case of neurotics. Psychoanalytical experience shows us, however, that in a number of instances one or other element disappears almost without trace, and as a result we find a whole spectrum, having the normal, positive Oedipus complex at one end and the inverted, negative one at the other, while the middle sections reveal variants of the complete form with unequal proportions of the two components. On the dissolution of the Oedipus complex, the four tendencies contained within it will combine in such a way that they give rise to a father-identification and a mother-identification. The father-identification will retain the mother-object of the positive complex, and at the same time replace the father-object of the inverted complex;[52] the same – in reverse – will be true of the mother-identification. One of the two identifications will be more marked than the other, and this will reflect the unequal distribution of the two sexual elements in the individual's make-up.

We can thus postulate that the most pervasive result of the sexual phase dominated by the Oedipus complex is that it leaves its imprint on the ego, manifest in the creation of these two identifications that are in some way harmonized with one another. This ego-alteration retains its special status and actively opposes the rest of the ego as the 'ego-ideal' or 'super-ego'.

The super-ego is not purely and simply the residuum of the id's earliest object-choices, however, but also signifies a vigorous reaction-formation directed against those same object-choices. Its relationship to the ego does not reside solely in the injunction 'You *shall* behave thus (like your father)', but also includes the prohibition 'You *must not* behave thus (like your father) – that is, you must not do *all* that he does, for some things remain his sole preserve.' This dual visage of the ego-ideal derives from the fact that the latter was brought into play in order to repress the Oedipus complex, indeed owes its very existence to this critical turn of events. The repression of the Oedipus complex was clearly no easy task. Since it was the parents, particularly the father, who were identified as the obstacle preventing the child's Oedipus wishes from being realized, his infantile ego gained the strength to accomplish the repression by erecting that same obstacle within itself. It borrowed the requisite strength from the father, so to speak – and to incur this loan is to incur the most momentous consequences: the super-ego retains the character of the father; and the stronger the Oedipus complex was, and the faster it was repressed (by dint of authority, religious doctrine, schooling, reading) – the more strictly the super-ego subsequently rules the ego as its conscience, and perhaps as an unconscious sense of guilt. The question arises as to where it gets the power so to rule – that power of compulsion which manifests itself as a categorical imperative; and I shall propose a possible answer to this question at a later stage.

Looking once again at the genesis of the super-ego as described above, we can see that it is the result of two extremely important biological factors: the long duration of the childhood period of helplessness and dependence in human beings, and the fact of their Oedipus complex, which we have of course attributed to the interruption of libido development caused by the latency period, and hence to the *diphasic onset* of human sexual life.[53] According to one psychoanalytical hypothesis, this latter phenomenon, which appears to be specific to humans, is a heritage of the enforced process of cultural development brought about by the ice age.[54] That being so, the super-ego's differentiation from the ego was by no means a chance event: it reflects the most significant developmental features of both the individual and the species; indeed, by giving lasting expression to the influence of the parents, it perpetuates the existence of the factors to which it owes its origins.

Psychoanalysis has been accused on countless occasions of failing to concern itself with man's higher, moral, suprapersonal side. This accusation is doubly unjust: unjust in *historical* terms because we argued from the very beginning that the ego's moral and aesthetic tendencies are the driving force behind repression; unjust with regard to *method* because our accusers refused to recognize that – unlike some tidy philosophical system – psychoanalytical research could not come bounding onto the stage with a complete and fully fashioned set of doctrines, but had to forge its way step by step towards an understanding of the complexities of the psyche by means of painstaking analysis of both normal and abnormal phenomena. We had no need to share the tremulous anxiety of others as to the precise location of the 'higher element' in human beings so long as we were busily studying the workings of the repressed in their inner souls.[55]

But now that we are venturing to analyse the ego, we can say to all those who, shaken to the very core of their moral consciousness, have pleaded that there must surely be a higher presence in man: 'There is indeed, and this higher presence is the ego-ideal or super-ego, the representamen[56] of our relationship to our parents. As little children we knew, admired and feared these higher presences, and later assimilated them into our own selves.'

The ego-ideal is thus heir to the Oedipus complex, and as such an expression of the id's most powerful impulses and most important libidinal experiences. By erecting the ego-ideal, the ego asserted control over the Oedipus complex – and simultaneously subordinated itself to the id. Whereas the ego is essentially a representative of the world without, of reality, the super-ego is contraposed to it as advocate of the world within, of the id. As of course we have meanwhile come to expect, conflicts between the ego and the ideal are ultimately going to reflect the antithesis of 'the objective' and 'the psychical' – the world without, and the world within.

By forming an ideal, the ego takes unto itself everything in the id that has been created by biology or left behind by the travails of the human race, and re-experiences it on an individual level. As a result of the way it is formed, the ego-ideal has the most abundant links to the phylogenetic acquest, the archaic inheritance, that is intrinsic to everyone. Thanks to the forming of an ideal, those elements within the individual psyche that once belonged to the deepest depths become – in terms of our scheme of values – the very loftiest aspects of the human soul. It would be a futile undertaking, however, to seek to *localize* the ego-ideal in anything like the way that we have done in respect of the ego, or to make it fit any of the metaphors and images that we have used in our efforts to delineate the relationship between the ego and the id.

It is easy to demonstrate that the ego-ideal meets all the expectations that we tend to have of the 'higher presence' in man. As a surrogate for the individual's longing for the father, it contains the germ from which all religions have evolved. The sense of inadequacy we feel when comparing our ego with our ideal gives rise to that religious feeling of humility that the yearning believer depends on.

As each child grows up, the role of the father is taken over by teachers and other authority figures, whose commandments and prohibitions remain powerfully alive in the ego-ideal – and in due course exercise moral censorship in the guise of *conscience*. The tension between what our conscience demands and what our ego actually does is experienced as *guilt feeling*. Our social feelings rest on identifications with other people on the basis of the same ego-ideal.

Religion, morality and a social sense – these chief constituents of man's higher nature[57] – were originally one and the same. According to the hypothesis I set forth in *Totem and Taboo*, they were acquired phylogenetically as a result of the father-complex – religion and moral restraint deriving from the process of overcoming[58] the Oedipus complex itself, and social feelings arising from the need to overcome the rivalry still remaining amongst the members of the younger generation. The male sex appears to have led the way in the acquisition of all these moral attributes, cross inheritance then transmitting them to females as well. Even today, social feelings develop within individuals as a construct serving to overbuild their jealous feelings of rivalry *vis-à-vis* their siblings.[59] Since their hostile impulses cannot be gratified, an identification with their erstwhile rival comes into being. Evidence gained from observing mild cases of homosexuality lends support to the supposition that this identification, too, is a surrogate for an affectionate object-choice, and has taken the place of the earlier stance of aggression and hostility.[60]

The mention of phylogenesis, however, raises new problems so challenging that one is tempted to choose discretion over valour and avoid them altogether. But we don't really have any choice: we must venture to resolve them, even though we fear that in the process the inadequacy of our entire enterprise may stand revealed. The question is this: was it the *ego* of primitive man that at some point acquired religion and morality as a consequence of the father-complex, or was it his *id*? If it was the ego, then why not simply describe the hereditary process as operating *within* the ego itself? If it was the id, how does that accord with the character of the id? Or are we wrong to suppose that the ego, super-ego and id became differentiated at such an early stage? Or shouldn't we admit in all honesty that our whole conception of the ego and its processes contributes nothing to our understanding of phylogenesis, and is altogether irrelevant to it?

Let us attempt the easiest answers first. We are obliged to attribute the differentiation of ego and id not merely to primitive man, but to organisms that are far simpler still, since it is a necessary manifestation of the influence exerted by the external world. As for the super-ego, we described it as having its very origins in the experiences that led to totemism; the question whether it was the ego or the id that underwent those experiences and acquired moral attributes quickly proves to be pointless. The next consideration that presents itself to our mind is that the id cannot experience or undergo any external pattern of events except via the *ego*, the sole representative of the external world that it possesses. None the less, we cannot in fact claim that there is a hereditary process operating directly within the *ego*. What we encounter here is the yawning gulf between actual individuals, and our notion of the species. Furthermore, we must not view the difference between the ego and the id in unduly rigid terms; we must not forget that the ego is part of the id, albeit differentiated from it in a special way.[61] The ego's experiences seem to be lost to heredity to begin with; however, if they recur often and strongly enough in numerous successive generations of individuals, they transform themselves so to speak into id experiences, and their impact is then preserved through heredity. The heritable id accordingly harbours within it remnants of countless numbers of previous egos, and when an individual ego evolves its super-ego from the id it is perhaps merely bringing older ego forms back to light, and back to life.

The manner in which the super-ego comes into being makes it readily comprehensible that early conflicts of the ego with the object-cathexes of the id can be continued later on in conflicts with their successor, the super-ego. If the ego has botched the task of overcoming the Oedipus complex, then its[62] energy-cathexis, which derives from the id, will reassert itself in the reaction-formation of the ego-ideal. The abundant communication between the ego-ideal and these *Ucs* drive-impulses serves to explain the puzzling fact that the ideal itself can remain largely unconscious, and inaccessible to the ego. The battle that had previously raged in the nether depths, but had never come to any final resolution through a rapid process of sublimation and identification, is now carried on at a higher level, rather as in Kaulbach's painting of the Battle of Châlons.[63]

IV

The Two Types of Drives

We have already made the point that our proposed division of the psyche into an id, an ego and a super-ego can only signify a real advance in our knowledge if it also proves to be the means to a deeper understanding and more accurate description of the dynamic relations at work in the life of the psyche. We have also come to appreciate that the ego is particularly subject to the influence of perception, and that in broad terms one can say that perceptions have the same significance for the ego that drives have for the id. At the same time, however, the ego is also susceptible to the influence of drives, just like the id – of which, of course, it is but part, albeit a specially modified one.

On the subject of drives, I have recently (in *Beyond the Pleasure Principle*) elaborated a view that I shall first recapitulate, and then use as the basis for the next stages of the argument. On this view, we need to distinguish two types of drives, one of which – the *sexual drives*, or *Eros* – is far more conspicuous, and far more accessible to our knowledge and understanding. It includes not only the uninhibited sexual drive itself and the goal-inhibited and hence sublimated drive-impulses deriving from it, but also the self-preservation drive that we perforce ascribe to the ego, and that at the very outset of our psychoanalytical work we had good reason to regard as contrasting sharply with the sexual object-drives. Demonstrating this second type of drive caused us considerable difficulty; our solution in the end was to regard sadism as representative of it. On the basis of theoretical considerations underpinned by biology, we posited a *death drive* charged with the task of causing animate organisms to revert to an inanimate state, whereas Eros pursues the goal of maximizing the complexity of life – and thereby of course preserving it – by an ever more catholic combination of the particles into which living matter had been fragmented. In pursuing their respective goals both drives behave in a strictly conservative manner, in that they seek the restoration of a state that was disrupted by the emergence of life. According to this view, the emergence of life is therefore the cause both of the urge to carry on living and, simultaneously, of the urge for death, while life itself is a battle and constant compromise between these two urges. Considered thus, the question as to the origin of life remains a cosmological one, while the question as to the purpose and intention of life is answered in *dualistic* terms.[64]

A particular physiological process is attributable – so the argument goes – to each of the two types of drive (anabolism and catabolism[65]); both drives are active in each and every piece of living substance, albeit in varying proportions, with the result that any such substance is capable of taking on the role of Eros.

Precisely *how* drives of the two types connect, combine and blend with each other remains entirely unimaginable – but *that* such a thing happens, routinely and on a very large scale, is a postulate crucial to our whole framework of ideas. We can hypothesize that as a consequence of the fusion of unicellular elementary organisms into multicellular organisms, the death drive in the individual cell was successfully neutralized, and its destructive impulses diverted to the external world through the mediation of a special organ, to wit the musculature; the death drive accordingly now finds expression – though in all probability only in part – as a *destruction drive* directed against the external world and other organisms.

Once we have accepted the notion of a merging of the two types of drives, we are then also confronted by the possibility of a – more or less complete – *de-mergence* of them. I would suggest that in the sadistic component of the sexual drive we see a classic example of a purposive *merging* of drives, while in sadism *qua* autonomous perversion we see an exemplary instance of *de-mergence*, albeit not one where the process has been taken to extremes.[66] This in its turn affords us fresh insight into a large mass of facts that have not previously been considered in this light. We can readily see that, in order to effect release, the *destruction drive* is routinely put at the service of Eros; we suspect that epileptic fits are produced by, and indicative of, a de-mergence of drives; and we are beginning to realize that amongst the effects achieved by certain serious neuroses, e.g. the obsessional neuroses, the de-mergence of drives and the appearance of the death drive deserve special consideration. By way of a rapid generalization: we are inclined to think that libido regressions, for instance regression from the genital to the sadistic-anal phase, are rooted essentially in a de-mergence of drives, and that, inversely, progression from the early to the definitive genital phase is dependent on an accession of erotic components. The question also arises whether ordinary *ambivalence* – which we so often find to be particularly marked in those who are constitutionally disposed to neurosis – should not be regarded as the result of a de-mergence; this latter process is so primal, however, that it must rate instead as a merging of drives that remained incomplete.

Our interest quite naturally turns to two particular questions: first, whether we shall not perhaps discover revealing connections between the structures we have postulated – the ego, super-ego and id – on the one hand, and the two types of drives on the other; second, whether we shall be able to show that the pleasure principle, the mechanism that controls psychic processes, stands in a firm and clear relationship to the two types of drives, and to the forms into which the psyche has differentiated. Before we enter upon this discussion, however, we need to deal with a doubt that challenges the very formulation of the question itself. While there can be no doubt about the pleasure principle, and whilst our division of the ego is soundly based on clinical evidence, yet our grounds for distinguishing between the two types of drives seem not altogether strong enough, and it seems quite possible that facts evinced by clinical analysis might rob them of all credibility.

There does appear to be just such a fact. We might reasonably substitute the polarity of love and hate for the antithesis constituted by the two types of drives. Whereas of course we have no problem showing how Eros is represented, it comes as quite a relief that we are now able to identify the destruction drive – which takes its lead from hate – as representing the highly elusive death drive. Clinical observation, however, clearly shows us not only that hate is an unexpectedly regular accompaniment of love (ambivalence), and is very often its precursor in human relationships, but also that in certain circumstances hate changes into love, and love into hate. If this transformation involves anything more than just temporal succession, that is, one thing simply taking the place of the other, then clearly we are left with no basis for making such a fundamental distinction as that between erotic drives and death drives – a distinction premised on the notion of physiological processes that run directly counter to one another.

Now cases where we first love someone and then hate them (or *vice versa*) because they themselves have occasioned the change, clearly have no bearing on our problem; nor do those cases where love that has not yet become manifest reveals itself first through hostility and a tendency to aggression, for here the destructive component may simply have run on ahead during the process of object-cathexis, before being joined in due course by the erotic component. But a number of cases are known to us from the psychology of neuroses in which there are much stronger grounds for supposing that a transformation does indeed take place. In *paranoia persecutoria* the patient resists an excessive homosexual attachment to a particular individual in such a way that this most deeply loved individual turns into a persecutor against whom the often dangerous aggression of the patient is directed. We can legitimately interject that a previous phase had served to convert the love into hate. Regarding the genesis of homosexuality, indeed also of desexualized social feelings, psychoanalytical study has only recently revealed to us the existence of intense feelings of rivalry leading to aggressive tendencies, feelings that have to be overcome before the hated object can become the loved object, or become the object of an identification.[67] The question arises whether we can assume that in these cases the hate is converted directly into love. After all, it is a matter here of purely internal changes, precipitated in no way by any change in behaviour on the part of the object.

However, another possible mechanism is familiar to us from our psychoanalytical study of the change that occurs in paranoia. Here, an ambivalent attitude is present from the outset, and the transformation is brought about through a reactive displacement of cathexis, whereby energy is withdrawn from the erotic impulse, and added to the hostile one.

Something very similar, albeit not quite the same, happens in the process that leads to homosexuality, namely the overcoming of hostile feelings of rivalry.[68] Hostility is an attitude with no prospect of gratification, and in consequence – for economic reasons, in other words – it is replaced by the attitude of love, which offers better prospects of gratification, that is, the possibility of release. In neither of these cases, therefore, do we need to assume a direct transformation of hate into love, which would be incompatible with the notion of a qualitative difference between the two types of drives.

It has not escaped our notice, however, that in drawing on this other mechanism whereby love changes into hate, we have tacitly made a further assumption – one that deserves to be made fully explicit. We have based our argument on the supposition that there exists within the psyche – whether in the ego or the id is still uncertain – a displaceable energy which, though indifferent in itself, can join forces with a qualitatively differentiated erotic or destructive impulse and increase its overall cathexis. We simply cannot get anywhere without positing a displaceable energy of this kind. But we are still left wondering where it comes from, who[69] it belongs to, and what it signifies.

The problem of the *quality* of drive-impulses, and how that quality is maintained throughout the sundry vicissitudes that drives are prone to, remains decidedly obscure, and to date barely any attempt has been made to tackle it. In the case of the sexual partial drives, which lend themselves particularly well to observation, one can see a number of processes that follow a similar pattern. Thus, for instance, the partial drives to some extent communicate with each other; a drive originating from one erogenous source is capable of surrendering its intensity in order to reinforce a partial drive originating from another; the gratification of one drive can serve another in place of the latter's own. Further similarities could be cited – all of which inevitably encourages us to venture certain kinds of hypotheses.

In this present discussion, too, I can offer not proof but only a hypothesis. It seems plausible to suppose that this displaceable and indifferent energy, active very probably in both the ego and the id, derives from the store of narcissistic libido, and is thus desexualized Eros; indeed, the erotic drives in general seem to us to be more plastic, more divertible, more displaceable than the destruction drives. That being so, we can quite logically go on to suggest that this displaceable libido operates on behalf of the pleasure principle, by preventing any undue build-up and facilitating release.[70] In so doing it clearly displays considerable indifference as to which particular pathway is adopted by the release process, provided that the actual process itself takes place. We know this trait to be typical of the cathexis processes in the id. It is evident in erotic cathexes, where a marked indifference is displayed with regard to the object; and it is very marked indeed in the transferences that occur in analysis – transferences that *have* to be effected, regardless of who happens to be their object. Rank has recently produced some splendid examples demonstrating that neurotic acts of revenge tend to be directed against the wrong people. This type of behaviour on the part of the unconscious inevitably reminds us of that comic little story of the three village tailors, one of whom is due to be strung up because the village's sole blacksmith has done a dastardly deed that calls for a hanging.[71] *Someone* has to be punished, even if it's not the guilty party. This same disregard first came to our attention in the displacements characteristic of the primary process in dream-work.[72] Whereas in that instance it was the *objects* that were apparently deemed to be of only secondary importance, in this present context it is the *pathways* utilized by the release process. If the ego were involved, we would expect to find an insistence on greater precision in the choice of both object and pathway.

If this displaceable energy is desexualized libido, then it may also be termed *sublimated*, for it would still be firmly adhering to Eros's central objective of being a unifying and binding force, by serving to bring about that unity which – or at least the striving for which – is the ego's most distinctive feature. If we include thought processes in the broader sense amongst these displacements, then of course thinking, too, may be seen to be covered by the sublimation of erotic energy.

This brings us back to a possibility that we touched on earlier, namely that sublimation routinely takes place via the medium of the ego.[73] Another circumstance that we might recall here is that this same ego deals with the initial object-cathexes of the id – and no doubt later ones as well – by taking their libido into itself and annexing it to the ego-alteration brought about by identification. Needless to say, this conversion [of object-libido] into ego-libido entails a desexualization, an abandonment of sexual goals. At all events this affords us clear insight into an important function of the ego in its relationship to Eros. By thus commandeering the libido of the various object-cathexes, setting itself up as sole love-object, and desexualizing or sublimating the libido of the id, it operates directly counter to the designs of Eros; it puts itself at the service of the opposing drive-impulses. In respect of certain other object-cathexes pertaining to the id, it simply has to put up with them – to tag along, so to speak. We shall return later to a further possible consequence of this activity on the part of the ego.[74]

At this point we probably need to make an important addition to the narcissism theory. At the very beginning the entire libido is massed in the id, during the period when the ego is in the process of formation, or formed but still weak. The id sends forth part of this libido for the purpose of erotic object-cathexes, whereupon the ego, having meanwhile gained in strength, seeks to commandeer this object-libido and force itself on the id as a love-object. The ego's form of narcissism is thus a *secondary* one – one that has been withdrawn from objects.[75]

Again and again, we find that the drive-impulses that we are capable of monitoring turn out to derive from Eros. If it were not for the arguments set forth in *Beyond the Pleasure Principle*, and ultimately also the sadistic admixtures encountered in Eros, we would have difficulty in holding firm to our fundamental dualist position. But since we have no alternative, we are driven to the supposition that the death drives very largely remain silent, and that the clamour of life comes mostly from Eros.[76]

And also from the battle *against* Eros! There can be no denying the notion that the pleasure principle serves the id as a compass in its battle against the libido, which habitually disrupts the smooth process of life. If the constancy principle in Fechner's sense[77] does indeed govern life, which on that view is supposed to be a steady slide into death, then it is the demands made by Eros, that is by the sexual drives, which – manifesting themselves as the *needs* that drives give rise to – interrupt the downward slide and create new tensions. Guided by the pleasure principle or, to be precise, by the awareness of unpleasure, the id defends itself against them by a variety of means. It does so in the first instance by meeting the demands of the non-desexualized libido as rapidly as possible, that is to say by striving to give gratification to the directly sexual urges. But it does so on a far larger scale by using one particular form of such gratification in which all the constituent demands coincide, in order to rid itself of those sexual substances that are the supersaturated vehicle, so to speak, of the erotic tensions. The shedding of the sexual substances in the sex act corresponds in a sense to the separating-out of soma and germ-plasm.[78] This explains why the state that ensues upon full sexual gratification is similar to dying, while in certain lower animals death coincides with the act of procreation. Reproduction is the cause of these creatures' death in the sense that the death drive can effect its aims without let or hindrance once Eros has been removed from the picture through the act of gratification. And finally, as we have seen, the ego makes it easier for the id to assert control by sublimating parts of the libido for itself and its own purposes.

V

The Ego and its Forms of Dependence

The sheer complexity of the topic in hand will perhaps excuse the fact that not one of these chapters has a title that entirely matches its content, and the associated fact that whenever we set out to explore new avenues of investigation we revert again and again to matters that we have already dealt with at an earlier stage.

Thus we have repeatedly stated that the ego very largely develops out of identifications which take the place of cathexes generated by the id and then abandoned, and that the first such identifications routinely assume the role of a special judgemental entity within the ego, and set about countering the ego[79] by behaving as a super-ego – whereas at a later stage the ego, having become stronger, may well show greater resistance to any such attempts on the part of identifications to exert influence over it. The super-ego owes its special position within – or counterposed to – the ego to a circumstance that needs to be appreciated from two distinct vantage-points: for one thing, it was the *first* identification, and it took place while the ego was still at a weak stage of its development; and secondly, it is heir to the Oedipus complex, and as such was responsible for introducing the most momentous objects into the ego. It relates to later ego-alterations rather as the primary sexual phase in childhood relates to the individual's later sexual life after puberty. Although it remains open to all the influences that subsequently play upon it, it still forever retains the particular characteristic that it acquired through its origins in the father complex, namely the ability to counter the ego and overmaster it. It is a monument to the erstwhile weakness and dependency of the ego, and it goes on to exert its dominance over the mature ego as well. Just as the child was subject to the compulsion that obliged it to obey its parents, so the ego submits to the categorical imperative of its super-ego.

However, the fact that the super-ego has its origins in the earliest object-cathexes of the id, and hence in the father complex, has other important implications for it as well: as we have already shown,[80] these origins link it to the phylogenetic acquirements of the id, and make it a reincarnation of previous ego forms that have left a residual imprint in the id. This means that the super-ego always has a very close relationship to the id, and can act as its representative *vis-à-vis* the ego. It secretes itself in the very depths of the id, and in consequence is further from consciousness than the ego.[81]

We can best appreciate these affinities if we turn our attention to certain clinical facts which, though by no means new, still await theoretical analysis.

There are people who behave in a very curious way in psychoanalysis. If you express any hope regarding the outcome of their treatment or show satisfaction over its progress, they do not seem the least bit gratified, and never fail to tell you that they feel worse than ever. At first you take this to be defiance, and an attempt to demonstrate to the physician their own superiority. Later, you arrive at a deeper and more just interpretation. You realize not only that such people cannot endure any form of praise or appreciation, but also that they react in directly inverse fashion to any progress in their treatment. Any element of the treatment that *ought* to produce an improvement or a temporary abeyance of symptoms, and in other cases does indeed produce such an effect, only serves to exacerbate their suffering, however briefly. Instead of getting better as the treatment proceeds, they get worse. They exhibit the phenomenon known as *negative therapeutic reaction*.

There can be no doubt that something within them actively resists recovery, and that the prospect of recovery is seen as a danger and feared as such. In the case of such people it tends to be said that the predominant factor is not the will to recover, but the need to be ill. Supposing we subject this resistance to analysis in the customary way, and supposing we manage to rid the patient of his attitude of defiance towards the doctor and his fixation on the various forms of illness-gain[82] – even then, most of the resistance stays firmly in place; and this always proves to be the most powerful single obstacle to recovery – more powerful even than those already familiar to us: narcissistic inaccessibility, a negative attitude to the doctor, and unwillingness to relinquish the illness-gain.

We finally come to realize that what is involved here is a 'moral' factor, so to speak: a guilt-feeling that finds its gratification in illness and refuses to forgo the punishment that suffering represents. Although this explanation is scarcely cheering, it is one that merits our unwavering support. However, this guilt-feeling remains entirely mute *vis-à-vis* the patient: it doesn't tell him he is guilty, and instead of feeling guilty, he feels ill. The guilt-feeling expresses itself solely as a resistance to recovery that can be attenuated only with great difficulty. It is particularly difficult, too, to convince the patient that this is the driving force making his illness persist; he will always cling to the explanation that more readily presents itself, namely that psychoanalysis is not the right treatment for him.[83]

This description relates specifically to what happens in the most extreme instances – but it probably applies, albeit to a lesser extent, to very many cases of neurosis, and perhaps to all of the more serious ones. Indeed we can go further: it may be precisely this factor – the behaviour of the ego-ideal – that chiefly determines the severity of a neurotic illness. This being so, we cannot really avoid offering one or two further comments on the way the guilt-feeling manifests itself in various different circumstances.

The normal, conscious, type of guilt-feeling (conscience) is easily understood: it has its basis in the tension between the ego and the ego-ideal; it is a manifestation of the fact that the ego has been condemned in some particular respect by the critical entity within it. The feelings of inferiority that are so familar in neurotics are probably not very far removed from this. In two disorders that are very well known to us, namely obsessional neurosis and melancholia, the guilt-feeling is excessively conscious; the ego-ideal displays particular severity in such instances and often attacks the ego in the most cruel way. Alongside this similarity, the two conditions also evince certain *dis*similarities that are no less significant.

In obsessional neurosis (or certain forms thereof), the guilt-feeling is strident in the extreme, but incapable of convincing the ego that it is justified. The patient's ego therefore strenuously refuses any imputation of guilt, and demands that the physician support him in his rejection of these guilt-feelings. It would be folly to yield to him, for any such attempt would inevitably fail. It then becomes evident in analysis that the super-ego is influenced by processes that occurred without the ego ever becoming aware of them. It really is possible to uncover the repressed impulses that account for the guilt-feeling. In this instance, the super-ego knew rather more than the ego about the unconscious id.

In melancholia there is an even stronger sense that the super-ego has seized control of consciousness. But in this case the ego does not dare to protest: it pleads guilty and submits to the punishments imposed.[84] We understand how this difference comes about: in obsessional neurosis it is a question of offensive impulses that have remained outside the ego; in melancholia, however, the object at which the super-ego's anger is directed has already been absorbed into the ego through identification.

The fact that guilt-feelings reach such an extraordinary pitch of intensity in these two neurotic disorders is certainly not easy to understand – but in fact the main problem confronting us in this situation resides elsewhere. We shall postpone discussion of it until we have dealt with the other cases in which guilt-feelings remain unconscious.

Needless to say, this latter form of guilt-feeling is mainly to be found in hysteria, and in states of the hysterical type. The mechanism causing it to remain unconscious is not difficult to divine. When threatened by a painful perception engendered by criticism on the part of its super-ego, the hysterical ego fends it off in just the same way as it is otherwise wont to fend off an unbearable object-cathexis – by an act of repression. It is thus the ego that is responsible for the fact that the guilt-feeling remains unconscious. We know that normally the ego carries out repressions as an obedient acolyte of its super-ego; here, however, we have an instance where it turns this selfsame weapon against its own lord and master. In obsessional neurosis the predominant phenomenon is of course reaction-formation in its various manifestations – but in this present instance the ego succeeds only in shutting out the material that the guilt-feeling relates to.

One can go further and venture the hypothesis that a large part of the guilt-feeling is normally bound to be unconscious since the genesis of conscience is intimately linked to the Oedipus complex, which itself belongs to the unconscious. If anyone were to advance the paradoxical proposition that normal human beings are not only much more immoral than they think, but also much more moral than they realize, then psychoanalysis – on whose findings the first half of this assertion is based – would also raise no objections to the second.[85]

It came as a surprise to discover that an intensification of this *Ucs* guilt-feeling can turn a person into a criminal – but this is undoubtedly the case. In many criminals, especially juveniles, we find clear evidence of a powerful guilt-feeling that was already in existence *before* their criminal act, and thus was not a consequence of it but rather the impetus behind it, as if they found it a relief being able to tie this unconscious guilt-feeling to something concrete and immediate.

In all these various circumstances the super-ego demonstrates its independence of the conscious ego, and its intimate rapport with the unconscious id. Now, with reference to the importance that we have ascribed to pre-conscious verbal residua in the ego,[86] the question arises whether the super-ego itself, assuming it is indeed *Ucs*, doesn't perhaps consist of such word-notions; and if not, then what *does* it consist of? One might tamely reply that the super-ego, too, cannot possibly deny that its roots lie in things *heard* – it is part of the ego, after all, and remains accessible to consciousness as a result of these word-notions (concepts, abstractions); but the *cathectic energy* delivered to these notions that make up the super-ego[87] derives not from auditory perception, not from the classroom, not from reading, but from sources within the id.

The question we deferred for later consideration is this: how is it that the super-ego very largely manifests itself as guilt-feeling (or

rather as criticism, since guilt-feeling is properly speaking the perception within the ego that corresponds to this criticism) and, in so
doing, brings such extraordinary harshness and severity to bear
against the ego? If we turn first to melancholia, then we find that the
excessively strong super-ego, having seized control of consciousness,
attacks the ego with unsparing savagery as if it had harnessed to its
own purposes the entire store of sadism available within that particular individual. Putting it in terms of our interpretation of sadism, we
would say that the destructive component has lodged itself in the
super-ego and then turned against the ego. What thereupon prevails
in the super-ego is not unlike a pure form of the death drive, indeed
it quite often succeeds in driving the ego to its death if the ego
doesn't manage in time to keep its oppressor at bay by switching
into mania.

The reproaches of conscience are similarly torturous and discomfiting in certain forms of obsessional neurosis, but the situation
here is less perspicuous. In contrast to melancholia, it is notable that
obsessional patients don't really ever tread the path of self-
destruction; they appear in effect to be immune to the danger of
suicide, and to be far better protected against it than hysterics are.
We can readily see that retaining the object is what guarantees
the safety of the ego. In obsessional neurosis, regression to the
pre-genital form of sexual organization makes it possible for love
impulses to turn into impulses of aggression towards the object.
Once again, the destruction drive is on the loose and wants to destroy
the object – or at least there is every semblance of there being such
an intention. The ego does not adopt these tendencies: it vigorously
resists them by means of reaction-formations and precautionary
measures, with the result that they remain in the id. The super-ego,
however, behaves as though the ego were responsible for them, and
at the same time shows us, through the utter seriousness with which
it combats these destructive intentions, that what is involved here is
a very real substitution of hate for love, and not a mere semblance
of it called forth by regression. Helplessly besieged on two fronts,
the ego battles in vain against the demands of the murderous id on
one hand, and the reproaches of its punitive conscience on the other.

All it can manage to do is to block the grossest depredations of both, and the outcome is, first, unending self-torment, which then develops into systematic tormenting of the object if and when it is accessible.

The dangerous death drives are dealt with in a variety of ways within each individual. Some of them are neutralized by being merged with erotic components, others are deflected into the outer world in the form of aggression, but in the main they undoubtedly continue their inner activities unchecked. How is it, then, that in melancholia the super-ego can turn into a kind of rallying-ground for the death drives?

Taking morality, the curbing of drives, as our parameter, we can summarize the position as follows: the id is wholly amoral; the ego tries hard to be moral; the super-ego can become hypermoral, and thereby show a degree of cruelty that only the id can match. It is a curious thing that the more a person curbs his aggression towards the external world, the more severe and hence more aggressive he becomes in his ego-ideal. Viewed in the customary manner, the situation appears to be quite the reverse: on this view it is the imperative of the ego-ideal that causes the aggression to be suppressed. The fact of the matter, however, is just as we have described it: the more a person succeeds in controlling his aggression, the more intense becomes his ego-ideal's aggressive disposition towards his ego. It is tantamount to a displacement, to the ego-ideal turning on the person's ego. But then even ordinary, normal morality is characterized by harsh restrictiveness and savage forbiddance. Indeed, it is from this that the conception arises of a higher being inexorably bent on meting out punishment.

Now I cannot expand any further on these matters without introducing a new hypothesis. The super-ego, as we know, resulted from an identification with the father *qua* paradigm. Every such identification is in the nature of a desexualization or even a sublimation. Now it seems that when such a conversion process occurs, a de-mergence of drives takes place as well.[88] After sublimation, the erotic component no longer has the strength to annex all the destructive capacity that has been added to it, and the latter becomes free-moving and manifests itself as an aggressive and destructive tendency. It is precisely from this de-mergence that the ideal presumably derives its harsh and cruel manner of dictating to the individual what he shall and shall not do.

Let us return for a moment to obsessional neurosis. Circumstances are different here. The de-mergence whereby love turns into aggression is not brought about by anything the ego does, but is the result of a regression that takes place in the id. But this process spills over from the id to the super-ego, which now becomes even more severe towards the innocent ego. In both cases, however [that is, in obsessional neurosis and in melancholia], it would seem that the ego, having taken control of the libido by means of identification, pays a heavy price for so doing by having to suffer the aggression that is mixed in with the libido as a punishment imposed by the super-ego.

Our ideas about the ego are beginning to settle, its various relations are becoming steadily clearer. We can now see the ego in all its strengths and weaknesses. It is entrusted with important functions: by virtue of its relation to the perceptual system it determines the temporal sequence of psychic processes and submits them to the 'reality-test'; by interpolating thought processes it is able to delay motor energy discharges,[89] and it controls the pathways to motor activity – though it must be admitted that this particular power is more formal than real: in its relationship to action the ego's position is somewhat akin to that of a constitutional monarch, without whose approval nothing can pass into law, but who would think extremely carefully before vetoing any bill laid before him by his parliament. The ego is enriched by all life experiences deriving from the external world – but the id is its *other* external world, which it seeks to subordinate to its own purposes. It withdraws libido from the id; it refashions the object-cathexes of the id into creations of the ego.[90] With the help of the super-ego, it draws – in some way as yet unclear to us – on the experiences of previous eras stored in the id.

There are two routes by which the content of the id can find its way into the ego. One is the direct route, while the other goes by way of the ego-ideal, and for some psychic activities it may well be crucially important which of these two routes they follow. As it develops, the ego first *perceives* drives, and later *controls* them; first *obeys* drives, and later *inhibits* them. This achievement is due in great measure to the ego-ideal, which is indeed itself to some extent a reaction-formation against the id's drive processes. Psychoanalysis is an instrument that is meant to enable the ego to defeat the id, and to go on defeating it.

On the other hand, however, we can see this same ego as a poor little creature subjected to servitude in three different ways, and threatened in consequence by three different dangers – one posed by the external world, one by the libido of the id, and one by the harshness of the super-ego. Corresponding to these three dangers are three different kinds of fear, for fear is the manifestation of a retreat from danger. As an entity located on the border between the world and the id, the ego seeks to mediate between them: it seeks to make the id tractable to the world; and by means of the muscle activity it instigates, it seeks to make the world match the wishes of the id. In fact it behaves rather as the physician does in psychoanalytic therapy: it commends itself, and its regard for the objective world, to the id as a potential libido-object, and seeks to divert the id's libido onto itself. It is not merely the id's adjutant, but a grovelling lackey desperate to win his master's love. It does its utmost to stay on good terms with the id; it dresses up the latter's *Ucs* commands in its own *Pcs* rationalizations; when reality wags its finger, it feigns obedience on the part of the id, even when the id has in fact remained obdurate and intransigent; it hushes up the id's conflicts with reality, and also, wherever possible, its conflicts with the super-ego. Positioned as it is between the id and reality, it yields all too often to the temptation to fawn, to lie, to do whatever may be opportune, rather like a politician who knows full well what he *ought* to do, but wants none the less to preserve his popularity in the eyes of the public.

The ego does not show impartiality in its dealings with the two types of drives. Through the work it does to bring about identifications and sublimations it helps the death drives to assert control over the libido, but it thereby runs the risk of itself becoming the object of the death drives and thus perishing. In order to provide such help, it must make itself replete with libido, thereby becoming a representative of Eros, keen to live and be loved.

However, since its sublimational work results in a de-mergence of drives and the unleashing of aggressive drives within the super-ego, its battle against the libido exposes it to the danger of suffering harm and death. If the aggression of the super-ego causes it to suffer or even perish, then its fate is analogous to that of the protista, which are destroyed by the products of their own catabolism. Viewed in economic terms, the morality operative within the super-ego seems to us to be just such a product of catabolism.[91]

Amongst the ego's various forms of dependence, the most interesting is probably its dependence on the super-ego.

The ego is of course the true locus of fear.[92] Threatened by dangers from three different directions, the ego displays the flight reflex by withdrawing its own cathexis from the perception of the threat or from the process within the id that is deemed to be posing the threat, and re-deploying it as fear. This primitive reaction is later superseded by the enactment of protective cathexes (the phobia mechanism). It is impossible to say precisely what the ego fears from the danger without, and from the libidinal danger within the id; we know it involves being overwhelmed or destroyed – but we cannot apprehend it analytically. The ego simply responds to the warning given by the pleasure principle. On the other hand it *is* possible to say what lies hidden behind the ego's fear of the super-ego, behind its consciential fear.[93] At some point in the past there was a threat of castration at the hands of the superior being that subsequently turned into the ego-ideal, and the fear of castration provoked by this is probably the core around which consciential fear subsequently accretes; consciential fear is the continuation of that castration fear.

The grandiloquent assertion that 'all fear is essentially fear of death' is more or less meaningless, and in any event impossible to justify.[94] On the contrary, it seems to me altogether right to distinguish fear of death from objective fear and neurotic libido-fear.[95] The fear of death poses a severe problem for psychoanalysis, for death is an abstract concept with negative content for which no unconscious correlative can be found. The mechanism behind the fear of death could only be that the ego very largely jettisons its narcissistic libido-cathexis, thus forsaking its own self in much the same way as it forsakes external objects in other fear situations. I rather think that the fear of death is something that evolves between the ego and the super-ego.

Fear of death arises, as we know, in two sets of circumstances (both incidentally directly analogous to those that apply in other instances where fear is generated): as a reaction to an external danger; and as an inner process, for instance in melancholia. Once again, the neurotic scenario may help us to understand the objective one.

There is only one possible explanation for the fear of death that arises in melancholia, namely that the ego gives up on itself because it feels itself to be hated and persecuted by the super-ego instead of loved. For the ego, therefore, 'to live' means the same as 'to be loved' – to be loved by the super-ego, which in this context, too, serves to represent the id. The super-ego plays the same protective, salvatory role as the father once did, and as providence or destiny will do later on. But the ego must inevitably draw the very same conclusion when confronted by a massive danger in the objective world that it believes itself powerless to overcome: it sees itself as deserted by all the forces that could have protected it, and lets itself die. Incidentally, this is the same situation as that which underlay the first great fear-state of birth and the fear-cum-longing[96] of infancy, namely separation from the protecting mother.

On the basis of these considerations, therefore, fear of death, like consciential fear, can be viewed as a modified form of castration fear. Given the enormous importance of guilt-feeling in neuroses, we cannot by any means dismiss the idea that ordinary neurotic fear may well be compounded in severe cases by the fear generated through the interaction between ego and super-ego (castration fear, consciential fear, fear of death).

The id – to which we finally return – has no means of showing the ego either love or hate. It cannot declare its will, for no single, unified will has ever lain within its means. Eros and the death drive do battle within it; we have already seen the various means that the two sets of drives deploy in their fight with each other. We could depict the id as being entirely under the control of the mute but mighty death drives, who seek peace and, prompted by the pleasure principle, seek to pacify Eros the troublemaker – but we fear that to do so would be to underestimate the part that Eros plays.

(1923)

*Inhibition, Symptom,
and Fear*

I

When we are describing pathological phenomena, ordinary linguistic usage allows us to distinguish between 'symptoms' and 'inhibitions', but attaches no particular significance to this distinction. We ourselves would scarcely muster any interest in differentiating the concepts of 'inhibition' and 'symptom' from one another if we did not encounter cases of illness obliging us to attest that they display no symptoms, only inhibitions, and if we did not wish to know the conditions that give rise to this.

The two concepts have different provenances. 'Inhibition' relates particularly to function, and does not necessarily signify anything pathological; we can just as well describe any *normal* restraint of a function as an 'inhibition' thereof.[1] 'Symptom', on the other hand, means something like 'indicator of a disease process'. Thus an inhibition, too, can be a symptom. The standard practice, then, is to speak of 'inhibition' where there is a straightforward diminution of any given function, and 'symptom' where the function in question shows unusual changes or behaves in some new way. In many cases it appears to be a matter of purely arbitrary choice as to whether one stresses the positive or the negative side of the pathological process and characterizes its outcome as 'symptom' or as 'inhibition'.[2] All this is really very uninteresting, and the problem as we initially formulated it turns out to offer very little promise.

Since inhibition is so intimately linked to function, one might usefully entertain the idea of investigating the different ego functions with a view to establishing the ways in which the disturbance of any of these functions manifests itself in the various neurotic disorders. For the purposes of this comparative study we have chosen the following areas: the sexual function, eating, locomotion, occupational work.

a) The sexual function is subject to disturbances of many different kinds, most of them displaying the characteristics of straightforward inhibitions. These are summarily termed 'psychic impotence'. The successful completion of normal sexual activity presupposes a highly complicated sequence of events, susceptible to disturbance at any point. In the male the principal manifestations of inhibition are successively as follows: blocking of the libido necessary for initiating the process (lack of desire at the psychic level); absence of physical preparedness (lack of erection); abbreviation of the act (premature ejaculation) – which can just as readily be described as a positive symptom; cessation of the act before its natural conclusion (lack of ejaculation); non-appearance of the appropriate psychic effect (i.e. of the pleasurable sensation of orgasm). Other disturbances result where the sexual function is combined with particular factors of a perverted or fetishistic nature.

It cannot escape our attention for very long that inhibition is related to fear.[3] Numerous inhibitions clearly consist in relinquishing a particular function because fear would result if it were to be carried out. In women, direct fear of the sexual function is common. We class this as a form of hysteria, as we also do in the case of the defensive symptom of disgust, which initially sets in as a post factum reaction to the passively experienced sexual act, and subsequently appears whenever the sexual act is visualized. In addition, a large number of compulsive acts turn out to be precautions and safeguards against sexual experience, and are accordingly phobic in nature.

This really doesn't add very much to our understanding. All we can do is to note that a great variety of means are deployed to disrupt the sexual function: 1) straightforward blocking of the libido – which more readily than anything else appears to produce what we term a pure inhibition; 2) spoiling the actual execution of the function; 3) rendering the function more difficult by adding special conditions, or modifying it by reorienting it towards different objectives; 4) averting it by dint of protective measures; 5) in cases where its inception can no longer be prevented: interrupting it by engendering fear; and finally 6) in cases where, despite everything, the function is carried through to its conclusion: provoking a post factum reaction that protests against what has occurred and seeks to undo it.

b) The most common disruption affecting the eating function is lack of interest in food due to withdrawal of libido. An *increased* interest in food is also not uncommon; the compulsion to eat is motivated by fear of starvation, and has been little researched. The symptom of vomiting is familiar to us as a hysterical defence against eating. Refusal to eat as a result of fear is a characteristic of psychotic states (delusional fear of poisoning).

c) Locomotion is inhibited in some neurotic disorders, both by lack of interest in walking and by physical weakness related specifically to walking. The disability is hysterical in nature, and operates by either paralysing the motor function of the leg muscles or inducing a specific suspension of this particular function (abasia). Especially characteristic is the process whereby locomotion is rendered more difficult by the introduction of special conditions, the non-fulfilment of which gives rise to fear (phobia).

d) Inhibitions affecting the ability to work – which so often present for treatment as an isolated symptom – reveal themselves to us in the form of diminished pleasure, inferior performance, or reactive phenomena such as tiredness, vertigo, nausea in cases where the person is forced to carry on working. Hysteria forces the person to stop working altogether by paralysing organs and functions in a way that makes it impossible for the work to be carried out. Obsessional neurosis disrupts the work process by making the person prone to constant distractions, and making him waste time by repeating and dwelling on things unnecessarily.

We could extend this brief survey to other functions as well, but we could not reasonably expect to gain anything by so doing, as we would not succeed in penetrating beyond the outer surface of things. Let us therefore settle without further ado on a hypothesis that rids the concept of inhibition of almost all its mystery. An inhibition is the manifestation of a *restriction of function in the ego*, which can itself have a whole variety of different causes. We are already very familiar with one general tendency displayed by this abnegation of function, and with some of its mechanisms.

The said tendency is more readily identifiable in the various specific inhibitions. In cases where piano-playing, writing and even walking are affected by inhibitions, psychoanalysis shows that this is caused by excessive eroticization of the organs involved, namely the fingers and the feet. We have already come to appreciate on a more general level that the ego function of an organ is impaired if there is an increase in its erogeneity, its sexual significance. If we might venture to use a somewhat farcical comparison: it behaves like the family cook who refuses to carry on working at the kitchen stove because the master of the house has started an affair with her. If writing – which consists in letting fluid flow from a tube onto a sheet of white paper – has acquired the symbolic significance of coitus, or if walking has become a symbolic surrogate for stamping on the body of mother earth, then both activities, writing and walking, are abandoned, since it would otherwise seem as if one were performing the forbidden sexual act. The ego abnegates its due functions in order to avoid having to carry out a fresh act of repression, in order to *avoid a conflict with the id*.

Other inhibitions clearly serve the purposes of self-punishment, as is not infrequently the case with those affecting work activities. These are things that the ego is not allowed to do because they would bring advantage and success, something that the stern super-ego has forbidden. The ego therefore refrains from these activities too – *in order not to enter into conflict with the super-ego*.

The more generalized inhibitions of the ego are subject to a different, very straightforward mechanism. If the ego is put under strain by particularly severe demands on the psyche, such as sorrow[4] for example, or a major suppression of emotion, or the need to stifle a constant welling of sexual fantasies, then it is left with so little spare energy that it has to stop expending it at numerous places all at once, like a speculator who is short of cash because he has tied it all up in his various projects. I was able to observe an instructive instance of such generalized inhibition, brief but intense, in the case of a patient suffering from obsessional neurosis, who fell into a paralysing torpor lasting anything from a day to several days in circumstances that clearly *ought* to have given rise to an explosion of rage. This must surely open the way to an understanding of the kind of generalized inhibition that characterizes depressive states, notably the most severe of these: melancholia.

By way of conclusion, therefore, we can say of inhibitions that they constitute a restriction of ego function, occurring either as a precautionary measure, or because so much energy has already been used up elsewhere. It is now easy to see in what way an inhibition differs from a symptom; and a symptom can clearly no longer be described as a process operating within, or acting upon, the ego.

II

We long ago made a study of the essential elements of symptom-formation, and offered a description of them that we hope is incontestable. On this view, a symptom is both sign and surrogate of a drive that has remained ungratified; it is a product of the repression process. The latter emanates from the ego, which – perhaps at the behest of the super-ego – refuses to go along with a drive-cathexis instigated within the id.[5] Repression enables the ego to prevent the notion serving as the vehicle of the disagreeable[6] impulse from entering consciousness – though psychoanalysis often shows it to have survived as an unconscious formation.[7] Everything seems clear enough up to this point; but as soon as we venture beyond it we encounter unresolved difficulties.

In our earlier descriptions of the repression process we emphatically stressed its success in keeping things from consciousness, but left various other matters open to doubt. One question that arose was this: what happens to drive-impulses activated within the id that seek gratification as their goal? Our answer was an indirect one, to the effect that the process of repression transforms the expected *pleasure* of gratification into *un*pleasure; and this left us facing the problematic question as to how the gratifying of a drive can possibly result in unpleasure. In the hope that this will clarify matters, we wish to argue in no uncertain terms that as a result of repression the excitatory process originally intended within the id does not in fact take place at all; the ego succeeds in inhibiting or deflecting it. If this is so, then we need no longer be puzzled by the 'transformation of affect'[8] brought about by repression. But at the same time we have conceded that the ego can exert a very considerable influence on events in the id, and we must accordingly learn to understand the means by which the ego is able to achieve this surprising degree of power.

I believe that the ego derives this influence from its very close links to the perceptual system, which indeed constitute its essence, and the grounds for its differentiation from the id. The function of this *Pcpt-Cs* system,[9] as we have termed it, is connected to the phenomenon of consciousness. The system receives excitations from within, as well as from without, and on the basis of the sensations of pleasure/unpleasure reaching it from that quarter it attempts to control the evolution of *all* psychic events in accordance with the pleasure principle. We so readily imagine the ego as being powerless against the id, but whenever it wants to resist a drive process within the id it need only give out a *signal of unpleasure* in order to achieve its ends, thanks to the assistance of the almost all-powerful agency of the pleasure principle. To consider this circumstance in isolation for a moment, we can illustrate it with an example borrowed from a different sphere. Let us suppose that in some state or other a certain clique is opposed to a measure which, if passed, would perfectly accord with the desires of the masses. This minority grouping therefore takes control of the press, uses it to manipulate 'public opinion' as the supreme political force, and thereby succeeds in ensuring that the proposed measure is not brought in.

This answer, however, raises further questions. Where does the energy come from that is used to generate the signal of unpleasure? We are offered a pointer by the notion that an unwanted process *within* is probably blocked in much the same way as a stimulus from *without*; that the ego takes the same course in defending itself against inner dangers as it does against external ones. In the case of external danger, living organisms do whatever they can to escape from the threat. First of all, they withdraw cathexis from their physical perception of the danger; then later they realize that a more effective remedy is to activate their muscles in such a way that perception of the danger, even supposing they choose not to shut it out, is no longer possible – in other words they retreat from the danger area. Repression, too, amounts to a similar attempt to escape from danger. The ego withdraws (pre-conscious) cathexis from the drive-representamen[10] that it wants to repress, and uses it to release unpleasure (fear). The question as to how fear arises in repression is doubtless not a simple one; none the less we can justifiably adhere to the notion that the *ego* is the true locus of fear, and reject the earlier view that it is the cathectic energy of the repressed impulse that is automatically transformed into fear. If I have expressed this view myself in the past, it is because I was offering a phenomenological rather than a metapsychological description.

On the basis of what has been said so far, a new question immediately presents itself: how is it possible, in terms of economy, for a mere withdrawal or release process such as that involved in the retracting of pre-conscious ego-cathexis to produce unpleasure or fear, which – according to all our assumptions – can only result from an *increase* in cathexis? My answer is that the explanation for this cause–effect relationship is not to be found in the economic realm at all; in repression, fear is not produced anew, but is *re*produced as a state of affect on the basis of a pre-existing memory-image. However, with the further question as to the *origin* of this fear – and of affects in general – we leave the realm that incontestably pertains to psychology, and enter the neighbouring terrain of physiology. States of affect are innate in the human psyche as the residue of primal traumatic experiences, and in analogous circumstances they are reawakened as memory-symbols. I believe that I was not mistaken when I equated them to attacks of hysteria, which arise at a later stage and on an individual basis, and when I described them as the normal paradigms for such attacks. In the case of humans and related species it appears to be the birth process which, as each individual's first experience of fear, gives the actual *expression* of the affect of fear its characteristic form. We must not attach undue importance to this nexus, however, and in acknowledging it we must not overlook the fact that an affect-symbol is a biological imperative for danger situations, and would have been created in any event. I also believe that there is no justification for supposing that in the case of every single attack of fear something occurs in the psyche amounting to a reproduction of the birth experience. It is not even certain whether attacks of hysteria, which start as traumatic reproductions of this kind, permanently retain this characteristic.

I have argued elsewhere that most repressions that we encounter in our therapeutic work are cases of *secondary* repression. They presuppose *primal* repressions that have taken place at an earlier stage and which exert a magnetic influence on the subsequent process. As yet far too little is known about these background factors and preliminary stages in respect of repression. One all too readily runs the risk of over-estimating the role of the super-ego in repression. It is currently impossible to judge whether it is not perhaps the emergence of the super-ego that marks the dividing line between primal and secondary suppression. One thing that is clear is that the first attacks of fear – which are extremely intense – occur *before* the super-ego differentiates. It is altogether plausible that *quantitative* factors, such as the excessive strength of an excitation and a sudden breaching of the protective barrier, constitute the most immediate cause of primal repressions.

Mention of the protective barrier serves as a cue reminding us that repressions occur in two different situations: when a disagreeable drive-impulse is aroused by perception of something *external*; and when it emerges *internally* without any such provocation from without. We shall return to this difference later on. Let us note, however, that the barrier gives protection only against external stimuli, not against internal pressures exerted by drives.

If we continue to focus our attention on the ego's attempts to escape from danger, we shall not get very far with respect to symptom-formation. A symptom arises out of a drive-impulse that has been obstructed by a repression. If by use of the unpleasure signal the ego achieves its goal of suppressing the drive-impulse completely, then we learn nothing about how this process happens. We can learn only from cases where the repression can be said to have *failed* to some greater or lesser degree.

In such cases it generally transpires that, despite the repression, the drive-impulse contrived to come through in surrogate form – but a severely stunted, displaced, inhibited one. Furthermore there is no hint of gratification about this surrogate. No sensation of pleasure is produced when it is carried into effect; instead, this latter event exhibits the character of a compulsion. In the course of thus debasing the gratification process to the level of a mere symptom, however, repression demonstrates its power in another respect as well. Wherever possible, the surrogation process is prevented from achieving release through motor activity; and even where it is not so prevented, it is forced to use up all its energy procuring changes within the body, and is not permitted to extend its activities to the world outside; it is denied any opportunity to convert itself into action. As we know, in repression the workings of the ego are subject to the influence of external reality, and it therefore ensures that any successes of the surrogation process do not obtrude upon that reality.

It is the ego that determines what enters consciousness, and likewise determines what makes the transition into action *vis-à-vis* the external world – and in repression it deploys its power in *both* directions. This exercise of its power is felt on the one hand by the drive-representamen, on the other by the drive-impulse itself. This being so, it is apposite for us to ask how this acknowledgement of the might of the ego can possibly accord with the description of the ego's status that we adumbrated in our study *The Ego and the Id*. In that work we depicted the ego's dependence on both the id and the super-ego; we exposed its impotence and its apprehensiveness *vis-à-vis* both, and its travails in maintaining its air of superiority. This view has since met with a highly positive response in psychoanalytical literature. Numerous voices have emphatically stressed the weakness of the ego *vis-à-vis* the id, of rationality *vis-à-vis* the daemonic element within us, and are busily turning this theory into one of the central pillars of a psychoanalytical 'world view'. Shouldn't their sheer awareness of how repression actually works deter psychoanalysts in particular from so enthusiastically embracing such an extreme and partisan position?

I am not at all in favour of concocting world views.[11] This is a preoccupation best left to philosophers, who avowedly find it impossible to accomplish life's journey without a Baedeker[12] of this sort to guide them at every turn. Let us humbly accept the scorn with which philosophers look down upon us from their vantage point of superior exigence.[13] Since we too can no more deny our narcissistic pride than anyone else, we shall seek consolation in the thought that all these grand 'Guides to Life' rapidly go out of date; that it is precisely our own myopically narrow focus on small details that makes it necessary for them to be rewritten; and that even the most modern of these Baedekers are merely attempts at filling the shoes of the old, so comfortable, so all-embracing catechism. As we well know, science has so far managed to shed precious little light on the riddles of the world, and philosophers for all their sound and fury will change this not one jot; the only thing that can slowly, steadily procure change is patient perseverance in the kind of work that subordinates everything to the single imperative of certainty. When the traveller sings in the night he may well close his eyes to his anxiety[14] – but it certainly doesn't help him to see things more clearly.

III

To return to the problem of the ego: our sense of a contradiction arises from the fact that we are too rigid in our approach to abstractions, and in the face of complex arguments have eyes now for this side, now for that, but never for both. Distinguishing the ego from the id appears entirely justified, indeed various circumstances compel us so to do; on the other hand, however, the ego is part and parcel of the id, being simply a specially differentiated portion thereof. Supposing that in our mind we envisage this part in contradistinction to the whole, or supposing that the two have split apart in actual reality, then the weakness of the ego is instantly evident to us. But if the ego remains at one with the id, and indistinguishable from it, then its strength is immediately apparent. Much the same is true of the ego's relationship to the super-ego. In many contexts we see the two as blending into each other; generally speaking we can only distinguish one from another when a tension or conflict has arisen between them. So far as repression is concerned, the decisive factor is that the ego is an organization,[15] whereas the id is not; in fact the ego is the organized part of the id. It would be quite wrong to imagine the ego and the id as being like two opposing armies, as if a repression entailed the ego setting out to squash a section of the id, whereupon the remainder of the id comes rushing to the rescue and pits its strength against the ego. Things may often end up this way, but it is certainly not the situation when the repression first begins; as a rule the drive-impulse that is due to be repressed remains completely isolated. While the act of repression shows us the strength of the ego, it bears witness at the same time to its impotence, and its inability to influence or control any of the id's individual drive-impulses; for once the process has been turned into a symptom by the repression, it henceforth carries on its existence *outside* the ego-organization, and independently of it. And this same privilege of what we might term 'exterritoriality' is enjoyed not only by the process itself, but also by any offshoots that it subsequently produces; and it seems altogether conceivable that if these latter happen through association to come into contact with elements of the ego-organization, they will win them over to their own side and, thus fortified, expand at the ego's expense. To use an analogy familiar to us from the past: we can think of a symptom as resembling a foreign body that constantly generates stimuli and reactions in the tissue in which it has become embedded. It is true that the attempt to fight off the disagreeable drive-impulse is sometimes brought to a successful conclusion by symptom-formation (so far as we can see, this occurs most readily in conversion hysteria). As a rule, however, things take a very different course: after the initial act of repression a protracted or indeed never-ending sequel ensues in which a battle against the symptom carries on where the battle against the drive-impulse left off.

This secondary defensive battle shows us two distinct faces – bearing contradictory expressions. On the one hand, the very nature of the ego obliges it to undertake what we can only regard as an attempt at restoration or reconciliation. The ego is an organization; its very essence lies in the fact that all its component elements enjoy freedom of movement and scope to influence each other; its desexualized energy declares its origins not least in its constant striving to bind and to unify – and the stronger the development of the ego, the stronger this synthesizing compulsion becomes. Thus we can readily understand the fact that the ego *also* attempts to put an end to the alien and isolated status of the symptom, by exploiting every possible opportunity to bind it to itself in some way, and by means of such bonds incorporate it into its own organization. We know that this kind of aspiration is already at work in the very act of symptom-formation. A classic instance of this is afforded by those symptoms of hysteria that we have come to realize constitute a compromise between the need for gratification and the need for punishment. In as much as they fulfil a demand made by the super-ego, such symptoms are part and parcel of the ego from the outset – while at the same time they also signify the positions taken up by whatever has been repressed, and the breaches through which it has made incursions into the ego-organization; they are, so to speak, border-posts occupied by troops from both sides. Whether all primary symptoms of hysteria are formed in this way is a question that merits careful examination.

As regards the subsequent course of events, the ego behaves as if guided by the reflection that 'Like it or not, the symptom is there and can't be got rid of; the best thing now is to learn to like the situation, and extract the maximum possible advantage from it.' The ego does something that it normally only achieves in respect of the objective world without: it adjusts to the alien element *within* that is represented by the symptom. There is never any shortage of opportunities for so doing. The existence of the symptom may result in a certain reduction in performance, which can prove useful in mitigating any requirement imposed by the super-ego or rejecting any demand asserted by the external world. Thus the symptom is gradually entrusted with the task of representing important interests; it comes to play a considerable role in the assertion of the self, merges ever more intimately with the ego, and becomes ever more indispensable to it. Only in very rare instances does the process of assimilating a foreign body meet with this kind of success. It is also quite easy to exaggerate the significance of this secondary process of adjustment to the symptom by asserting that the ego only procured the symptom in the first place in order to enjoy the advantages it brings. That is just as right or just as wrong as arguing that the wounded soldier only had his leg shot off in the war so that he could live off his disability pension and avoid having to work.

Other symptom types, namely those of obsessional neurosis and paranoia, prove themselves particularly valuable to the ego not because they bring advantages, but because they bring narcissistic gratification that otherwise it has to go without. The systems that typically form in obsessional neurotics flatter their self-love by giving them the illusory belief that they are better than other people by virtue of being especially clean or especially conscientious; the delusions of paranoia give the wit and imagination of the patient a whole new realm of activity for which no substitute can easily be found. The outcome of all these various factors is the phenomenon known to us as the (secondary) *illness-gain*[16] of neurosis. This gain helps the ego in its efforts to incorporate the symptom, and reinforces the latter's fixation. If we then attempt in the course of psychoanalysis to assist the ego in its battle against the symptom, we find that these reconciliatory bonds between the ego and the symptom operate to the advantage of the resistances – and that it is by no means easy for us to undo them. It is indeed the case that the ego's two methods of dealing with the symptom directly contradict one another.

The second method is less cordial in nature, for it consists in continuing along the very same course as the repression. It seems clear, however, that it would not be right for us to accuse the ego of behaving inconsistently. The ego is peaceable, and seeks to incorporate the symptom, to absorb it into its own system. It is the *symptom* that causes the problem: as the fully fledged surrogate and offshoot of the repressed impulse it carries on playing the latter's role, again and again renewing its bid for gratification, and thus forcing the ego to give out a signal of unpleasure and to adopt an aggressively defensive stance.

The secondary battle against the symptom takes many forms, takes place on many different levels, and uses a multiplicity of means. We will not be able to say very much about it unless we focus our investigation on individual instances of symptom-formation. In the process we shall have occasion to discuss the problem of fear, which we have long felt to be lurking in the background. We do best to begin with the symptoms brought about by hysterical neurosis – for we are not yet in a position to appreciate the prior conditions that are necessary for symptom-formation to take place in the case of obsessional neurosis, paranoia and other neuroses.

IV

Let us look first of all at infantile hysterical animal phobia – a good example of which is the horse phobia of 'Little Hans',[17] a case that is surely typical in all essential respects. Even the briefest of glances at it is sufficient to make us realize that the circumstances in a real-life case of neurotic illness are far more complex than we might expect or imagine when we operate merely on the basis of theoretical abstractions. It takes quite a lot of work to determine which is the repressed impulse, what constitutes its surrogate, and where the motive force behind the repression is to be found.

Little Hans declines to go out into the street because he is afraid of horses. That is our raw material. What, then, constitutes the symptom here: the process of fear-generation,[18] the choice of fear-object, the surrendering of the freedom to move, or some combination of these? Where is the gratification he refuses to allow himself? Why is he driven to this refusal?[19]

It would be easy to reply that there is nothing very puzzling about this case. The child's unaccountable fear of horses is the symptom; the inability to go out into the street is a manifestation of inhibition, a restriction that the ego imposes on itself in order not to arouse the fear symptom. The correctness of this latter point is immediately clear to us, so we shall simply ignore the inhibition element as we proceed with our discussion. As for the supposed symptom, however, our first brief acquaintance with the case does not even enable us to recognize the real manner in which it expresses itself. As we discover once we probe more deeply, it is a matter not of a generalized fear of horses on Little Hans's part, but of a specific fearful expectation – namely that a horse will bite him. This underlying notion is keen to stay out of the realm of consciousness, however, and seeks a surrogate in the form of a generalized phobia reflecting the fear and its object, but nothing else. Is it perhaps this underlying notion, then, that constitutes the real nub of the symptom?

We will not get a single step further unless we look at the entire psychic situation of the child as revealed to us in the course of our psychoanalytical work with him. He is possessed of a jealous and hostile Oedipus attitude to his father, whom he none the less dearly loves – at any rate so long as his mother, as the cause of the rift, remains out of the picture. What we have, then, is a conflict caused by ambivalence: well-founded love and equally justified hate, both directed at the same person. His phobia must be an attempt to resolve this conflict. Ambivalence conflicts of this kind are very common – and we are familiar with another typical outcome that they can have, whereby one of the two competing impulses, generally the affectionate one, becomes enormously intensified, while the other disappears. It is only the inordinate extent and compulsive nature of the love that tells us that this is not the sole psychic attitude involved and that it is always ready to leap into action to keep its rival thoroughly suppressed, and which also allows us to postulate the operation of a process that we might describe as repression through *reaction-formation* (within the ego). Cases such as that of Little Hans show no sign of any such reaction-formation; there are clearly various different ways of coping with ambivalence conflicts.

There is one thing, however, that we established beyond doubt: the drive-impulse that was being subjected to repression was a hostile impulse directed against the father. Proof of this came in the course of analysis, when we were trying to track down the origins of the idea of the biting horse. Hans had seen a horse fall down, and he had also seen a playmate with whom he was playing horses fall over and hurt himself. Analysis gave us good grounds for postulating a wish-impulse in Hans to the effect that he wanted his father to fall over and injure himself like the horse and his playmate. Links with a particular episode that he had witnessed, involving the departure of someone from his street, lead us to think that his wish to be rid of his father had also found more forthright expression. Such a wish, however, amounts to an *intention* to get rid of him himself; it amounts to the murderous impulse of the Oedipus complex.

We have not so far discovered any direct connection between the repressed drive-impulse and its putative surrogate in the shape of the horse phobia. Let us therefore now simplify the psychic situation presented by Little Hans, by taking away the elements of infancy and ambivalence; let us imagine him for instance as a young servant who is in love with the mistress of the house and enjoys certain favours bestowed by her. The element we *don't* take away is that he hates the – far stronger – master of the house, and would like to be rid of him. Given this scenario, it is the most natural thing in the world for him to dread his master's vengeance, and to be seized by an abiding state of fear with regard to him – altogether similar to Little Hans's phobia with regard to horses. This means that we cannot describe the fear element in this phobia as a 'symptom'. If Little Hans, being in love with his mother, were to exhibit plain, straightforward fear of his father, we would have no right to impute a neurosis, a phobia, to him; we would be looking at a thoroughly comprehensible emotional reaction. It is a quite different feature that alone turns this reaction into a neurosis: the substitution of the horse for the father. It is accordingly this displacement that produces what might properly be called a symptom. Displacement thus constitutes that alternative mechanism referred to earlier, which allows ambivalence conflicts to be dealt with *without* the help of reaction-formation. It is made possible, or at any rate easier, by the fact that at this tender age the traces of totemistic thinking innate in all of us are still easily rekindled. The divide between man and beast is still not acknowledged at this age, and certainly not as over-emphasized as it is later on. The full-grown man, admired yet feared, is still seen in the same perspective as the large animal, whom the child envies in so many respects, but against whom he has also been warned because it can turn dangerous. The ambivalence conflict is thus not resolved in relation to the actual person concerned, but is so to speak circumvented, in that the subject foists a *different* person on one of his impulses by way of a surrogate.

In all these respects the picture makes perfect sense to us – but in another respect the analysis of Little Hans's phobia brought downright disappointment: the deformation that the process of symptom-formation consists in is effected *not* on the representamen (i.e. the perceived notion) of the drive-impulse that is being repressed, but on a quite different one corresponding merely to a *reaction* to the disagreeable element itself. Our expectations would have been more readily satisfied if, in place of his *fear* of horses, Little Hans had developed an inclination to ill-treat or beat them, or if he had clearly displayed his desire to see them fall down, injure themselves, and perhaps even die with much jerking of limbs ('making a racket with their legs'). Something of this kind did indeed become apparent in the course of the analysis, but it was by no means a prominent element in his neurosis. And strangely enough, if he really *had* developed this sort of hostility as his main symptom, but directed it at horses instead of his father, then we would certainly not have deemed him to be suffering from a neurosis. There is something wrong, then – either with our interpretation of repression, or with our definition of a symptom. One thing strikes us at once, of course: if Little Hans really *had* exhibited such behaviour towards horses, it would have meant that the repression process had not altered the *character* of the objectionable, aggressive drive-impulse, but had merely changed its object.

There are quite certainly cases of repression where this, and no more than this, is achieved – but in the genesis of Little Hans's phobia more unquestionably *did* happen. Just how much may be gathered from another piece of analysis altogether.

We have already seen that according to Little Hans the gist of his phobia lay in the notion he harboured of being bitten by a horse. Now it so happens that we later investigated the genesis of another case of animal phobia; wolves were the fear-object here – but they, too, played the role of father-surrogates.[20] As a direct consequence of a dream (which we were able to elucidate in analysis), this particular boy developed a fear of being eaten by a wolf, like one of the seven little billy-goats in the fairy-tale. The well-established fact that Little Hans's father had played horses with him was surely the decisive factor in his choice of fear-object; and in the same way, it turned out to be at the very least highly probable that in the child-hood games of my Russian patient (whom I did not come to analyse until he was already in his twenties), his father had pretended to be a wolf and had playfully threatened to eat him up. Since then I have encountered a third case, involving a young American man, and although in this case an animal phobia did *not* materialize, it is precisely its non-appearance that helps us to understand the other cases. His sexuality had been kindled by a fantastical children's story that had been read to him, about an Arabian chieftain who goes chasing after a character made of edible matter (the 'gingerbread-man') in order to eat him. He identified himself with this edible manikin, the chieftain was easily recognizable as a father-surrogate, and this fantasy became the initial basis for his autoerotic activities.

The notion of being gobbled up by one's father is a typical piece of ancient child lore, however; and we are all familiar with the relevant analogies in mythology (Cronus) and in the animal world. But while this knowledge might ease our path a little, the notion remains so deeply alien to us that we can concede its presence in a child only with incredulity. We also don't know whether it really means what it appears to mean, and we don't understand how it can come to be the stuff of a phobia. Our psychoanalytical experience, however, *does* provide us with the requisite information. It teaches us that the notion of being eaten by one's father is a regressively debased manifestation of a passive affectionate impulse that consists in a craving to be the object – in the genital-erotic sense of the term – of the father's love. Once we follow the history of the case all the way through, we are left in no doubt as to the correctness of this interpretation. Needless to say, the genital impulse no longer betrays any sign of its affectionate intent when it is manifested in the language of the transitional phase – already successfully concluded – from oral to sadistic organization of the libido. Incidentally, is it a question here merely of the *representamen* being replaced by a regressive *manifestation*, or is there an actual regressive debasement of the genitally oriented impulse in the id? It does not seem at all easy to determine this. The case history of the Russian 'Wolf-man' argues very strongly for the latter, more grave possibility, for his behaviour following the all-important dream was 'bad', cruel, sadistic, and he very soon developed a thorough-going obsessional neurosis. At any rate, we do come to realize that repression is not the only means available to the ego for warding off disagreeable drive-impulses. If it succeeds in making the drive regressive, then it has in effect confuted it even more thoroughly than would have been possible through repression; though of course in some cases it first forces a regression, then follows this up with a repression.

The situation in the case of the Wolf-man, and the rather more straightforward one in the case of Little Hans, are such as to trigger all sorts of further reflections, but two unexpected insights are afforded to us straightaway. There can be no doubt whatever that the drive-impulse that is repressed in these phobias is hostile to the father. One can reasonably say that it is repressed by being transformed into its opposite: the subject's aggression towards the father is replaced by the aggression – or vengeance – of the father towards the subject. Since in any case aggression of this kind has its roots in the sadistic phase of the libido, it needs very little debasement for it to descend to the oral stage, which in Hans's case is merely hinted at by his fear of being bitten, but is graphically clear in the Wolf-man's fear of being devoured. In addition, however, analysis establishes beyond all doubt that *another* drive-impulse fell prey to repression at the same time – an opposite one consisting in a passive affectionate impulse in favour of the father, which had already attained the genital (phallic) level of libido organization. This latter impulse even appears to be the more significant one as regards the ultimate outcome of the repression process: it undergoes more extensive regression, and it plays the key role in determining the content of the phobia. Thus whereas we began by tracking down the repression of just *one* drive, we find ourselves having to acknowledge that *two* such processes run in tandem with each other; the two drive-impulses involved – sadistic aggression towards the father, and passive affection for him – constitute a duo of opposites. And that's not all! If we interpret Little Hans's story correctly, we see that the formation of the phobia also served to nullify his affectionate object-cathexis in respect of his mother, even though the phobia itself betrays no sign of this. What is involved in Hans's case (things are much less clear in the case of my Russian patient) is a repression process that affects almost *all* the components of his Oedipus complex – his hostile and affectionate impulses in respect of his father, and his affectionate impulse in respect of his mother.

These are unwelcome complications for us, given that we set out to study only *simple* cases of symptom-formation caused by repression, and to this end deliberately addressed ourselves to the earliest and seemingly most transparent neuroses of childhood. Instead of finding just one repression, we encountered a whole mass of them, and for good measure we also found ourselves dealing with regression. Perhaps we have added to the confusion by wanting to treat the two available analyses of animal phobias – those of Little Hans and of the Wolf-man – as if they were altogether identical. In fact, however, we are struck by various differences between them. Only in Little Hans's case can one say with certainty that he manages through his phobia to deal with the two chief impulses of the Oedipus complex: the aggressive one *vis-à-vis* his father, and the over-affectionate one *vis-à-vis* his mother. The affectionate impulse in respect of his father is undoubtedly also present (it plays its own particular role in the repression of its opposite); but there is no evidence that it is strong enough to provoke a repression itself, or that it is subsequently neutralized. Hans just seems to have been a normal boy with a so-called 'positive' Oedipus complex. It is quite possible that the factors that appear to be missing in his case *were* in fact fully operative, but we can produce no evidence of this: there are simply too many gaps in the material uncovered by even the most searching parts of our analysis; the documentation is just not full enough. In the case of our Russian patient the deficiency lay elsewhere: his relationship to women was damaged as a result of his having been seduced at an early age; his passive, feminine side was very pronounced; and while the analysis of his 'wolf dream' revealed little sign of deliberate aggression towards his father, it yielded wholly unambiguous proof that the repression bore on his passive attitude of affection towards him. The other factors may have been involved here, too, but there is no evidence of them.

If despite these various differences – amounting almost to a direct antithesis – the two cases ultimately produce very nearly the same outcome in their respective phobias, then the explanation for this phenomenon must be sought elsewhere. We find it, in fact, in the second of the two insights afforded by our brief comparative survey. For we believe we know what constitutes the motor driving the repression in both cases, and we see its role confirmed by the way in which the two children's development proceeded. It is the same in both cases: fear of imminent castration. It is fear of castration that makes Little Hans give up his aggression towards his father; and the full meaning underlying his fear of being bitten by a horse is easy to see: he is afraid that a horse will bite off his genitals, will castrate him. But it is likewise fear of castration that makes our young Russian relinquish his wish to be loved by his father as a sexual object, the realization having dawned on him that the prerequisite of such a relationship would be the sacrifice of his genitals, i.e. of that which makes him different from a woman. *Both* forms of the Oedipus complex – the normal, active one and the inverted one – come to grief because of the castration complex. It is true that the young Russian's fear of being devoured by a wolf contains nothing specifically suggesting castration (oral regression has carried it too far from the phallic phase for that to be possible); but more than enough proof is provided by the analysis of his dream. Moreover, it constitutes a resounding triumph on the part of the repression that the phobia no longer contains even the merest hint of castration.

This, then, is our unexpected insight: in both cases, fear of castration is the motor driving the repression. The particular *notions* attaching to the individuals' fear[21] – the notion of being bitten by a horse, or devoured by a wolf – are deformational surrogates for the notion of being castrated by the father. This latter notion is what actually undergoes repression. In the case of the young Russian it was the expression of a wish that could not possibly hold its own against the rebellion of his masculinity; in Hans's case it was the expression of a reaction that converted his aggression into its antithesis. However, the *affect* of fear that constitutes the very essence of the phobia derives not from the repression process, not from the libidinal cathexes of the repressed impulses, but from the agent of repression itself; the fear in animal phobia is unconverted fear of castration, in other words objective fear,[22] fear of a danger that is actual and imminent, or at any rate perceived as such. As we can see here, it is fear that causes repression – and not, as I used to believe, repression that causes fear.

It gives me no pleasure to think back on it, but it would be futile for me to deny that I have often argued the hypothesis that repression causes the drive-representamen to be deformed, displaced etc., while causing the libido of the drive-impulse to be converted into fear. However, our investigation of the two phobias, which ought to have provided a perfect opportunity for proving this hypothesis, has clearly *not* confirmed it; rather, it appears to directly contradict it. The fear in animal phobias is the ego's fear of castration; the fear in agoraphobia – which has been less thoroughly studied – appears to be fear of temptation, which indeed must be connected in its origins with fear of castration. So far as we know at the present time, most phobias stem from a fear of this kind on the part of the ego – fear of the demands made by the libido. It is invariably the case that the ego's attitude of fear comes first, and triggers the repression; it is *never* the case that the fear arises out of the repressed libido. If in my earlier writings I had contented myself with saying that following the repression a quantum of fear appears in place of the expected manifestation of libido, then I should have no reason to take anything back today. That is an accurate description of what happens, and a match such as I postulated probably does indeed exist between the strength of the impulse that is to be repressed, and the intensity of the resulting fear. But I confess that I believed I was giving more than a mere description: I thought I had identified a metapsychological process consisting in a direct conversion of libido into fear. This is plainly not a view that I can hold to today; and even when I did propound it, I was quite unable to say how such a conversion might occur.

So where did I get the idea of this conversion in the first place? From my study of the 'actual' neuroses,[23] undertaken long before we learned to differentiate between processes in the ego and processes in the id. I found that attacks of fear and a generalized state of apprehensiveness are precipitated by certain sexual practices such as coitus interruptus, frustrated arousal and enforced abstinence – in other words, whenever sexual excitement is inhibited, checked or deflected before it has achieved gratification. Since sexual excitement is the manifestation of libidinal drive-impulses, it did not seem rash to suppose that disruptions of this kind have the effect of converting the libido into fear. And this observation is still valid today. Then again, it cannot be denied that the libido of the id-processes suffers disruption instigated by the repression; accordingly it may still be right to suppose that when repression takes place, fear is produced by the libido-cathexis of the drive-impulses. But how are we to reconcile *this* conclusion with our other conclusion that the fear present in phobias is an ego-fear,[24] that it arises in the ego, that it does not *emerge* from the repression but *causes* the repression? This appears to be a contradiction, and one that is not easy to resolve. It is no simple task to reduce these two sources of fear to a single one. One might attempt to do so by hypothesizing that in situations such as coitus interruptus, arousal without gratification or enforced abstinence, the ego senses danger, and responds to this danger with fear; but this supposition gets us nowhere. On the other hand, it seems that our analysis of the phobias in question cannot be faulted. *Non liquet*[25] is the only possible verdict!

V

Our aim was to study symptom-formation and the ego's secondary battle against the symptom, but in choosing phobias we clearly didn't strike lucky. The fear that is such a predominant feature in this particular condition now seems to me to be an unnecessary complication that obscures the issue. There are plenty of neuroses that exhibit no signs of fear. True conversion hysteria[26] is one such: we encounter not the slightest tinge of fear in even its gravest symptoms. This fact alone ought to warn us not to posit too close a connection between fear and symptom-formation. In all other respects phobias are so closely akin to conversion hysterias that I have thought it right to regard the former as a sub-group of the latter, under the heading 'fear-hysteria'. But no one has yet been able to say what circumstances determine whether a particular case takes the form of a conversion hysteria or a phobia; in other words, no one has fathomed the circumstances that lead to the development of fear in cases of hysteria.

The most common symptoms of conversion hysteria – motor paralyses, contractures, involuntary actions or energy-discharges,[27] pains, hallucinations – are either permanently established or intermittent cathexis processes, and this circumstance confronts us with yet more difficulties in our attempts to find an explanation. We don't really know a great deal about these symptoms. Through psychoanalysis we can discover which particular disrupted excitation process they are substituting for. It mostly transpires that they themselves are part and parcel of this process, rather as if its entire energy were focused on this one element. Thus, for instance, the patient's pain turns out to have been present in the situation in which the repression first occurred; his hallucinations started out as actual perceptions; his motor paralysis arose as a means of defence against an action that was supposed to be carried out at that same juncture, but was inhibited; his contracture is usually the displacement of a muscle innervation that was meant to happen then, but in some other part of the body; his spasms are the outward mark of an explosion of affect that has escaped the control normally exercised by his ego. There is a quite remarkable variation in the sensations of unpleasure that accompany the appearance of these symptoms. In the case of permanent symptoms that are displaced onto motor activity, such as paralyses and contractures, there are generally no such sensations at all: the ego behaves in their regard as though entirely uninvolved. In the case of intermittent symptoms and those relating to the sensory sphere, marked sensations of unpleasure are usually experienced, which in respect of pain symptoms can intensify to an extreme degree. It is very difficult in the midst of this multiplicity to establish which particular factor makes for such disparities, and yet allows us to see how they all hang together. We also find little trace in conversion hysteria of the ego's battle against the symptom once it has actually formed. Only when the sensitivity to pain of a particular part of the body has turned into a symptom is it enabled to play a dual role. When this part of the body is touched *externally*, the pain symptom manifests itself just as surely as it does when the pathogenic situation it represents is associatively activated *internally*, whereupon the ego takes precautionary measures to prevent the symptom from being aroused through external perception. We are clearly incapable of fathoming the origins of the peculiar obscurity that attaches to symptom-formation – but this gives us a good reason to abandon this unfruitful terrain without delay.

We turn now to obsessional neurosis, in the expectation that we shall learn rather more here about symptom-formation. The symptoms of obsessional neurosis are generally of two kinds, which tend in opposite directions. They consist on the one hand in prohibitions, precautions, penances – i.e. they are negative in nature; on the other hand, and in sharp contrast, they consist in surrogate gratifications, very often in symbolic guise. Of these two groups, it is the negative, defensive, punitive one that arises first; as the illness proceeds, however, the gratifications proliferate markedly, mocking all efforts to fight them off. It is a particular triumph of symptom-formation when it manages to merge the prohibition element into the gratification element, so that the injunction or prohibition originally active as a defence mechanism ends up itself taking on the character of a gratification – a process in which highly artificial associative pathways are frequently called upon. This achievement displays the proclivity to synthesis that we have already noted in the ego. In extreme cases the patient gets to the point where the great majority of his symptoms not only have their original significance, but also a directly contrary one – clear evidence of how powerful the ambivalence is that plays such a major role in obsessional neurosis (though we do not yet know why). In very extreme cases the symptom shows two distinct phases: an action having been carried out in accordance with some particular precept, a second immediately follows that cancels or reverses the first, without as yet daring to effect its complete opposite.

This very brief overview of obsessional symptoms gives rise to two distinct impressions. The first is that a constant battle is being waged here against whatever has been repressed – a battle in which the forces of repression are driven ever further back; the second is that the ego and super-ego are involved in the symptom-formation process to a particularly marked degree.

Obsessional neurosis may be the most interesting and most rewarding object of scrutiny within the purview of psychoanalysis – but as a problem it none the less remains unresolved. If we aim to delve deeper into its essence, then we have to acknowledge that we cannot yet manage without continued recourse to shaky assumptions and unproven conjectures. Obsessional neurosis presumably arises out of exactly the same circumstance as hysteria does, namely the imperative need to fight off the libidinal demands of the Oedipus complex. Moreover, the nethermost layer of every obsessional neurosis appears to consist of hysterical symptoms that were formed at a very early stage. Its subsequent development, however, is decisively altered by a constitutional factor. The genital organization of the libido turns out to be weak and insufficiently resistant. Thus when the ego commences its defensive battle, the first success it achieves is that the genital organization (of the phallic phase) is wholly or partially forced back to the earlier sadistic-anal phase. This regression remains a determining influence on everything that ensues.

Another possibility also merits consideration. Perhaps the real factor causing the regression is not constitutional but temporal. On this hypothesis the regression is made possible not because the genital organization of the libido is too puny in its development, but because the ego's defensive response begins too early, while the sadistic phase is still in full flourish. I would not venture to come to a definite decision on this point either – but it is not a supposition that is supported by psychoanalytical observation. On the contrary, the latter tends to show that by the time the shift towards obsessional neurosis occurs, the phallic stage has already been attained. Furthermore, this neurosis sets in at a later age than hysteria does (that is, in the second period of childhood, following the onset of the latency period). Indeed in one case that I was able to study, in which the disorder developed at a particularly late stage, it became very clear that it was a specific impairment of the patient's previously unscathed genital life that created the conditions conducing to regression and the emergence of his obsessional neurosis.[28]

The metapsychological explanation of regression appears to me to lie in a 'de-mergence' of drives, in the elimination of those erotic components that supervened at the beginning of the genital phase and thereby compounded the destructive cathexes of the sadistic phase.[29]

In forcing a regression to occur, the ego scores its first success in its campaign of defence against the demands of the libido. It is expedient here for us to draw a distinction between 'defence', as a more generalized activity, and 'repression', which is just one amongst the various mechanisms that the defence process makes use of. It is perhaps even clearer to us in cases of obsessional neurosis than in normal and hysterical cases that the *driving force* behind the defence process is the castration complex, its *target* the busy pretensions of the Oedipus complex. We are dealing here with the beginning of the latency period, which is characterized by the dissolution of the Oedipus complex, the creation or consolidation of the super-ego, and the erection of ethical and aesthetical barriers in the ego. In obsessional neurosis, these processes carry on well beyond the norm: in addition to the destruction of the Oedipus complex there is also regressive debasement of the libido; the super-ego becomes particularly harsh and unbending; and the ego in its obedience to the super-ego produces strong reaction-formations in the shape of conscientiousness, compassion and cleanliness. The temptation to carry on with early infantile masturbation is renounced and reviled with implacable severity, albeit not always with success – masturbation that now draws on regressive (sadistic-anal) imaginings, but none the less represents that portion of phallic organization that remains unbeaten and unbowed. There is an inherent contradiction in the fact that for the very purpose of safeguarding masculinity (castration fear), every least hint of masculine activity is forestalled; but this contradiction, too, is already part and parcel of the normal routine for getting rid of the Oedipus complex, and is remarkable in obsessional neurosis only for its excessiveness. The axiom that excess always bears within it the seeds of its own dissolution is borne out not least by obsessional neurosis, in that the suppressed masturbation forces its way in the guise of obsessional acts ever closer to gratification.

The reaction-formations that take place in the ego of obsessional neurotics, which we have identified as exaggerated versions of normal character-formation, may reasonably be described as a *new* defence mechanism by comparison with regression and repression. They appear to be absent or very much weaker in hysteria. Looking back, then, we can make a conjecture as to what constitutes the distinguishing feature of the defence process in hysteria: it appears to confine itself to repression, in that the ego turns away from the disagreeable drive-impulse, leaves it to run its course in the unconscious, and takes no further part in its destiny. True, this cannot be wholly and invariably correct, for of course we know of cases where a hysterical symptom simultaneously represents the fulfilment of a call for punishment pronounced by the super-ego;

but it may serve to describe a general characteristic of the ego's behaviour in cases of hysteria.

One can either simply accept it as a fact that the super-ego takes on such a harsh form in obsessional neurosis, or else one can suppose that the fundamental trait of this disorder is libido regression, and then attempt to posit a connection between this and the severity exhibited by the super-ego. It is certainly the case that the super-ego, which itself derives from the id, cannot just ignore the regression and the de-mergence of drives that have occurred there. It would scarcely be surprising if the super-ego for its part did not become harsher, colder, more pitiless than it is when there is normal development.

During the latency period, fighting off the temptation to masturbate appears to be treated as the paramount task. This battle produces a whole range of symptoms that recur in typical form even in very different individuals, and are by and large ritualistic in character. It is very much to be regretted that they have not yet been catalogued and systematically analysed: as the earliest by-products of neurosis they would be likely to shed more light than anything else on the mechanism of symptom-formation involved here. Even at this early stage they exhibit signs of the traits that will come to the fore in such a dire way once the illness becomes severe: the tendency to repeat and dwell on things becomes apparent; and ordinary, everyday activities – going to bed, washing and dressing, going from A to B – reflect their influence in the form of habits that are later to become practically automatic. Why this happens is by no means fully understood as yet; but the sublimation of anal-erotic components clearly plays a role in it.

Puberty marks a decisive watershed in the development of obsessional neurosis. The process of genital organization broken off earlier in childhood now reasserts itself with tremendous force. We know, however, that the pattern of sexual development in early childhood also determines the direction that things take in this new beginning represented by the pubertal period. Thus on the one hand the aggressive impulses of infancy awaken afresh, and on the other hand a pretty substantial proportion of the *new* libidinal impulses – in severe cases all of them – are obliged to follow the paths already marked out by the regression process, and to emerge as aggressive and destructive tendencies. Because of this camouflaging of the person's erotic urges, and because of the powerful reaction-formations that occur in the ego, the battle against sexuality is now waged under the banner of ethics. The ego recoils aghast from the cruel and violent demands transmitted to its consciousness from the id, without realizing that in so doing it is actually fighting off erotic desires, including some to which under normal circumstances it would have raised no objection. The hyper-severe super-ego insists even more emphatically on the suppression of this sexuality because of the fact that it has assumed such repellent forms. The conflict thus proves to be doubly exacerbated in obsessional neurosis: the forces doing the fighting off become even more intolerant, while the forces needing to be fought off become even more intolerable. Both developments are the result of a single factor: the regression of the libido.

One might consider a number of our suppositions to be contradicted by the very fact that the disagreeable notion informing the obsession ever enters consciousness in the first place. There can be no doubt, however, that before doing so it has first gone through the process of repression. In most cases the ego is completely oblivious of the real purport of the aggressive drive-impulse, and a good deal of psychoanalytical work is required in order to make the patient aware of it. As a rule, the only thing that manages to make its way into consciousness is a deformed surrogate that is either blurred and dreamlike in its lack of definition, or so absurdly disguised as to be unrecognizable. Even if the repression has not gnawed away at the actual content of the aggressive drive-impulse, it will certainly have got rid of the attendant element of affect. The ego accordingly perceives the aggression not as an active impulse, but – as patients tend to say – as a mere 'thought', something that ought to have no effect whatever on the emotions. What is most extraordinary is that this is not in fact the case. For the affect that is kept out of the picture as regards the subject's perception of the notion behind his obsession *does* make its appearance after all – but in a different location. The super-ego behaves as if no repression had taken place, as if it were familiar with both the precise purport and the whole affective nature of the aggressive impulse, and treats the ego on the basis of these assumptions. On the one hand the ego knows itself to be guiltless, but on the other hand it necessarily experiences guilt-feelings and a sense of blame that it simply cannot explain. The puzzle that this confronts us with is not as big as it first seems, however. The behaviour of the super-ego is altogether understand-able; as for the contradiction within the ego, it simply proves to us that it has shut itself off from the id by means of the repression, while remaining entirely open to any influences emanating from the super-ego.[30] The further question as to why the ego does not similarly abstract itself from the torment of the super-ego's criticism becomes otiose once we realize that this does indeed happen in a great number of cases. Furthermore, there are obsessional neuroses that exhibit no guilty conscience at all: the ego has avoided all cognizance of it, so we believe, by summoning up a whole new set of symptoms, penances and self-punishing restrictions. At the same time, however, these symptoms represent the gratification of masochistic drive-impulses, which the regression process has likewise served to reinforce.

Obsessional neurosis displays such enormous diversity in its mani-festations that no amount of effort has ever succeeded in producing a coherent synthesis of all its variations. Our one aim is to identify connections and correlations typical of the disorder, yet we are worried all the time lest we overlook other recurrent features that are no whit less important.

I have already described the general tendency characteristic of symptom-formation in obsessional neurosis. It amounts to giving ever more scope for surrogate gratification, hence ever *less* scope for refusal.[31] Thanks to the ego's proclivity to synthesis, the same symptoms that originally signified restrictions subsequently also acquire the significance of gratifications, and it is clear that this latter role gradually becomes the more influential of the two. An extremely restricted ego that is entirely dependent on symptoms for its gratifi-cation: that is the eventual result of this process, which gets ever closer to marking the total failure of what began as a defensive battle. This shift in the balance of forces in favour of gratification can lead ultimately to the dreaded phenomenon of a complete paralysis of will in the ego, which, when facing any kind of decision, experiences almost as strong an impetus from the one side as from the other. The unduly fierce conflict between the id and the super-ego that dominates the disorder from the outset can proliferate to such an extent that *all* activities of the ego – itself quite incapable of mediating between the two – are irresistibly drawn into it.

VI

In the course of these battles one can observe two symptom-forming activities on the part of the ego that merit particular attention, since they are clearly surrogates for repression and therefore ideally placed to throw light on its purpose and technique. Perhaps we may also regard the appearance of these auxiliary and surrogate techniques as proof that the substantive repression process encounters difficulties when put into operation. The fact that repression manifests such a variety of forms will perhaps seem more readily comprehensible to us when we consider that in obsessional neurosis the ego is so much more a locus of symptom-formation than it is in hysteria; that it clings tenaciously to its relationship to reality and to consciousness, and devotes its entire intellectual capacities to that end; that indeed the whole process of thought appears hyper-cathected and eroticized.

The two techniques referred to are *obliteration of past events*,[32] and *isolation*. The first of these is applied across a very large area, and reaches far back into the past. It is negative magic, so to speak; rather than targeting merely the *consequences* of an event (of something experienced or witnessed), it seeks by means of motor symbolism[33] to make the event itself 'vanish into thin air'. By using this latter expression we want to point up the role that this technique plays not only in neurosis, but also in magic, folk-lore and religious ritual. In obsessional neurosis one encounters the obliteration phenomenon first of all in the two-phase symptoms mentioned earlier, where the second action in effect cancels the first, as though it had never happened, whereas in reality *both* have happened. Obliteration also constitutes the second of the two root objectives underlying ritual behaviour in obsessional neurosis, the first being prevention, that is the adoption of precautionary measures to ensure that a particular event does not happen, or does not recur. The difference between the two is easy to see: the precautionary measures are rational; the 'cancellations' by means of obliteration are irrational and magical in nature. One must naturally suppose that this second root objective is the older one, dating from when the world around was seen in animistic terms. In normal behaviour the tendency to obliteration appears in modified form in the determination to treat an event as if it had never happened – but one then takes no further action on the matter, bothering neither about the event nor its consequences, whereas the neurotic seeks to cancel the past itself, to repress it through motor processes. This same proclivity may also account for the compulsion to repeat so common in obsessional neurosis, the actual enactment of which then becomes the rallying point for a variety of conflicting purposes. Anything that did not happen in the way the person wanted it to happen is obliterated by being subjected to repetition in a *different* way – which prompts all the various motive forces to appear on the scene and join in for the duration of the repetitions. As the neurosis proceeds, a marked tendency to obliterate a specific traumatic experience often reveals itself to be a major motive force causing symptoms to form. Thus we unexpectedly gain insight into a new defensive technique involving motor processes – or, as we may say with rather more precision here, a new *repressive* technique.

The other technique being described here for the first time is that of *isolation*, a process peculiarly appropriate to obsessional neurosis. It, too, relates to the motor sphere. What happens is that directly after a disagreeable event, and likewise after any activity on the part of the subject himself that is significant within the context of the neurosis, a pause is interpolated during which nothing else may happen; no sensory perceptions are made and no actions are carried out. Although puzzling at first, this response soon reveals its connection to repression. In hysteria, as we know, it is possible to have a traumatic experience 'swallowed up' by amnesia. In obsessional neurosis this has often not been fully accomplished; the experience is not forgotten – but it is shorn of its affect, and its associative connections are suppressed or interrupted, with the result that it exists in isolation, so to speak, and furthermore is not reproduced in any thought processes. Now the outcome of isolating the experience in this way is the same as that attained by repression involving amnesia. This latter technique is thus reproduced in the isolation processes of obsessional neurosis, but at the same time it is also intensified at the motor level in order to produce the requisite magic effect. The elements that are thus kept apart from each other are precisely those that belong associatively together; motor isolation is intended to guarantee that the links remain broken whenever thinking is going on. This neurotic procedure is offered a useful pretext by the normal phenomenon of concentration, which ensures that the process of taking in any particular impression or carrying out any particular task that seems significant to us remains undisturbed by the intrusion of alien thought processes or activities. But even in normal behaviour, the device of concentration is used for protection not only from whatever is irrelevant and extraneous, but also and especially from whatever is unsuitable and antipathetic. What is felt to be most intrusive of all is any combination of things that originally belonged together but were subsequently wrenched apart as development progressed – for instance, if the ambivalence of the father-complex finds expression in the context of our relationship to God, or if our excretory organs make themselves felt in the midst of erotic arousal. The isolating process thus constitutes a major task that the ego routinely accomplishes in controlling the sequence of thoughts; and as we know, in our psychoanalytical practice we have to train the ego to relinquish this particular function for the time being, thoroughly justified though it is in itself.

We have all had experience of the fact that obsessional neurotics find it particularly difficult to adhere to the basic rule of psychoanalysis. Their ego is more vigilant, and more stringent in its use of isolation, probably as a result of the high degree of antagonistic tension between their super-ego and their id. While they are engaged in thinking, their ego has too many things to fight off – the intrusion of unconscious fantasies, the emergence of the various ambivalent tendencies lurking within. It cannot afford to relax; it must be constantly ready for battle. It then backs up this compulsion to concentrate and isolate by means of those 'magical' acts of isolation that acquire such prominence and practical significance as *symptoms*, while being in themselves quite useless, of course, and in the nature of mere ritual.

In thus seeking to prevent associations and thought-connections, however, the ego is obeying one of the oldest and most fundamental imperatives of obsessional neurosis: the taboo on *touching*. If we ask ourselves why the avoidance of touch, contact, contagion plays such a major role in this particular neurosis, and is made the focus of such complex systems, then we find our answer in the fact that touch, bodily contact, is the immediate goal of both the aggressive and affectionate forms of object-cathexis. Eros seeks physical contact because it strives for union, for the removal of any barriers of distance between ego and love-object; but destruction of an enemy – which prior to the invention of remote weapons could only be accomplished at close quarters – in principle also presupposes physical contact, that is, one person getting his hands on the other. To 'touch up' a woman is the standard euphemism for treating her as a sexual object; 'Don't touch your penis' is the standard form of words forbidding autoerotic gratification. Obsessional neurosis being relentlessly hostile to touching, first in its erotic form and then, once regression has occurred, in its guise as aggression, there is nothing it deems so utterly despicable and reprehensible, nothing that is so well suited to becoming the pivot of a whole system of prohibitions. Isolation, however, removes any *opportunity* for touching; it is a device for preventing something from coming into any form of contact with anything else. Thus when a neurotic isolates a particular experience or activity by interpolating a pause, he is giving us symbolically to understand that he does not want to let his thoughts on the matter in question come into associative contact with any others.

Our investigations into symptom-formation take us thus far, but no further. There is little to be gained by summarizing them: they remain inconclusive, their results are meagre, and they have produced very little that we didn't already know. It would be futile to look at symptom-formation in other disorders besides phobias, conversion hysteria and obsessional neurosis, as too little is known about it. But even the very act of dealing jointly with these three neuroses raises a severe problem that has to be faced without further delay. The starting-point for all three neuroses is the destruction of the Oedipus complex; in all of them, we assume, fear of castration is the motor driving the ego's vigorous resistance. But fear of this kind is actually *apparent* only in the phobias; only here is it openly avowed. What has become of it in the other two disorders? How has the ego saved itself from fear of this sort? The problem becomes even more acute when we reflect on the possibility – mentioned earlier – that the fear arises, via a kind of fermentation process, out of the libido-cathexis itself when the ordinary progression of the latter is interrupted. And on top of that: is it absolutely certain that fear of castration is the *sole* motor of repression (of the defence process)? We are bound to doubt this if we turn our mind to women's neuroses: even though a castration complex is plainly observable in their case, we certainly can't speak of a *fear* of castration – in any proper sense of the word – where castration is already a *fait accompli*.

VII

Let us return to the topic of infantile animal phobias – after all, we understand these cases better than any others. Here, then, the ego has to take action against a libidinal object-cathexis on the part of the id (whether involving the positive or the negative form of the Oedipus complex), because it is convinced that giving in to it would incur the risk of castration. We have already dealt with this in some detail, but would like to take this opportunity to resolve a doubt that still remains from that earlier discussion. In the case of Little Hans (that is, of a positive Oedipus complex), are we to suppose that it is the affectionate impulse in favour of his mother, or the aggressive impulse directed against his father, that provokes the ego into mounting its defence? From a practical point of view this might seem immaterial, particularly since the two impulses are conditional upon each other; but the question is interesting in theoretical terms, since only the affectionate feeling for the mother can be regarded as a purely erotic one. The aggressive feeling towards the father is essentially dependent on the destruction drive, and we have always supposed that in neurosis the ego defends itself against the demands of the libido, not of the other drives. And we do indeed find that once the phobia had formed, Little Hans's affectionate attachment to his mother to all intents and purposes disappeared, having been comprehensively dealt with by the repression process, whereas his aggressive impulse showed full-scale symptom-formation (formation of a surrogate). The situation is rather more straightforward in the case of the Wolf-man: the repressed impulse really is an erotic one – his feminine attitude to his father – and it is here, too, that symptom-formation takes place.

It is almost enough to make us feel ashamed that for all our protracted labours we still encounter difficulties in trying to understand the most fundamental phenomena; but we are determined to simplify nothing and conceal nothing. If we are incapable of seeing things clearly, we do at least wish to see with absolute clarity what is *un*clear. What is impeding us here is plainly some kind of flaw in the way we have developed our theory of drives. Initially, we tracked the forms of libido oganization through their various stages from the oral via the sadistic-anal to the genital and, in so doing, represented the components of the sexual drive as being all on the same footing as each other. Later, however, sadism appeared to us to represent a different drive altogether, and one antithetical to Eros. This new conception envisaging *two* groups of drives seems on the face of it to demolish the earlier theory of *successive phases* of libido organization. But we have no need to invent some new explanation to help us out of this difficulty, for the solution presented itself to us long ago, to the effect that we practically never find ourselves dealing with pure, unalloyed drive-impulses, but invariably with combinations of both kinds of drives in varying proportions. Thus a sadistic object-cathexis also has a perfect right to be treated as a libidinal one, the aggressive impulse directed against the father has just as much right to become an object of repression as the affectionate impulse in favour of the mother – and there is accordingly no need for us to revise our view of the various forms of libido organization. All the same, let us note for later consideration the possibility that repression is a process that has a particular affinity with the genital phase of libido organization, and that the ego resorts to different methods of defence when it has to fight off the libido in its other organizational phases. Let us also add that a case like Little Hans's does not allow us to resolve the issue one way or the other: here, an aggressive impulse is indeed dealt with by means of repression, but at a point when genital organization has already been attained.

We do not want to lose sight this time of the fear nexus. We mentioned earlier that as soon as the ego becomes aware that there is a danger of castration it gives out a fear signal, and then – in some way that we do not understand beyond the fact that it involves the agency of the pleasure/unpleasure principle – inhibits the cathexis process within the id that is threatening it. At the same time, the relevant phobia takes shape. The fear of castration acquires a different object and a deformational form of expression: it becomes fear of being bitten by a horse (eaten by a wolf), instead of being castrated by the father. The forming of a surrogate has two obvious advantages. First, it avoids an ambivalence conflict (the father being at one and the same time an object of love). Second, it allows the ego to stop any further fear being generated; for the fear pertaining to phobias is *facultative*,[34] appearing only when its object is directly perceived. That is quite right, too, for only then is the danger situation actually present; if the father is absent, there is no need to fear castration at his hands. The father cannot be got rid of, however: he can reappear whenever he chooses. But if he is substituted by an animal, then one need only avoid the sight – i.e. the presence – of the animal in order to remain free of danger and fear. Little Hans therefore imposes a restriction on his ego; he produces the inhibition stopping him from going out of doors, in order not to encounter any horses. Things are even easier for our young Russian: he loses precious little by not looking at a particular picture-book any more. If his naughty sister didn't keep showing him the picture of the wolf standing on its hind legs that appears in this book, he would be able to feel completely safe from his fears.

I once characterized phobias as being in the nature of a projection, in that they substitute a danger perceived in the world *without* for a danger posed by drives *within*; this has the advantage that one can protect oneself from an external danger by fleeing from it, or avoiding all sight of it, whereas flight is quite useless if the danger emanates from within.[35] My assertion was not wrong, but it certainly didn't get to the heart of the matter. After all, the pressure exerted by a drive is not a danger in itself, but only because it brings with it a real external danger, namely that of castration. When it comes down to it, therefore, what actually happens in a phobia is simply that one external danger is replaced by another. The notion that in phobias the ego has only to take avoiding action, or deploy a symptom of inhibition, in order to keep fear at bay, accords extremely well with the proposition that this fear is merely a signal of affect, and that the economic situation has not changed in any way.

On this view, then, fear in animal phobias is an affective reaction to danger on the part of the ego, and the danger being signalled here is that of castration. The sole difference between this and the objective fear normally manifested by the ego in danger situations is that the content of the fear remains essentially unconscious, entering consciousness only in the guise of a deformation.

I rather think that this same view will prove to be valid in respect of adults' phobias, too, even though a much greater wealth of material is processed by the neurosis in such cases, and even though various additional factors besides symptom-formation come into the picture. The pattern is basically the same. The agoraphobe imposes a restriction on his ego in order to escape a danger posed by his drives. This danger resides in the temptation to give in to his erotic desires, which would result in him once again conjuring up the fear of castration (or some analogous fear), just as in his childhood. As a straightforward example of this, I would cite the case of a certain young man who became agoraphobic because he was afraid of yielding to the allurements of prostitutes and catching syphilis as a punishment.

I am well aware that many cases show a more complicated structure, and that many other repressed drive-impulses can feed into the phobia, but these latter are only auxiliary in nature, and for the most part impinge on the core of the neurosis at a relatively late stage. The symptomatology of agoraphobia is complicated by the fact that the ego is not entirely satisfied by simply avoiding something: it takes other action as well in order to remove the danger from the situation. This additional action commonly consists in a temporal regression into infancy (in extreme cases right back into the womb, to a period that afforded protection from the danger that now threatens), and this then becomes the sole condition under which the avoidance mechanism remains in abeyance. Thus the agoraphobe can go out into the street provided that – like a small child – he is accompanied by someone he trusts. By the same token he may also be able to go out alone, provided he does not go further than a certain distance from his home, or does not go into areas that are unfamiliar to him or where people don't know him. In his choice of such provisos he reveals the influence of the infantile factors that dominate his life through his neurosis. One particularly clear example – even in the absence of any such infantile regression – is the phobia involving fear of being alone, the essential purpose of which is to avoid the temptation to indulge in solitary masturbation. Needless to say, infantile regression can only occur in individuals who are no longer children.

As a rule, a phobia only emerges after the individual has first been stricken by fear in a particular set of circumstances, for example when he is in the street, or in a train, or on his own. The fear is thereupon shut out, but reappears whenever the protective stratagem cannot be maintained. The phobia mechanism does splendid service as a means of defence, and tends to exhibit marked stability. In many cases – though not in all – the defensive battle is carried a stage further, being henceforth directed against the symptom.

What we have learnt about fear in the context of phobias also remains relevant to obsessional neurosis. It is not difficult to reduce the overall situation characteristic of obsessional neurosis to that characteristic of phobias. Here, the motor driving all subsequent symptom-formation is plainly the ego's fear *vis-à-vis* the super-ego. The hostility of the super-ego constitutes the danger situation that the ego must fight shy of. There is not the least semblance of projection here: the danger is wholly internalized. But if we ask ourselves what the ego is so fearful of suffering at the hands of the super-ego, then we are compelled to conclude that the punishment threatened by the latter is simply a refined version of the punishment of castration. Just as the super-ego is the father in depersonalized form, so too the specific fear of being castrated by him has changed into an indefinite social or consciential fear.[36] But this fear remains latent; the ego keeps it at a safe distance by obediently carrying out whatever commands, prescriptions and penances are imposed upon it. If it is prevented from so doing, then the most extreme discomfiture immediately ensues, which we may reasonably regard as the equivalent of fear, and which patients themselves equate with fear.

We thus arrive at the following conclusion: fear consists in a reaction to a particular danger situation; the ego saves itself from this fear by taking action to withdraw from the situation or avoid it altogether. Now one might be tempted to say that symptoms are produced in order to avoid any fear being generated in the first place – but this does not really get us very far. It is more accurate to say that symptoms are produced in order to avoid the *danger situation* signalled by the fear that has already been generated. In the cases considered so far, however, this danger lay in castration or in something that can be traced back to castration.

If fear is the ego's reaction to danger, then it may seem logical to construe traumatic neurosis – which so often ensues where the individual has survived a life-threatening danger – as a direct result of fear of death or fear for life and limb,[37] thereby disregarding castration and the dependent status of the ego.[38] This indeed is what most of those with clinical experience of the traumatic neuroses of the last war[39] have done, and the triumphant cry has gone up that we now have proof positive that a threat to the self-preservation drive can produce a neurosis without any involvement on the part of sexuality, and without paying the slightest heed to the complex processes posited by psychoanalysis. It really is extremely regrettable that there exists not a single reliable analysis of a traumatic neurosis. Our regrets relate not to the denial of the aetiological importance of sexuality, for any such denial has long since been refuted by the introduction of the concept of narcissism, which places libidinal cathexis of the ego in the same category as object-cathexes and stresses the libidinal nature of the self-preservation drive; rather, we regret this analytical deficit because we have thereby lost a priceless opportunity to gain crucial information about the relationship between fear and symptom-formation. In the light of everything we know about the more straightforward neuroses of everyday life, it seems highly unlikely that any neurosis could be brought about solely by the presence of objective danger, without any involvement on the part of the deeper unconscious layers of the psychic apparatus. However, there is nothing within the unconscious capable of giving substance to our notion of the extinction of life. Whereas castration is rendered imaginable to us by our daily experience of being separated from the contents of our bowels, and by the loss of the maternal breast that we experience when weaned, experiences akin to death have never happened to us, or else – like fainting-fits – have left no identifiable trace. I therefore hold to the supposition that the fear of death has to be understood as an analogue of the fear of castration, and that the situation to which the ego reacts is that of being abandoned by its guardian the super-ego – that is, by the forces that rule our destiny – and hence deprived for ever of the shield safeguarding it from dangers all and sundry.[40] It also needs to be borne in mind that in experiences leading to traumatic neurosis the barrier that normally provides protection against external stimuli is breached, and excessive quanta of excitation descend upon the psychic apparatus; this means that here we encounter a *second* possibility, namely that fear is not only *signalled* as an affect, but is also *created anew* out of the economic conditions of the situation.

In asserting just now that the ego becomes habituated to the notion of castration by regularly experiencing object-loss, we have arrived at a new concept of fear. Whereas hitherto we have regarded fear as a signal of affect indicating danger, it now appears to us – since it so often involves the danger of castration – to constitute reaction to a loss, a separation. While numerous considerations might instantly seem to gainsay this conclusion, we none the less cannot help being struck by a most remarkable similarity: birth constitutes the first experience of fear, at any rate for human beings, and in objective terms signifies separation from the mother; it might therefore be likened to castration of the mother (based on the equation 'child = penis'). Now it would be highly gratifying if fear were subsequently to be repeated as a symbol of separation every time an actual separation occurred; unfortunately, however, we cannot build an argument on this similarity given the fact that birth is of course not *subjectively* experienced as separation from the mother, the thoroughly narcissistic foetus being altogether unaware of the mother as object. A further objection can also be raised – namely that the affective reactions to separation are well known to us, and that we experience them as pain and sorrow, not as fear. At the same time, however, we are mindful that in our discussion of sorrow we were at a loss to understand why it should be so painful.[41]

VIII

It is time for us to pause for thought. What we are looking for is plainly some decisive insight that will reveal to us the whole nature of fear, a clear perspective on the problem that will neatly separate truth from error. But that is difficult to achieve; fear is not easy to pin down. So far we have managed to come up with nothing but contradictory possibilities, none of which could be preferred over any other except on the basis of prejudice. I suggest that we now take a different approach: let us impartially rehearse all our arguments on the subject of fear, and in so doing abandon any expectation of arriving at an all-embracing new synthesis.

Fear, then, is first and foremost something that is *felt*. We call it a 'state of affect', even though we don't actually know what an affect is. This feeling is blatantly unpleasurable in nature, but that is not a sufficient description of it, for not every form of unpleasure may be termed fear. There are other feelings of an unpleasurable kind, such as tension, pain and sorrow – and fear must accordingly have other characteristics besides this quality of unpleasure. Question: will we ever succeed in understanding the differences between these various unpleasurable states of affect?

None the less there is one thing we *can* deduce from the feeling of fear: its quality of unpleasure appears to have a distinct character of its own (although probable, this is difficult to prove, as there would seem to be nothing very obvious to go on). But quite apart from this special quality of unpleasure that is so difficult to isolate, we also perceive more specific *physical* sensations when fear is present, which we connect with specific organs. Since the physiology of fear is not our concern here, it will be sufficient for us to mention just one or two representative examples of these sensations, the most frequent and most obvious being those involving the respiratory organs and the heart. They afford us proof that motor innervations, in other words release processes, play a part in the overall phenomenon of fear. Our analysis of the state of fear thus reveals the following features: 1) a specific quality of unpleasure; 2) actions involving release; 3) perception of these actions.

Straightaway, points 2 and 3 show us a distinct difference between fear and other states, e.g. those of sorrow and pain. In these latter cases, any motor manifestations that happen to occur are not directly integral to the phenomenon itself; where they exist, they clearly stand out as being *not* constituent elements of the whole process, but consequences of it or reactions to it. Fear is thus a particular state of unpleasure, with release actions that follow specific pathways. In accordance with our general philosophy in these matters we are inclined to think that the root of fear lies in an increase in excitation that on the one hand generates unpleasure of a particular kind, and on the other hand relieves it by means of the above-mentioned release processes. This purely physiological summary is scarcely going to satisfy us, however: we are tempted to suppose that a *historical* factor is at work here, linking the sensations and innervations of fear firmly together. Our supposition, in other words, is that the state of fear constitutes the reproduction of a prior experience containing the necessary conditions for such an increase in stimulus and for release via specific pathways, and that this is how the unpleasure of fear acquires its specific character. In the case of human beings, birth suggests itself to us as being just such a paradigmatic experience, and we are accordingly disposed to regard the state of fear as a reproduction of the trauma of birth.[42]

In saying this we have adduced nothing that might serve to grant fear a special place amongst the states of affect. We take the view that the other affects are also reproductions of ancient, perhaps pre-individual events of life-and-death importance, and may be regarded as universal, typical, inborn hysterical attacks, in contradistinction to the attacks characteristic of hysterical neurosis, which develop at a much later stage and on an individual basis, and whose genesis and significance as memory-symbols have become clear to us thanks to psychoanalysis. It would be highly desirable, of course, if we could substantiate this hypothesis in respect of a whole series of other affects – but at present we are still very far from achieving this.

Our contention that fear may be traced back to the experience of birth obliges us to deal with a number of self-evident objections. Fear is a reaction that is probably common to *all* organisms, at any rate all the higher ones, but birth is experienced by mammals alone, and it is questionable whether birth is traumatic for all of the latter. Fear thus exists *without* the paradigm of birth. But this objection ignores the boundaries dividing psychology from biology. Precisely because fear – as the reaction to danger – fulfils a biologically indispensable function, it may well be differently constituted in different organisms. Furthermore, we do not know whether it has the same repertoire of sensations and innervations in organisms far removed from human beings as it does in humans themselves. This accordingly presents no obstacle to the supposition that in human beings the paradigm for fear is the birth process.

If the structure and origins of fear are indeed thus, then the question immediately arises: what is its function, and in what circumstances is it reproduced? The answer seems both obvious and compelling: fear arises in the first place as a reaction to a *danger situation*, and is then regularly reproduced whenever a situation of the same kind recurs.

This calls for further comment, however. The innervations involved in the original state of fear were probably also senseful and purposive, just as the muscle actions in an initial hysterical attack are. So if we want to understand the hysterical attack, then of course we simply need to look for a situation in which the relevant movements formed part of some apt and necessary set of actions. We accordingly find that during birth the innervation process, by being directed at the respiratory organs, probably served to prepare the lungs for action, while the acceleration of the heart-beat was intended to counteract any potential poisoning of the bloodstream. Needless to say, this purposive element does not come into the picture whenever the original fear-state is subsequently reproduced as an affect, just as it is also conspicuously absent whenever the initial hysterical attack is repeated. Therefore if an individual encounters a *new* danger situation, it can easily be counter-purposive for him to respond by reproducing the original fear-state – namely the reaction to a previous danger – instead of reacting in a manner appropriate to the current one. The purposive element re-emerges, however, if the danger situation is perceived as impending rather than present, and is duly signalled by an attack of fear. More appropriate responses can then instantly take the place of this fear. It thus becomes clear at once that fear can emerge in two quite different ways: one that is counter-purposive, where there is a new situation of *actual* danger, and one that is purposive, namely one aimed at signalling an *impending* danger and preventing it from becoming a reality.

But what constitutes a 'danger'? In the birth process there is an objective danger to life; we know what that means in terms of physical reality – but in psychological terms it means nothing at all. The danger posed by birth does not at the time impinge in any way on the psyche. We surely cannot attribute to the foetus any knowledge whatsoever that the process might end in the extinction of its own life. All that the foetus is capable of registering is a massive upset in the economy of its narcissistic libido. Large quantities of excitation come surging into it, producing unpleasurable sensations of a new kind; various organs peremptorily achieve increased cathexis, which amounts to a sort of prelude to the process of object-cathexis that is soon to commence. But which element in all of this will be put to use as a marker indicative of a 'danger situation'?

Unfortunately we know far too little about the psychic make-up of the newborn to be able to answer this question directly. I cannot even vouch for the validity of the description I have just offered. It is easy enough to assert that the newborn child will repeat the affect of fear in all subsequent situations that remind it of its birth; the crucial issue, however, is the question as to what serves to remind it, and what it is reminded of.

There is really only one course open to us, and that is to study the circumstances in which babies and somewhat older children show a readiness to generate fear. In his book *Das Trauma der Geburt* [*The Trauma of Birth*] (1924), Rank tried very hard to prove a link between the earliest phobias in children and their experience of the birth process – but in my view he did not succeed. One can offer two objections to his argument. The first is that it rests on the supposition that in the course of their birth children receive specific sense impressions, particularly visual ones, any recurrence of which can call forth the memory of the birth trauma and therewith the associated fear reaction. This assumption is totally unproven and highly improbable: it is simply not credible that children retain any sensations from the birth process other than tactile ones and ones of a very generalized nature. Thus if a child subsequently exhibits fear of small animals that disappear down holes or emerge from them, this is due in Rank's view to its perception of an analogy, but one of which it necessarily remains unaware. The second objection is that in his analysis of these subsequent fear situations Rank picks and chooses according to the needs of his own argument in deciding which is the operative factor in any given case – the child's memory of its blissful intra-uterine existence, or its memory of the traumatic disruption of that existence. To do this is to open the floodgates to sheer arbitrariness of interpretation. Some instances of childhood fear are flatly unamenable to the application of Rank's principle. If a child is put on its own in a dark place, then on Rank's view we might expect it to welcome this restoration of its situation in the womb, whereas it is precisely in such circumstances that it reacts with fear – and when we hear this being attributed to the child's memory of the disruption of uterine bliss by the birth process, we can no longer fail to recognize the factitiousness of this would-be explanation.

I have to conclude that the phobias of very early childhood cannot be directly attributed to the experience of birth, and indeed have so far defied all attempts to account for them. A certain degree of apprehension[43] is unmistakably evident in babies. Rather than – say – being at its strongest just after birth and then slowly abating, it only manifests itself later on, when the psyche begins to develop, and carries on throughout a certain period of the individual's childhood. If early phobias of this kind persist *beyond* that period, then we tend to suspect the presence of a neurotic disorder, even though we have no idea what its relationship might be to the later and clear-cut neuroses of childhood.

The manifestation of fear in young children is readily comprehensible to us only in very few circumstances, and these are the ones we need to focus on – as when the child finds itself alone, or in darkness, or faced with a stranger instead of the person intimately familiar to it (that is, its mother). These three circumstances boil down to a single determining factor: distress at the absence of the loved (and longed for) person. Once we appreciate this, however, we are well on the way to achieving a real understanding of the phenomenon of fear, and to resolving the apparent contradictions connected to it.

The memory-image[44] of the longed-for person no doubt becomes intensely cathected, at first probably in a hallucinatory manner. But this does not produce the desired result, and it seems as if this longing then changes abruptly into fear. This fear conveys a strong sense of being an expression of utter bewilderment on the child's part, as if this still very undeveloped creature knew no better way of giving vent to its highly cathected longing. Fear thus emerges as a reaction to the distressing absence of the object – and at this point two parallels come forcefully to mind: the fact that in castration fear, too, the issue is separation from a highly prized object; and the fact that the very first manifestation of fear, namely the 'primal fear' of birth, arises out of separation from the mother.

Our next consideration takes the argument beyond this specific focus on object-loss. The fact that babies want their mother within sight is surely for the sole reason that they already know from experience that she will instantly gratify all their needs. The situation that the child registers as 'dangerous', and from which it seeks to be protected, is accordingly that of non-gratification, of an *increase in the tension caused by unmet needs*, in the face of which it is entirely powerless. To my mind, everything falls neatly into place once considered in this perspective. The situation of non-gratification, in which the quanta of stimulation reach an unpleasurable level without being brought under control through processes of psychic utilization and release, must seem to the baby directly analogous to the experience of being born; it must seem to be a repetition of that same danger situation. The common factor in both is the economic disruption caused by the sudden increase in the quanta of stimulation demanding urgent processing; this factor is accordingly the real nub of the 'danger'. Fear presents itself as a reaction in both circumstances – and in the case of the baby, too, proves to be just as purposive as before, in that its form of release via the respiratory and vocal muscles causes the mother to come and attend to the child's needs, much as it caused its lungs to become active on parturition in order to get rid of the internal stimuli. There is no reason whatever to suppose that a child retains anything from its birth other than this means of identifying danger.

With the child's realization that an external, directly apprehensible object can put an end to the dangerous situation that harks back to its birth, the burden of the danger accordingly shifts from the economic situation to the factor determining it, namely loss of the object. It is now the distressing absence of the mother that constitutes the danger, and the baby gives out a fear signal as soon as this danger presents itself, even *before* the economic situation it so dreads has come into being. This change represents the first major step forward in the self-preservation regime of the child, in the process embracing the transition from a state whereby fear recurs automatically and involuntarily, to a state whereby it is *intentionally* reproduced as a signal of danger.

In both respects – as an automatic phenomenon and also as a rescue signal – fear is manifestly a product of the infant's psychic helplessness, which is self-evidently the counterpart of its biological helplessness. The striking symmetry whereby fear during birth and fear in the baby once it is born are both determined by separation from the mother requires no psychological interpretation: a perfectly straightforward biological explanation resides in the fact that the mother, having first satisfied the entire needs of the foetus by means of her own bodily mechanisms, then carries on precisely this same function *after* parturition as well, while drawing to some extent on other means too. Intra-uterine life and the initial phase of childhood are much more of a continuum than the very marked caesura of the birth process might lead us to suppose: the child's *psychic* situation of having the mother as its object amply takes the place of its *biological* situation in the womb – though this should not cause us to forget that the mother was not an object for the child in its intra-uterine life, and indeed that no objects at all existed at that stage.

It is plain that there is no scope in this context for abreacting the birth-trauma, and that the sole identifiable function of the child's fear is to serve as a signal in order to prevent a potential danger situation. However, object-loss as the determinant of this fear has very considerable further repercussions. For the next form of fear that ensues, namely the fear of castration that emerges in the phallic phase, likewise consists in fear of separation, and entails this same determinant. The danger here is that of being separated from one's genitals. An altogether plausible hypothesis of Ferenczi's permits us to see very clearly how this links back to the subject's earlier perceptions[45] of the danger situation. The high narcissistic value placed upon the penis can be attributed to the fact that possession of this organ guarantees reunification with the mother (in the form of a mother-surrogate) through the act of coitus. To be robbed of it is tantamount to being separated from the mother all over again, and thus it also means becoming the helpless victim of unpleasurable tension caused by an unmet need – just as happened during birth. As before, the individual is afraid that the need will intensify – but the need is now a specific one, namely that of genital libido, and no longer a generalized one as was the case in infancy. I would add here that the *fantasy* of returning to the womb represents the coitus-substitute of the impotent (those inhibited by the threat of castration). Taking Ferenczi's lead, we can say that such individuals, having previously sought a vicarious return to the womb by means of their genital organ, now regressively substitute their entire person for that organ.

The steady progression in the child's development, his increasing independence, the ever clearer separation of his psychic apparatus into several areas with distinct responsibilities, the emergence of new needs – these factors inevitably influence his perception of the danger situation. We have already seen how it changes from 'loss of the mother as object' to 'castration' – and we can now go on to see how the next step in the process is brought about by the power of the super-ego. With the increasing depersonalization of the parental voice – the quarter from which, so one feared, castration would come – the danger becomes less specific. Fear of castration evolves into *consciential* fear, into *social* fear.[46] It is no longer quite so easy to say what this fear is afraid of.[47] The formula 'separation – exclusion from the horde' relates only to that later element of the super-ego that develops on the basis of social paradigms, and not to the central core of the super-ego, which represents the parental voice in introjected form. To express it in more general terms: in the estimation of the ego, the potential danger – which it responds to by giving out a fear signal – resides in the possibility that the super-ego might visit wrath or punishment upon it, or withdraw its love. The final variant of this fear of the super-ego, so it seems to me, is the fear of death (or of life)[48] – fear, that is, of the super-ego in projected form busily determining the forces that rule our destiny.[49]

I once attached considerable importance to the view that it is the cathexis withdrawn in the course of repression that is utilized for the release of fear. Today this notion seems to me scarcely worthy of any attention. The difference lies in the fact that whereas in those days I believed that in every case without exception fear arose *automatically* as the result of an economic process, our present conception of fear as an intentional signal deployed by the ego in order to exert influence on the pleasure/unpleasure matrix[50] shows us to be independent of that economic automatism. Needless to say, no objection can be raised to the supposition that it is indeed precisely the energy freed up by being withdrawn during the process of repression that is utilized by the ego in order to generate the requisite affect; but the question as to which particular portion of energy is involved has become entirely irrelevant.

Another erstwhile proposition of mine that needs re-examining in the light of our new conception of fear is my assertion that the ego is the true locus of fear.[51] I rather think this will prove to be correct. We certainly have no reason to attribute any manifestation of fear whatsoever to the super-ego. If on the other hand there is mention of 'fear within the id', then one has to say that this notion is clumsily expressed rather than downright wrong. Fear is a state of affect, which of course can only be felt by the ego. Unlike the ego, the id is incapable of experiencing fear; it is not an organization,[52] and cannot make judgements as to whether or not there is a danger situation. However, it is an altogether common occurrence for processes to take place, or take shape, in the id that prompt the ego to generate fear; in fact the repressions that probably happen earliest of all are activated precisely by this kind of fear on the ego's part of individual processes within the id – as are the majority of those that happen later on. Here again we have every reason to draw a clear distinction between two different cases: one in which something occurs in the id that activates one of the various danger situations for the ego, and thereby causes it to give out a fear signal in order to trigger an inhibition; and another in which a situation analogous to the trauma of birth constitutes itself within the id, and automatically gives rise to a fear reaction. We can bring these two cases somewhat closer together by emphasizing the point that the second one corresponds to the original, primal danger situation, while the first corresponds to one of the fear-determinants derived at a later stage from that primal situation. Or to relate them to the disorders specifically manifested by patients: the latter case is operative in the aetiology of the 'actual' neuroses, while the former remains a characteristic feature in that of the psychoneuroses.

We can thus see that we have no need to jettison our earlier findings, but merely to adjust them in line with our more recent insights. It is an undeniable fact that in circumstances of sexual abstinence, or when sexual excitation is improperly disrupted or deflected from the processing due to it in the psyche, fear arises directly out of libido; in other words, in the face of excessive tension caused by unmet needs a state of helplessness is induced in the ego that culminates – as in the birth process – in the generation of fear. And it is altogether possible, though of no particular moment, that it is precisely the surplus quantity of unutilized libido that finds release in the generation of fear. We can see that psychoneuroses develop particularly easily on the basis of these 'actual' neuroses, which presumably means that the ego, having already learned how to keep fear temporarily in abeyance, makes various attempts to evade it altogether and annex it by means of symptom-formation. Analysis of traumatic war neuroses – albeit a term that embraces a very wide variety of disorders – would probably have shown that a number of them share characteristics particular to the 'actual' neuroses.

In describing how the various danger situations evolved out of their paradigm in the birth process, we by no means intended to argue that each subsequent fear-determinant simply cancels out the preceding one. However, as the development of the ego progresses, this does indeed tend to help to diminish and marginalize earlier danger situations, so that we might reasonably say that each stage of development has its own appropriate fear-determinant. The danger of psychic helplessness befits the period of life in which the ego is still immature – and by the same token the danger of object-loss befits early childhood and the dependent status it entails, the danger of castration befits the phallic phase, fear of the super-ego befits the latency period. But it is perfectly possible for all these danger situations and fear-determinants to go on existing side by side with each other and to trigger a fear reaction in the ego at a later juncture than is appropriate to them; alternatively, several of them may become operative at the same time. There may well also be quite a close connection between the danger situation that happens to be operative, and the form of neurosis that follows it.[53]

When we had occasion earlier in this study to note that the danger of castration is of significance in quite a number of neurotic disorders, we none the less admonished ourselves not to overestimate the importance of this particular factor, since it clearly cannot play a decisive role in the case of women – who are surely more prone to neurosis than men are. There is now clearly no danger of our declaring fear of castration to be the sole motor driving the defence processes that lead to neurosis. I have shown elsewhere how in the development of young girls the castration complex directly conduces to affectionate object-cathexis.[54] It is precisely in women that the danger situation of object-loss appears to have remained most effective. As regards the fear-determinant in this particular case, we might add the minor modification that it is no longer a matter of the actual loss of the object itself or distress at such loss, but rather the loss of the object's love. Given the well-established fact that hysteria has a stronger affinity to femaleness, just as obsessional neurosis has a stronger affinity to maleness, we may readily suppose that loss of love plays the same kind of role as a fear-determinant in hysteria as the threat of castration does in the phobias, and fear of the super-ego in obsessional neurosis.

IX

All that now remains for us to do is to deal with the relationship between symptom-formation and fear-generation.

There seem to be two very widely held opinions on this matter. One regards the fear element as being itself a symptom of the neurosis, while the other believes the two to be far more closely and subtly connected.[55] According to this latter view, *symptom-formation is undertaken wholly and solely for the purpose of evading fear*: the symptoms serve to annex the psychic energy that would otherwise find release as fear. In this perspective fear is the core phenomenon in the neurosis, and its chief problem.

That this second approach is at least partly justified may be demonstrated by some telling examples. If, having accompanied an agoraphobe out into the street, we then abandon him to his own devices, he will produce an attack of fear; if we stop an obsessional neurotic from washing his hands after he has touched something, he will become prey to almost unbearable fear. It is thus clear that the proviso of venturing out only if accompanied, and the obsessional procedure of hand-washing, are intentional – and successful – mechanisms for preventing such attacks of fear. Considered in this light, *every* inhibition that the ego imposes on itself can be termed a symptom.

Having argued earlier that fear-generation is attributable to the danger situation, we prefer to say that *symptoms are created in order to extricate the ego from the danger situation*. If symptoms are prevented from forming, then the danger becomes an actual reality; that is, a situation arises, analogous to birth, in which the ego finds itself helpless in the face of ever-increasing demands asserted by the drives – the first and most primal of all the fear-determinants. On our particular view of things, the connection between 'fear' and 'symptom' proves to be less close than was supposed – a result of the fact that we have interposed another factor between them, namely the 'danger situation'. In addition, we would contend that fear-generation is the prelude to symptom-formation, indeed a necessary prerequisite of it, for if the ego didn't jolt the pleasure/unpleasure matrix into action by generating fear, it would not acquire the power to halt the process that was instigated in the id and that now threatens danger. At the same time there is an unmistakable tendency on the part of the ego to limit itself to generating the bare minimum of fear and to use it only as a signal, for otherwise the unpleasure threatened by the drive process would simply be felt somewhere else instead – an outcome that would certainly not count as a success in terms of the pleasure principle, but is none the less a common enough occurrence in neuroses.

Symptom-formation thus really does succeed in neutralizing the danger situation. There are two aspects to this process: one remains entirely hidden from us and consists in producing the change in the id by means of which the ego is removed from danger, while the other openly displays what it has brought about in place of the deflected drive-process – namely the formation of a surrogate.

We ought to express ourselves more accurately, however: what we have just said about symptom-formation should instead be applied to the defence process, while the term 'symptom-formation' should be treated as synonymous with 'surrogate-formation'. It then seems plain that the defence process is analogous to the act of flight whereby the ego escapes an *external* danger, and indeed itself represents an attempt at flight in the face of the [internal] danger posed by a drive. The misgivings prompted by this comparison will help us to clarify matters further.

First, it might be countered that object-loss (or loss of the object's love) and the threat of castration are external dangers just as much as, say, a ravening animal is, and are therefore not dangers that emanate from drives. But the situation is clearly not the same. The wolf would probably attack us anyway, regardless of how we behaved towards it; but the loved person would not withdraw their love from us, nor would we be threatened with castration, if we did not harbour certain feelings and intentions within us. These drive-impulses thus become the determinants of external danger, and as such become dangerous themselves – with the result that we can now fight the danger without, by means of measures directed at the dangers within. In the case of animal phobias the danger appears still to be experienced as a wholly external one, just as it likewise undergoes external displacement in the relevant symptom. In obsessional neurosis the danger is much more internalized: that part of an individual's fear of the super-ego that is *social* fear represents the ongoing inner surrogate of an external danger, while the other part, i.e. *consciential* fear, is entirely endopsychic.[56]

A second objection is that in attempting to flee from an external danger we are purely and simply increasing the physical distance between ourselves and whatever is threatening us; we don't try to defend ourselves, nor do we seek to alter the status of the danger itself – as would be the case if we set about the wolf with a big stick or shot at it with a gun. But what the defence process does seems to amount to *more* than a mere attempt at flight: it engages with the drive process that is threatening it, suppresses it in some way, deflects it from its goal, and thereby renders it harmless. This objection seems irrefutable, and we must take due account of it. We believe that in all probability there are indeed defence processes that can reasonably be compared to an attempt at flight, while in others the ego responds far more aggressively and takes energetic counter-measures. Unless of course the comparison between flight and the defence process is altogether vitiated by the fact that both the ego and the drive within the id are parts of one and the same organic whole, not separate entities like the wolf and the child, with the result that *any* kind of behaviour on the part of the ego is bound to affect the drive process as well, and alter it in some way.

By dint of studying the determinants of fear we have inevitably seen the ego's behaviour in the defence process bathed, as it were, in the clear light of rationality. Each danger situation corresponds to a particular stage of life or to a particular phase in the development of the psychic apparatus, and seems to be appropriate to it. A very young child really *isn't* equipped to assert psychic control over large quanta of excitation arriving from without or within; what really *does* matter most at the relevant stage of an individual's life is that the people he is dependent on do not withdraw their loving care. If, as a boy, he perceives his mighty father as a rival *vis-à-vis* his mother, and becomes aware of his aggressive inclinations towards the one and sexual intentions towards the other, then he is perfectly justified in being afraid of his father, and his fear of punishment can easily be phylogenetically reinforced and manifest itself as fear of castration. Once he begins to enter social relationships, then fear of the super-ego, or conscience, becomes an absolute imperative, and any lapsing of this factor becomes the source of severe conflicts and dangers etc. However, a new problem is raised by precisely this circumstance.

Let us try for a moment to replace the affect of fear by another one, for instance the affect of pain. We regard it as entirely normal for a girl to weep pain-racked tears at the age of four if one of her dolls breaks, at age six if her teacher scolds her, at sixteen if her beloved pays her too little attention, at twenty-five perhaps if she has to bury her own child. Each of these pain-determinants has its own particular time, and vanishes once that time has passed; the last of them, the definitive ones, then remain in force throughout the rest of the individual's life. However, we would find it striking indeed if as a woman and mother this same girl were to sob over a broken knick-knack. But that is exactly how neurotics behave. All the various systems for taking control of stimuli across a very broad area have long since become fully established in their psychic apparatus; they are adult enough to be able to gratify most of their needs; they learned long ago that castration is not used as a punishment any more. And yet they behave as if the old danger situations still existed; they hold fast to all the earlier fear-determinants.

Finding the answer to this puzzle will take quite a while. The essential first step is to look carefully at the facts. In a great many cases the old fear-determinants are indeed relinquished, having already generated neurotic reactions. The phobias of very young children with respect to strangers, the dark, and being on their own

– phobias that can almost be termed normal – generally fade away within a few years; to use a phrase often applied to other childhood disorders, children simply 'grow out of them'. Animal phobias, common as they are, share the same destiny, and many of the childhood conversion hysterias show no recurrence in later years. Ritual behaviour is an extremely common phenomenon in the latency period, but only a very small percentage of such cases later develop into full-blown obsessional neurosis. So far as we are able to judge on the basis of our experience of white urban children subject to quite sophisticated socio-cultural expectations, childhood neuroses in general are passing phases that occur routinely in the course of children's development – although too little attention is paid to them, now as ever. There is never a single adult neurotic who does not show the telltale signs of childhood neurosis, whereas by no means all children who display such signs become neurotics in later life. It must thus be part and parcel of the maturation process for fear-determinants to be relinquished, and for danger situations to lose their importance. A further consideration is that some of these danger situations manage to survive into a much later period by modifying their fear-determinant to suit it. Thus for instance fear of castration carries on in the guise of syphilis phobia, the subject having discovered that while castration may no longer be customary as a punishment for indulging sexual desire, severe diseases have replaced it as the danger threatening anyone who plays free with their drives. Other fear-determinants, such as fear of the super-ego, are not destined for oblivion at all, but are meant to accompany us throughout the whole of our life. What differentiates neurotics from normal people, therefore, is that their *reactions* to these dangers are excessively intense. Finally, even adulthood does not offer sufficient protection against the return of the primal traumatic fear-situation; it seems likely that everyone has a limit beyond which their psychic apparatus is no longer capable of controlling the quanta of excitation that require urgent processing.

These minor adjustments to our argument are by no means intended to detract from the basic fact at issue here, namely that so many people remain infantile in their response to danger, and fail to put fear-determinants behind them once their time has passed. To deny this would be to deny the very fact of neurosis, for such people are precisely those we term 'neurotics'. But how is this possible? Why aren't *all* neuroses just passing phases in a person's development, phases that end once the next begins? What makes these reactions to danger so enduring? What gives the affect of fear the advantage that it seems to enjoy over all the other affects, namely the ability to call forth reactions which stand out from the others as plainly abnormal, and which are counter-purposive in obstructing the steady flow of life? We find ourselves, in other words, unexpectedly confronted once again with the same old conundrum: Where does neurosis come from? What is the force that ultimately and particularly drives it?[57] Despite decades of exertions in the field of psychoanalysis, this problem still looms before us, just as inviolate[58] as it was at the beginning.

X

Fear is the reaction to danger. Given that the affect of fear is able to commandeer a special position for itself in the psychic economy, it is surely plausible to suppose that this has to do with the nature of danger itself. But dangers are common to all mankind, they are the same for each and every individual. What we need – yet do not have – is some key factor that will explain how those particular individuals are selected who are able to subordinate the affect of fear to their normal psychic processes despite its special status; or, alternatively, a factor that determines which individuals are doomed to fail in this task. To the best of my knowledge, two attempts have so far been made to uncover such a factor (understandably enough, *any* attempt in this direction can expect a sympathetic reception, since it promises to relieve an agonizing need). The two attempts are complementary to each other, in that they approach the problem from opposite directions. The first was undertaken more than ten years ago by Alfred Adler. Reduced to its bare essentials, his argument is that those who fail to master the task that danger poses them, do so because the inferiority of their organs is such as to cause them insurmountable difficulties. If only we could put our faith in the adage *simplex sigillum veri*,[59] then we should have to hail Adler's solution as the answer to all our prayers. On the contrary, however, the critiques that have appeared over the last decade have irrefutably demonstrated the total inadequacy of this account – which, moreover, blithely ignores the entire wealth of material that has been discovered thanks to psychoanalysis.

The second attempt was undertaken by Otto Rank in 1923 in his book *Das Trauma der Geburt* [*The Trauma of Birth*]. It would be unfair to compare Rank's attempt to Adler's in any respect other than the one highlighted here, for it remains entirely within the realm of psychoanalysis, builds on its ideas, and deserves recognition as a legitimate bid to solve its problems. Taking the 'individual'/ 'danger' relation as a given, Rank shifts attention away from the individual and the frailty of his organs, and focuses instead on the variable intensity of the danger. The birth process is the first danger situation; the economic upheaval that it causes becomes the paradigmatic fear reaction. We earlier traced the line of development that links this first danger situation and fear-determinant to all the subsequent ones, and we saw that they all share a common factor, in that they all in one sense or another signify separation from the mother, at first only in biological terms, then in terms of object-loss – *direct* object-loss to start with, and *indirect* later on. The discovery of this crucial linkage is an undisputed merit of Rank's hypothesis. Now the trauma of birth affects different individuals with differing degrees of intensity, and as the intensity of the trauma varies, so too does the intensity of the fear reaction; according to Rank, it is the degree of fear thus generated at the very beginning that determines whether an individual will ever be able to assert control over it – that is, whether he will become neurotic or normal.

It is not our concern here to offer a detailed critique of Rank's ideas, but merely to consider whether they can help us find a solution to our specific problem. Rank's proposition – that people become neurotics because the intensity of their birth trauma is such that they never succeed in fully abreacting it – is highly questionable from a theoretical point of view. It isn't at all clear what is meant by 'abreacting the trauma'. If we take it literally, then we arrive at the untenable proposition that the neurotic will get closer and closer to being healthy the more frequently and more intensively he reproduces the affect of fear. Indeed, it was precisely because it thus contradicted reality that I had by that time already abandoned the abreaction theory, which played such a major role in the practice of catharsis.[60] Rank's emphasis on the variable intensity of the birth trauma takes no account of the perfectly sound aetiological credentials of hereditary constitution; and yet it is an organic factor that behaves in a quite random way by comparison with the constitution, and is itself dependent on numerous other factors that can only be termed random, such as the timely advent of help during the birth process. Rank's theory leaves both constitutional and phylogenetic factors completely out of account. But any attempt to accommodate the importance of the constitution – for instance by modifying the argument to the effect that what matters is rather the extent to which the individual reacts to the variable intensity of the birth trauma – simply robs the theory of its entire impact, and relegates the new factor introduced by Rank to a secondary role. The key factor that determines whether an individual ultimately develops neurosis thus lies in some other realm after all – and one that remains, as before, quite unknown to us.

The fact that the birth process is common both to humans and to the other mammals, whereas a special propensity for neurosis is a human privilege not vouchsafed to animals, is hardly likely to dispose anyone very favourably to Rank's theory. The chief objection to it, however, is that it is all up in the air, instead of being based on sound empirical evidence. There is no reliable body of research to show whether there is any clear correlation between a difficult and pro-tracted birth, and the development of neurosis, or indeed whether it is exclusively children born in such circumstances that exhibit the characteristic signs of early infantile anxiety[61] longer or more intensely than the norm. The point might be made that induced births, and births that are easy for the mother, *may* possibly mean severe trauma for the child; but this does not detract from the proposition that births involving asphyxia are *certain* to show the purported consequences. Rank's aetiology arguably does have a particular advantage in that it gives pre-eminence to a factor that can be tested against the empirical evidence; until it has indeed been tested in this way, it is impossible to form a judgement as to the real value of his hypothesis.

At the same time, I cannot share the view that Rank's theory contradicts the long-established tenet of psychoanalysis as to the aetiological importance of the sexual drives, for it bears solely on the individual's relationship to the danger situation, and leaves us to come to our own conclusions on the uplifting proposition that anyone incapable of dealing satisfactorily with the dangers that occur at the beginning of their life is also bound to fail in the situations of sexual danger that arise later on, and thus fall prey to neurosis.

I do not believe, then, that Rank's attempt provides us with the answer to our question as to *why* neurosis arises, and while it clearly does contribute to a solution, I think it is still too early to say just how significant that contribution may be. If research reveals that a difficult birth does *not* have a significant effect on the individual's susceptibility to neuroses, then Rank's contribution will have to be considered slight. It is very much to be feared that our need for a tangible and coherent 'ultimate cause' of nervous disorders will never be satisfied. The ideal answer – and one that doctors probably aspire to even today – would be to identify a bacillus that could be isolated and pure-cultured, and on inoculation would produce the same specific disorder in each and every individual. A somewhat less fantastical answer would be to identify particular chemical substances, the administering of which would induce or dispel specific neuroses. But solutions of this sort are not very likely.

What psychoanalysis enables us to say is less simple and less satisfying. I have nothing new to add here: I can only repeat what has long been known. If the ego succeeds in warding off a dangerous drive-impulse, by means of the repression process for instance, then it certainly inhibits and impairs the relevant part of the id – but at the same time it also grants it a certain element of independence, and forgoes a certain portion of its own sovereignty. This is an inevitable consequence of the very nature of repression, which in essence is an attempt at flight. The repressed element is now at large 'beyond the pale': excluded from the grand organization of the ego, and subject only to the laws that prevail in the realm of the unconscious. If the danger situation now alters in such a way that there is nothing motivating the ego to take defensive action against a *new* drive-impulse similar to the repressed one, then the consequences of the ego's restriction become apparent. The course of the new drive-impulse proves subject to automatism – or, as I should prefer to say, to the compulsion to repeat – and thus follows the same path as the earlier, repressed one, as if the danger situation that had already been successfully overcome were still in existence. The fixating factor in repression is thus the unconscious id's compulsion to repeat, which is normally neutralized only by free-moving[62] ego function. Now the ego may occasionally succeed in breaking down the barriers of repression that it has itself erected, thus enabling it to reassert its influence on the drive-impulse and control the course of the *new* one in accordance with the changed danger situation. But the fact of the matter is that it generally fails in this respect and is unable to reverse its repressions. The quantitative ratios involved may be the decisive factor in determining the outcome of this conflict. Our impression is that in quite a number of cases there is only one possible outcome: the regressive attraction exerted by the repressed impulse and the force of the repression itself are so great that the new impulse has no choice but to obey the compulsion to repeat. In other cases we see the effect of a different interplay of forces: the *attraction* of the repressed original impulse is reinforced by the *repulsion* generated by the objective difficulties that hinder the new impulse from following any other course.

That this is indeed the way in which the subject comes to be fixated on the repression, and to hold to a danger situation that no longer exists, is clearly borne out by the sheer fact of psychoanalytic therapy, which, though modest enough in itself, is enormously significant in theoretical terms. When in the course of psychoanalysis we give the ego the requisite help that enables it to lift its repressions, it recovers its power over the repressed id, and can get the drive-impulses to pursue their course as if the old danger situations no longer existed. Our achievements in this regard are fully in accord with the limited scope of our powers in medicine generally. In our therapeutic practice, after all, we must be content as a rule to achieve the same benign outcome that would have materialized anyway given the right circumstances – but to do so more rapidly, more reliably, and with less fuss.

Our deliberations thus far have shown us that it is the *quantitative* ratios of the various factors involved – ratios that cannot be directly demonstrated but only indirectly inferred – which determine whether old danger situations are perpetuated, whether repressions effected by the ego are maintained, whether childhood neuroses are continued in later life. Among the factors that are involved in the causation of neuroses – having created the conditions in which the various psychic forces do battle with each other – three in particular seem to us to stand out: a biological one, a phylogenetic one, and a purely psychological one.

The biological factor is the very lengthy period during which the young of the human species remain in a state of helplessness and dependence. The intra-uterine existence of human beings appears somewhat abbreviated by comparison with that of most animals, and they come into the world less able to cope. As a result, the objective external world exerts a more powerful influence on them, and the ego is encouraged to differentiate from the id at a very early stage; furthermore, the dangers posed by the external world become more significant, and the importance of the object – the only thing that can protect them from these dangers and make up for the loss of their intra-uterine existence – is vastly increased. This biological factor thus produces the first danger situations in each child's life, and generates the need to be loved – a need that stays with him throughout his life.

The second, phylogenetic, factor is merely a supposition on our part – but one forced upon us by a very curious aspect of libido development. We find that the sexual life of man does not develop along a steady path from birth to maturity, as does that of most animals closely related to him, but abruptly breaks off after an initial flourish lasting until the fifth year of life, then starts again at puberty, picking up where it left off in its infantile beginnings. We rather think that at some point during the shaping of mankind's destiny some momentous event must have occurred that left its mark in the form of this break in human sexual development.[63] The pathogenic significance of this factor is clearly demonstrated by the fact that most of the demands asserted by the drives in infantile sexuality are treated by the ego as dangers and duly warded off, with the result that the later sexual impulses of puberty, which ought to be ego-accordant,[64] are at risk of succumbing to the attraction of the paradigmatic impulses of infancy, and following them into repression. Here we find ourselves face to face with the most direct cause of neurosis. It is striking that the human being's early contact with the demands of sexuality affects the ego in much the same way as does his over-early contact with the external world.

The third, psychological, factor is to be found in a certain imperfectness of our psychic apparatus that has to do precisely with its differentiation into an ego and an id, and is thus ultimately also due to the influence of the external world. By dint of paying due attention to the dangers posed by objective reality, the ego is compelled to take defensive action against certain drive-impulses in the id, and to treat them as dangers. But the ego cannot protect itself against the dangers posed by its own inner drives as effectively as it can against a threat posed by external reality. Being itself intimately bound up with the id, it can fight off the danger posed by a drive only by restricting its own organization and accepting symptom-formation as the price it has to pay for obstructing the drive. If the rejected drive subsequently renews its assault, then the ego finds itself beset by all those difficulties that constitute the affliction familiar to us as 'neurosis'.

And that, I rather think, is about as far as we have managed to get for the time being in our quest to understand the nature and causation of neurosis.

XI

Addenda

In the course of this discussion various topics have been raised which then had to be all too quickly abandoned. These topics are now brought together here so that they can receive the full measure of attention that they deserve.

A *Modification of Previously Expressed Views*

a) Resistance and counter-cathexis

It is an important element of the theory of repression that it does not consist in an isolated, one-off process, but requires the continuous application of effort. If this effort were to cease, then the repressed drive, which is constantly replenished by its original well-springs, would make a further advance along the same path from which it had previously been ousted: the repression would either fail, or have to be repeated over and over again. It is thus the continuous nature of the drive that makes it necessary for the ego to devote itself unceasingly to its defence campaign in order to ensure its success. It is this sustained activity aimed at safeguarding the repression that we encounter in our therapeutic ministrations as *resistance*. Resistance presupposes the phenomenon that I have termed *counter-cathexis*.[65] Such a phenomenon is palpably present in obsessional neurosis, where it takes the form of an ego-alteration, that is, a *reaction-formation* within the ego, due to an intensification of whatever stance is antithetical to the thrust of the drive that is being repressed (e.g. compassion, conscientiousness, cleanliness). These reaction-formations in obsessional neurosis are all simply an exaggerated form of normal character traits that develop during the latency period. It is far more difficult to produce evidence of counter-cathexis in the case of hysteria, where in theoretical terms we would expect it to be just as indispensable. Here, too, there is unmistakable evidence of a certain degree of ego-alteration as a result of reaction-formation; indeed this is so marked in some circumstances that it forces itself on our attention as the principal symptom of the condition. It is in this way that the ambivalence conflict in hysteria is resolved, for instance: feelings of hatred towards a loved person are suppressed by dint of exaggerated affection and anxious concern for them. However, it needs to be emphasized that, in contradistinction to obsessional neurosis, such reaction-formations do not exhibit the generalized nature typical of character traits, but are confined to quite specific interactions. For instance, if a hysterical woman displays excessive affection towards her own children, while in truth hating them, this does not mean that she will *in general* be any more loving than other women, or indeed any more affectionate towards other children. In hysteria, reaction-formation sticks doggedly to a particular object, and does not turn into a general tendency on the part of the ego – whereas it is precisely such a generalizing process, a freeing-up of object relationships, an increase in the scope for displacement with regard to object-choice, that characterizes obsessional neurosis.

There is another form of counter-cathexis that does seem rather more appropriate to the particular nature of hysteria. The repressed drive-impulse can be activated (re-cathected) from two different directions: firstly from within, due to an intensification of the drive brought about by its own internal sources of excitation, and secondly from without, due to perception of an object that the drive finds desirable. Hysterical counter-cathexis, however, is largely directed *outwards*, and against any perception that might pose a danger. It takes the form of a special vigilance which, by means of restrictions of the ego, avoids situations in which such a perception might occur, or, if it occurs anyway, succeeds in preventing the subject from paying any attention to it. Certain French writers (notably Laforgue) have recently highlighted this feature of hysteria by giving it the special name 'scotomization'.[66] This particular technique of counter-cathexis is even more marked in the phobias, where the subject's whole focus of interest is to remove himself ever further from any situation that might involve the perception he so dreads. Although it is not an absolute one, the complete contrast in the direction of the counter-cathexis in hysteria and phobias on the one hand, and in obsessional neurosis on the other, appears to be significant. It invites us to suppose that there is a rather more intimate connection between repression and external counter-cathexis, as also between regression and internal counter-cathexis (ego-alteration due to reaction-formation). The task of warding off a dangerous perception is incidentally common to all neuroses. In obsessional neurosis, sundry 'dos' and 'don'ts' are intended to serve this same purpose.

We established on an earlier occasion that the resistance that we have to overcome in psychoanalysis is produced by the ego, which doggedly persists in its counter-cathexes.[67] The ego finds it hard to turn its attention to perceptions and notions which it has hitherto made it a rule to avoid, or to acknowledge as its own certain impulses blatantly antithetical to those it is wont to think its own. It is just such a view of this resistance that forms the basis of our attempts to overcome it in analysis. Where, on account of its affinity with the repressed drive-impulse, the resistance is unconscious – as is frequently the case – we make it conscious; once it has become conscious, we put up logical arguments against it; we promise the ego rewards and advantages if it abandons its resistance. There is thus no call to doubt or modify the notion of 'resistance' by the ego. None the less, the question arises whether it is sufficient on its own to account for the actual facts of the matter as presented to us in psychoanalysis. We find that the ego still has difficulty in undoing the repressions, even after it has resolved to relinquish its resistances, and we have used the term 'working through' to describe the phase of strenuous endeavour that follows this laudable resolve. We now need to recognize the dynamic factor that makes this working-through process both necessary and understandable. It must surely be the case that, even when the resistance of the ego has been removed, there is still something else to be overcome – namely the powerful compulsion to repeat, the attraction of the unconscious paradigms acting upon the suppressed drive process; and there could be no objection to our terming this factor the *resistance of the unconscious*.

We must not let ourselves get upset about such emendations: they are distinctly desirable if they bring us new knowledge, and by no means shameful if, rather than discrediting our old knowledge, they serve to refine it, perhaps by narrowing down a generalization that is somewhat broad, or broadening an interpretation that is rather too narrow. However, we cannot assume that by making this particular emendation we have attained to a comprehensive overview of all the different types of resistance confronting us in psychoanalysis. On the contrary, we find on closer examination that we have altogether five kinds of resistance to contend with, arising from three distinct directions, that is, from the ego, the id and the super-ego. The ego turns out to be the source of three of them, each having a different dynamic. The first of these three resistances on the part of the ego is the one we have just dealt with, namely *repression* resistance, and there is very little that we can add here. Although similar in nature, *transference* resistance none the less belongs in a separate category: it manifests itself differently and much more distinctly in analysis, since it contrives to establish a relationship with the analytic situation or with the person of the analyst, and thereby to rekindle a repression that was meant to be merely recollected. A further form of ego resistance, but one of a very different nature, is that predicated on *illness-gain*, which essentially involves assimilating the symptom into the ego. It corresponds to a fervent unwillingness to refrain from any gratification or other relief. As for the fourth type of resistance, namely that of the *id*, we have just seen how it is this that makes the 'working-through' process necessary. The fifth kind of resistance, that of the *super-ego* – the last to be recognized and the most obscure, though not always the least powerful – appears to stem from the subject's sense of guilt or need for punishment; it puts obstacles in the way of any form of success – including, of course, the subject's own recovery through psychoanalysis.[68]

b) Fear arising from transformation of libido

The interpretation of fear put forward in this essay diverges to some extent from the one that I previously thought correct. I used to regard fear as a general reaction on the part of the ego in circumstances of unpleasure; I always sought to account for its appearance in economic terms, and on the basis of my investigations into the 'actual' neuroses I assumed that any libido (sexual excitation) rejected or not utilized by the ego finds direct release in the form of fear. There is no overlooking the fact that these various findings do not accord well with each other, or at the very least do not follow logically from one another. Furthermore, they foster the impression of a particularly intimate link between fear and libido, something that once again does not accord with the general nature of fear as a reaction denoting unpleasure.

The objection to this previous interpretation stemmed from my argument making the ego the sole locus of fear, and was thus one of the results of my attempt in *The Ego and the Id* at a taxonomy of the psychic apparatus. The earlier interpretation tended to regard the libido of the repressed drive-impulse as the source of the fear; according to the later one, however, this fear was the ego's responsibility. 'Ego-fear' or 'drive-(id-)fear' – that is the question. Given the fact that the ego operates with desexualized energy, the new version also posits a much less intimate connection between fear and libido. I hope I have at least succeeded in making the contradiction clear, and in precisely delineating the area of uncertainty.

Rank's insistence that the affect of fear is indeed – as I myself initially maintained – a consequence of the birth process, and a repetition of the situation then experienced, obliged me to take a fresh look at the fear problem. I was unable to get anywhere with Rank's own interpretation, according to which birth is a trauma, the state of fear is the reaction to that trauma giving the requisite release, and each new affect of fear is an attempt to 'abreact' the trauma ever more completely. It became necessary to go back a stage and look at the *danger situation* underlying the fear reaction. The introduction of this factor enabled us to view things in a new perspective. We now saw birth as the paradigm for all the danger situations that subsequently arise in the new circumstances created by changes in the subject's form of existence and by the progressive development of his psyche; but we also saw its own significance as being restricted to this paradigmatic role with regard to danger. The fear experienced at birth now became in this perspective the paradigm of a state of affect that necessarily shared the destiny of other affects. On the one hand the affect of fear, having been purposive in the original danger situation, automatically reproduces itself as a *counter*-purposive form of reaction in situations analogous to those in which it first arose; on the other hand, the *ego* reproduces it, having managed to gain power over it, and uses it as a warning of the impending danger and as a means of jolting the pleasure/ unpleasure mechanism into action. The biological importance of the affect of fear received its due, in that fear was recognized as being the universal reaction to a danger situation; the role of the ego as the locus of fear was confirmed, in that it was acknowledged as being a function of the ego to produce the affect of fear in accordance with its own particular needs. The fear that manifests itself in all the later phases of life was thus seen as originating in two distinct ways: one – invariably justifiable in economic terms – that occurs involuntarily and automatically whenever a danger situation arises that is analogous to that of birth; another that is specifically produced by the ego as a preventative measure whenever there is simply the *threat* of such a situation arising. In this latter case, the ego was seen as subjecting itself to fear as if to a vaccine, so to speak, thus accepting a mild dose of illness in order to avoid a full-blown attack. It is as if the ego deliberately summons up a vivid picture of the danger situation – with the unmistakable purpose of restricting this painful experience to a mere hint or signal. We have already shown in considerable detail how in the process the various danger situations develop separately, one after another, yet remain genetically linked. We shall perhaps manage to penetrate a little further in our understanding of fear once we tackle the problem of the relationship between neurotic fear and objective fear.

Our earlier hypothesis of a direct transformation of libido into fear is now of less interest to us – but if we take stock of it all the same, then we need to distinguish between several different sets of circumstances. It is certainly not applicable where fear serves as a signal to alert the ego, and it is thus also not applicable to any of those danger situations that prompt the ego to initiate a repression. As is most plainly evident in the conversion hysterias, the libidinal cathexis of the repressed drive-impulse finds uses other than being transformed into fear, or released as fear. In our further discussion of danger situations, however, we shall come upon a particular form of fear-generation that probably needs to be viewed rather differently.

c) Repression and defence

In the context of these discussions on the problem of fear I have reverted to a concept – or to put it more modestly, a term – that I used exclusively at the start of my work thirty years ago, and then subsequently abandoned. I mean the term 'defence process'.[69] In due course I replaced it with the term 'repression', but the relation-ship between the two remained imprecise. I now think that it is distinctly advantageous to hark back to the old concept of 'defence', provided it is clearly established that it is intended to serve as the general designation for *all* the techniques used by the ego in its various conflicts, any of which may lead to neurosis, while 'repression' remains the name of one particular such mechanism that we have first become more familiar with because of the direction our investigations happen to have taken.

Even a purely terminological innovation requires to be justified; it needs to reflect a new perspective or a new insight. And indeed, the resumption of the concept of 'defence', and the narrowing of the concept of 'repression', gives due recognition to a fact that has long been known but has acquired extra significance thanks to various more recent discoveries. We first learned about repression and symptom-formation in the context of hysteria. We saw that the perceptions attaching to excitatory experiences and the notions attaching to pathogenic trains of thought are forgotten and thus excluded from reproduction within the subject's memory, and we therefore concluded that keeping certain things from consciousness is one of the chief characteristics of hysterical repression. We later studied obsessional neurosis and found that in this particular disorder the pathogenic events are *not* forgotten. They remain conscious, but are 'isolated' in some way not yet comprehensible to us, so that much the same outcome is achieved as in the case of hysterical amnesia. None the less, the difference is large enough to justify our view that the process whereby demands on the part of drives are rebuffed in obsessional neurosis cannot be the same as that in hysteria. Further investigations have taught us that in obsessional neurosis the vigorous resistance of the ego causes the drive-impulses to regress to an earlier libidinal phase, and while this does not render a repression superfluous, it is clearly similar to repression in its effect. In addition, we have seen that counter-cathexis – a process we can also assume to be operative in hysteria – plays a particularly important role in protecting the ego in obsessional neurosis by means of reactive ego-alteration; we have become aware of an 'isolation' process – albeit without yet being able to explain how it works – that finds direct expression at the symptomatic level; and we have also become aware of the 'obliteration of past events', a procedure we can only call magical, which unquestionably has a defensive function, but bears no further resemblance to the process of 'repression'. These findings are reason enough to reintroduce the old concept of *defence* – which can readily embrace all these processes with their common purpose of protecting the ego against challenges on the part of drives – and to subsume repression under it as a special sub-category. The importance of using nomenclature of this sort becomes even greater if we take into account the possibility that in digging ever deeper in our researches we may well find that there is an intimate connection between particular forms of defence and specific disorders, for instance between repression and hysteria. Furthermore, we expect that there is a real possibility of our discovering another, equally significant pattern of dependence: it may well be that *prior* to the sharp differentiation of the ego and the id and the formation of the super-ego, the psychic apparatus uses different methods of defence from those it uses *after* attaining these stages of organization.

B *Fear: Supplementary Remarks*

The affect of fear exhibits certain characteristics the investigation of which promises to bring us further enlightenment. For one thing, fear is unmistakably associated with *expectation*; it is fear *of* something. For another, it is in the very nature of fear to be *non-specific* and to *have no object*. In proper linguistic usage it even changes its name if it acquires an object, the word 'fear' being replaced by the word 'dread'.[70] Furthermore, fear is not only associated with danger but also with neurosis, a topic we have long been struggling to elucidate. The question arises: why aren't *all* fear reactions neurotic, and why do we regard so many of them as normal? It is high time we undertook a thorough appreciation of the difference between objective fear and neurotic fear.

Let us take as our starting point the problem we have just been dealing with. The progress we made consisted in the fact that we went back a stage and concentrated on the danger situation rather than the fear reaction. If we make the same shift with respect to the problem of objective fear, its solution becomes quite straightforward. Objective danger is a danger that we know, and objective fear is fear of such a danger, that is, one that is known. Neurotic fear is fear of a danger that we do *not* know. Thus we first have to work out what that neurotic danger consists in; and psychoanalysis has shown us that it is a danger posed by the drives. In bringing to consciousness this danger that was previously quite unknown to the ego, we blur the distinction between objective fear and neurotic fear and are thus able to treat the latter as if it were the former.

In the face of objective danger we display two reactions: an affective one, namely a surge of fear, and a practical one, for the purposes of self-protection. It seems likely that the same thing happens in the face of dangers posed by our drives. We are familiar with situations of purposive interplay between the two reactions, whereby one gives the signal that serves to trigger the other; but we are also familiar with the *counter*-purposive situation of fear-induced paralysis, whereby one reaction proliferates at the expense of the other.

There are certain cases that display a mixture of objective fear and neurotic fear. The danger is known and real, but the fear shown towards it is disproportionate, it is more than we think it ought to be. This excess over and above what is objectively appropriate clearly reveals the neurotic element. But such cases tell us nothing fundamentally new. Psychoanalysis reveals the fact that, linked to the known objective danger, there is an unrecognized danger emanating from the drives.

We can make further progress if we do more than step back just one stage from fear to danger and go on to ask what constitutes the real *core* of the danger situation, its most significant element. Clearly it is the process whereby we assess our own strength in relation to the magnitude of the danger, and acknowledge our helplessness in the face of it – physical helplessness in the case of objective danger, psychic helplessness in the case of danger emanating from our drives. In making this judgement we are guided by the actual experiences we have been through in the past; whether the judgement is right or wrong is immaterial to the outcome. Let us use the term 'traumatic' to designate this situation in which we experience a sense of helplessness; we then have good grounds for drawing a distinction between the *traumatic situation* and the *danger situation*.

Now it marks an important advance in our powers of self-preservation when this sort of traumatic situation of helplessness is not just passively awaited, but actively foreseen and expected. The situation that offers the requisite conditions for such expectation may be termed the 'danger situation', for it is here that the fear signal is given out. What this signal says is that I am expecting a situation of helplessness to arise, or else that I am reminded by the current situation of one of my previous traumatic experiences. I therefore *anticipate* the trauma, and so long as there is still time to ward it off I seek to behave as if it were already present. Fear is therefore on the one hand the *expectation* of future trauma, and on the other a *repetition* of past trauma in a mild form. The two characteristics of fear that attracted our attention thus have different origins. Its association with expectation appertains to the danger situation, whereas its non-specificness and lack of an object appertain to the traumatic situation of helplessness, itself anticipated in the danger situation.

Having set forth this sequence 'fear – danger – helplessness (trauma)', we can now summarize the position as follows. A danger situation is a situation of helplessness that we simultaneously recognize, remember and expect; fear is the original reaction to helplessness in the trauma that is then subsequently reproduced in the danger situation as a signal calling for help; the ego, having experienced the trauma passively, now actively repeats a reproduction of it in diluted form, in the hope of being able to keep control of the way it evolves. We know that children behave in precisely this way with respect to all the experiences they find distressing, in that they reproduce them in their play; by thus moving from a passive to an active role they seek to assert control in psychic terms over the experiences that life brings them.[71] If this is what 'abreacting the trauma' is supposed to mean, then we can't really raise any further objections to it.[72] The really crucial matter, however, is the initial displacement of the fear reaction from the *presence* of the situation of helplessness in which it originated, to the *expectation* of such a situation, that is, the danger situation. Thereafter ensue the various further displacements from the danger to the *determinant* of the danger, that is, loss of the object, and the modified forms of such loss mentioned earlier.[73]

The undesirable consequence of 'spoiling' a young child is that the danger of object-loss – the object being the means of protection against any and every situation of helplessness – becomes unduly magnified in comparison to all the other dangers. The individual is thereby encouraged to *remain* in the state of childhood, which is characterized by motor and psychic helplessness.

We have not so far had occasion to view objective fear any differently from the way we view neurotic fear. We know what the distinction between them is: an objective danger is one posed by an external object; a neurotic danger arises from demands made by the individual's own drives. In so far as these demands on the part of the drive are objectively real, neurotic fear, too, can be regarded as having an objective basis. We have seen that if fear and neurosis appear to be particularly intimately connected, this is simply because the ego uses the fear reaction to defend itself against dangers posed by the drives just as it does against external, objective dangers – but due to a certain imperfectness of our psychic apparatus the particular thrust of this defensive activity leads ultimately to neurosis. We have also come to the conclusion that the demands of the drives often pose an (internal) danger only because their gratification would give rise to an external danger, in other words because the *internal* danger represents an *external* one.

Equally, on the other hand, the external (objective) danger has to have been internalized in some way if it is to be of any significance to the ego; it has to have been recognized as bearing a relationship to a previously experienced situation of helplessness.[74] Human beings seem to have been endowed with little or no instinctive awareness of dangers that threaten from without. Young children constantly do things that endanger their life, and for that very reason cannot do without their protective object. In our relationship to a traumatic situation, where we find ourselves helpless, there is a convergence of external danger and internal danger – of objective danger, and the demands of a drive. No matter if in one case the ego experiences a pain that never ceases, while in another it experiences a build-up of need that can find no gratification: in both cases the economic situation is the same, and the subject's motor helplessness manifests itself in psychic helplessness.

The puzzling phobias of early childhood deserve further mention here. We found that some of them – fear of strangers, of darkness, of being alone – can be understood as reactions to the danger of object-loss. In other cases – fear of small animals, storms etc. – an answer to the conundrum might lie in the argument that they are the attenuated remnants of a congenital alertness to objective dangers, an alertness that is so strongly developed in other animals. The only part of this archaic inheritance that remains purposive for human beings is that relating to object-loss. Where these particular childhood phobias become fixated, increase in intensity and endure into later life, psychoanalysis clearly demonstrates that their content has let itself be coloured by the demands of the subjects' drives, and thus stands for internal dangers as well as external ones.

C *Fear, Pain, and Sorrow*

So little is currently known about the psychology of emotional processes that the remarks offered in all diffidence here deserve to be judged in a spirit of extreme tolerance. The problem, as we see it, arises out of our assertion that fear comes to be a reaction to the danger of object-loss. Now we already know of one such reaction to object-loss, namely sorrow. The question is: when does the one reaction set in, and when the other? We have already dealt with sorrow at some length in a previous context,[75] but one feature of it defied all understanding: its particularly painful nature. At the same time, it seems altogether understandable to us that separation from one's object should be painful. The problem thus becomes even more complicated: when does separation from an object produce fear, when does it produce sorrow, and when – if at all – does it produce only pain?

Let us admit straight away that there is no prospect of our providing answers to these questions. The best we can do is to draw some distinctions and offer some suggestions.

As our starting point, let us again take the one situation that we think we understand, namely that of the baby who finds himself confronted by a stranger instead of his mother, and thereupon displays the fear that we have thus far interpreted solely by reference to the danger of object-loss. But this fear is probably rather more complicated and merits closer examination. While there can be no doubting the baby's fear, his facial expression and his reaction of crying suggest that he is also feeling pain. It seems that various things that he will later differentiate from each other are at this stage all merged into one. He cannot yet tell the difference between temporary absence and permanent loss; if he fails just once to catch sight of his mother, he behaves as if he were never going to see her again, and only when repeated experiences to the contrary have brought him solace does he learn that such disappearances on the part of his mother are generally followed by her reappearance. His mother fosters this crucial insight by playing the familiar game of hiding her face from him, then, to his great delight, uncovering it again. This enables him to feel pangs of longing, as it were, that are not attended by despair.

Because he misunderstands it, the situation whereby he is distressed at his mother's absence is not a danger situation but a traumatic one. Or to put it more precisely: it is a traumatic one if at that particular moment he happens to be feeling a need that his mother is meant to gratify; if no such need is present, then it becomes a danger situation. The first fear-determinant that the ego itself introduces is accordingly loss of perception of the object, which it equates with loss of the object itself. There is no question of loss of love at this stage. Later on, experience teaches the child that his object can be present, but angry with him, and loss of the object's love then becomes the new and far more constant danger and fear-determinant.

The traumatic situation of distress at the mother's absence differs in one crucial respect from the traumatic situation of birth: at that point there was no object, and hence no possibility of distress at its absence; the only reaction that could arise was fear. In the meantime, however, repeated instances of gratification have made the mother the child's object, and whenever he experiences need this object undergoes intense cathexis that can be described as 'longing'. It is to this new development that we can relate the reaction of pain. Thus pain is properly speaking the reaction to object-loss, while fear is the reaction to the danger attendant on this loss and, by extension, to the danger of object-loss itself.

Pain, too, is something we know very little about. All we know for certain is that pain occurs – at any rate primarily and as a general rule – when a stimulus attacks somewhere on the periphery, penetrates the apparatus forming the protective barrier, and then produces just the same effect as if it were a continuous stimulus emanating from the drives – a process altogether proof against the muscle actions that are otherwise effective in removing the relevant part of the body from the stimulus attacking it.[76] The situation is no different if the pain stems from an internal organ rather than from a point on the surface of the skin; all that has happened is that a part of the inner periphery has taken the place of the outer one. There are clearly occasions when children experience pain quite independently of their experiencing need. But the circumstances that give rise to this kind of pain seem to bear very little resemblance to object-loss. Furthermore, peripheral stimulation – that defining feature of pain – is entirely absent from the situation of longing experienced by a child. And yet it cannot be wholly without rhyme or reason that language has coined the notion of inner, psychic pain, and treats the sensations caused by object-loss as being identical in all respects to physical pain.

Physical pain gives rise to an intense cathexis of the painful part of the body; this cathexis, which we may term narcissistic, grows ever more intense, and has an 'emptying' effect on the ego.[77] It is well known that when we suffer pain in our internal organs, we apprehend three-dimensional and other images or notions of parts of the body that never otherwise figure in our conscious mind at all. Moreover, the fact that the cathexis is concentrated on the *psychic representamen* of the painful part of the body explains the remarkable fact that if the psyche's attention is distracted by another interest of some sort, even the most intense physical pain simply does not materialize (it would *not* be correct in this context to say that it 'remains unconscious'). It seems to be precisely in *this* point that the analogy resides that allows the sensation of pain to be carried over into the psychic realm. The intense, ever-increasing cathexis of the absent (lost) object generated by the child's unassuageable longing creates exactly the same economic conditions as does the pain-generated cathexis of an injured part of the body, and thus makes it possible for the absence of the usual prerequisite of physical pain – an attack somewhere on the periphery – to be disregarded. The transition from physical pain to psychic pain corresponds to the change from narcissistic cathexis to object-cathexis. The subject's *notion* of his object, highly cathected by his needs, plays the same role as a part of the body cathected by an increase in stimulus. The continuous nature of the cathexis process and its insusceptibility to inhibition combine to produce the same state of psychic helplessness. If the resulting sensation of unpleasure shows the specific characteristics of pain (characteristics that do not permit of any more precise definition), instead of manifesting itself in the form of a fear reaction, then it seems reasonable to attribute this to a circumstance that we have made too little use of in our interpretations thus far: the fact that these processes leading to the sensation of unpleasure are enacted at a very elevated level of cathexis and annexion.

A further emotional reaction to object-loss is familiar to us, namely sorrow – but its explanation no longer presents any difficulties: the sorrowing process is triggered by the 'reality-test', which categorically insists that since our object no longer exists, we must separate ourselves from it;[78] the task of the sorrowing process is to carry out this withdrawal from the object in all those situations where the object was the focus of intense cathexis. The painful nature of this separation fully accords with our explanation, given the intense cathexis – caused by unassuageable longing – that occurs during the reproduction of the various situations in which the subject has to undo the ties that bound him to his object.

(1926)

Notes

On the Introduction of Narcissism

1. [The title given in the *Standard Edition* is *On Narcissism: an Introduction* – but this is a startling mistranslation of Freud's wording (*Zur Einführung des Narzissmus*). Far from introducing us to an apparently well-recognized phenomenon, as the *Standard Edition* mis-title implies, Freud is signalling the introduction of a whole new theory of narcissism (cf. the fifth paragraph of the essay!).]

2. [It is at once striking and instructive that the phrase 'with sexual pleasure' (*mit sexuellem Wohlgefallen*) is simply omitted from the *Standard Edition*.]

3. [Freud's term *Unterbringung der Libido* (in other contexts *Libidounterbringung*) is a metaphor that cannot be adequately replicated in English. The relevant verb (*unterbringen*) means 'house', 'accommodate', 'find an appropriate niche for'. The *Standard Edition* has 'allocation', but this suggests something quite different from Freud's original.]

4. Otto Rank (1911) ['Ein Beitrag zum Narzissismus' ('A Contribution on Narcissism')].

5. Regarding these propositions, cf. the discussion of the 'end of the world' in the analysis of Senate President Schreber (1911); cf. also Abraham (1908) [Freud deals with the Schreber case in 'Psychoanalytic Remarks on an Autobiographically Described Case of Paranoia (Dementia Paranoides)'; an English version of Abraham's treatise may be found in K. Abraham, *Selected Papers* (London 1927; New York 1953), Ch. 11].

6. ['Cathexis' is an ugly and opaque term – coined by James Strachey – that has nothing of the apparent simplicity of Freud's metaphor *Besetzung*. Unfortunately, however, Freud's word has no direct or uncontentious equivalent in English, and Strachey's well-established hellenism is therefore reluctantly retained throughout this present volume (together with the associated verb 'cathect').]

7. [The obfuscatory tendencies of the *Standard Edition* are epitomized by the fact that it renders Freud's *Zauberkraft* – a word that any child would instantly understand – as 'thaumaturgic force'!]

8. See the relevant sections of my book *Totem und Tabu* [*Totem and Taboo*] (1912–13). [See Chapter III.]

9. See Ferenczi (1913) [Sándor Ferenczi, 'Entwicklungsstufen des Wirklich-keitssinnes' ('Stages in the Development of the Sense of Reality', *First Contributions to Psycho-Analysis*, London, 1952, Ch. VIII)].

10. [See also *Beyond the Pleasure Principle*, below, p. 91. This idea will be revised later on, once Freud has evolved the notion of the 'id'; see *The Ego and the Id*, below, p. 121, and the corresponding note 45. The *Standard Edition* carries a lengthy Appendix by the editors on the 'considerable difficulty' attaching to this particular metaphor of Freud's.]

11. There are two mechanisms involved in this 'end of the world' scenario: when the entire libido-cathexis streams out onto the love-object, and when it all floods back into the ego.

12. [Cf. *OED*: 'The germ-plasm is the essential part of the germ-cell, and determines the nature of the individual that arises from it' (sample quotation dated 1890).]

13. [The first two German editions of the essay printed *ersterwählte* – the first hypothesis *chosen* – whereas subsequent editions printed *ersterwähnte* – the first hypothesis *mentioned*. The *Standard Edition* opts for the original version – but there seems little logic in this, given that Freud did indeed 'mention' this hypothesis just a few paragraphs earlier.]

14. [This curious term is Freud's own (*psychisches Interesse*).]

15. [Freud is referring to Ferenczi's review of Jung's *Wandlungen und Symbole der Libido* (published in English under the title *Psychology of the Unconscious*).]

16. [Freud's term is *Realfunktion*, derived from Pierre Janet's *la fonction du réel*.]

17. [Freud gives this phrase in English.]

18. [*Positionen*. This is a recurrent term of Freud's in connection with the libido, especially with regard to the loci that it comes to occupy as a result of cathexis.]

19. [*Ichveränderung*. See also below, *The Ego and the Id*, note 43.]

20. [See the *Longman Dictionary of Psychology and Psychiatry*, ed. Robert M. Goldenson, New York and London, 1985: '*actual neurosis* – a neurosis which, according to Freud, stems from current sexual frustrations, such as coitus interruptus, forced abstinence, or incomplete gratification, as contrasted with psychoneurosis, which stems from experiences in infancy or childhood. The term was applied primarily to anxiety neurosis, hypochondriasis, and neurasthenia, but is rarely used today.' See also the final paragraph of Chapter IV of *Inhibition, Symptom, and Fear* below.]

21. [*Angstneurose*. The long-established term 'anxiety neurosis' is reluctantly retained here but it should be noted that *Angst* means 'fear', and is normally used in precisely that sense by Freud. See also below, *Inhibition, Symptom, and Fear*, note 3.]

22. Cf. 'Über neurotische Erkrankungstypen' (1912) ['Types of Onset of Neurosis'].

23. [Freud's important but challenging term is *Versagung*, from the verb *versagen*, itself cognate with English 'forsake' – one now-obsolete meaning of which is 'To decline or refuse (something offered)' (*OED*). What he means by the term is rather more clearly shown by the opening sentences of 'Die am Erfolge scheitern' ('Those who Founder on Success'): 'Our work in psychoanalysis has presented us with the following proposition: People incur neurotic illness as a result of *refusal*. What is meant by this is that their libidinal desires are refused gratification' – i.e. by the savagely censorious entity within that oversees their every thought and deed. See also the penultimate sentence of this present essay: 'We can thus more readily understand the fact that paranoia is frequently caused by the ego being wounded, by gratification being refused within the domain of the ego-ideal.' The *Standard Edition* routinely and astonishingly mistranslates the term as 'frustration'.]

24. [The voice here is God's; the lines are from Heine's *Neue Gedichte* ('Schöpfungslieder', vii).]

25. ['Release' is used throughout this volume to render Freud's important but not readily translatable metaphor *Abfuhr* (the *Standard Edition* prefers 'discharge').]

26. [*Konversion*. See also below, *Remembering, Repeating, and Working Through*, note 3.]

27. [Freud's term – used here for the first time in his *œuvre* – is *Anlehnungstypus*. Alas, it cannot be rendered directly into English, and so 'imitative type' is necessarily an approximate rather than a precise translation (as are the two immediately preceding instances of 'imitate', both rendering words derived from the verb *sich anlehnen*). However, this is a considerable improvement on the *Standard Edition*, which goes seriously awry when it translates Freud's term as 'the "anaclitic" or "attachment" type'. 'Anaclitic' is a specially concocted word – but concocted on the basis of a startling misunderstanding of the German expression *sich anlehnen an*, as the footnote in the *Standard Edition* makes embarrassingly clear: the expression does *not* imply 'attach' or 'attachment'; it simply means that A 'is modelled on', 'is based on', 'follows the example of' B; thus one might typically say that Beethoven's early symphonies *lehnen sich an* the mature work of Mozart, or that Freud's theories *lehnen sich an* the ideas and visions of nineteenth-century German literature (in the *Introductory Lectures on Psychoanalysis: New Series* Freud himself notes that the term 'id' (*das Es*) was devised on the model of Nietzsche's linguistic practice – *in Anlehnung an den Sprachgebrauch bei Nietzsche*).]

28. [Freud's German is somewhat ambiguous; his wording is such that it could be understood to mean 'who have *partly* relinquished their own narcissism' (this is the interpretation preferred by the *Standard Edition*).]

29. [Freud cites the phrase in English, and is probably quoting the title of a painting exhibited in the Royal Academy, which depicted a baby being wheeled grandly across a busy London street while two policemen hold up the traffic.]

30. [*sein aktuelles Ich*.]

31. [*Idealbildung*. Freud is particularly fond of creating compound nouns ending in *-bildung*, the gerund of the verb *bilden*, 'to form' (cognate with English 'build'), e.g. *Reaktionsbildung*, *Symptombildung*, *Traumbildung*.]

32. [Freud's word is *Instanz* – a cardinal term in his vocabulary, but one that has no direct linguistic or indeed cultural equivalent in English, with the result that a number of different renderings are deployed in this present translation to match the relevant context. The key feature of the word is that it implies some kind of judicial or quasi-judicial authority making judgements about what is permissible and impermissible, acceptable and unacceptable – and doing so very often in implacably harsh and even sadistic terms involving 'guilt', 'condemnation', 'punishment' etc. This vision of the human psyche as a domain under constant surveillance by draconian but shadowy forces is fascinatingly similar to that of Freud's fellow Jew and Austro-Hungarian near-contemporary, Franz Kafka.]

33. Merely by way of conjecture I would add that the development and consolidation of this all-scrutinizing entity might also embrace the ultimate emergence of (subjective) memory and of the phenomenon whereby time holds no validity for unconscious processes.

34. [Having thus far used abstract nouns (*Instanz*, *Zensur*) to convey the policing of the psyche, Freud gives the process a far sharper edge here by suddenly personifying it (*Zensor*).]

35. I cannot here resolve the issue whether the differentiation of this censorial entity from the rest of the ego is capable of providing a psychological substantiation of the philosophical distinction between consciousness and self-consciousness.

36. [*Selbstgefühl*. The *Standard Edition* bizarrely renders this as 'self-regarding attitude'. For useful definitions and examples of 'self-feeling' as a technical term current in nineteenth and early twentieth-century thinking, see *OED*.]

37. [*Ichgerecht*. The *Standard Edition* has 'ego-syntonic', but this is misleading as well as obfuscatory given that the term *Syntonie* ('syntony') was not introduced into psychiatry (by Eugen Bleuler) until 1925 – more than a decade after Freud's *Narcissism* essay.]

38. [*Objektbefriedigungen*. This is one of Freud's more brutalist compounds. As the ensuing paragraphs make clear, it is elliptical for 'gratifications *pertaining to* objects'.]

39. [*Zensor*. See above, note 34.]

40. [On the face of it, Freud's German (*Perversionen wiederherzustellen*) means 'restore' or 'reinstate' the individual's perversions (the *Standard Edition* duly translates it in this sense); but it is more plausibly an elliptical usage highlighting love's benignly restorative effect on the individuals themselves (*wiederherstellen* is a standard expression for 'restore to health').]

41. [*Massenpsychologie*. In the *Standard Edition* this term is routinely translated as '*group* psychology'.]

42. [In *Inhibition, Symptom, and Fear* Freud will draw an important distinction between 'consciential fear' and 'social fear'; see below, *Inhibition, Symptom, and Fear*, note 56.]

43. [*Umbildung*.]

Remembering, Repeating, and Working Through

1. [*Abreagieren*. The term, together with the attendant therapeutic concept, was introduced by Freud and Breuer in their *Studien über Hysterie* (*Studies on Hysteria*, 1895). 'Abreaction' is defined in the *OED* as follows: 'The liberation by revival and expression of the emotion associated with forgotten or repressed ideas of the event that first caused it. Hence "abreact", to eliminate by abreaction'. In *Inhibition, Symptom, and Fear* (published twelve years after *Remembering, Repeating, and Working Through*), Freud was to comment that he had long since 'abandoned the abreaction theory' (see below, p. 219).]

2. [This paragraph and the three that follow – all printed in smaller type than the rest of the text when first published in 1914 – amount to an extended parenthesis, interpolated between two paragraphs that essentially belong together.]

3. [*Konversionshysterien.* 'Conversion' in Freud's sense is defined in the *OED* as 'The symbolic manifestation in physical symptoms of a psychic conflict'; the *OED* entry also includes the following quotation from Freud's disciple Ernest Jones: 'The energy finds an outlet in some somatic manifestation, a process Freud terms "conversion".']

4. [*Deckerinnerungen.* The *deck-* element of the neologism means 'cover', 'conceal'.]

5. [*Kindheitsamnesie.* 'Childhood amnesia' in Freud's sense is amnesia *concerning* childhood – not amnesia *during* childhood.]

6. ['Relationary processes' is more a guess than a translation. Freud's neologism is *Beziehungsvorgänge* – and there is no clue as to which of the various meanings of the word *Beziehung* he had in mind. The *Standard Edition* offers 'processes of reference'.]

7. ['Thought-connections' is also a guess – all the wilder for the fact that in itemizing the various 'psychic processes', Freud chooses a word (*Zusammenhänge*) that cannot by any stretch of the imagination be used to describe a 'process' . . .]

8. [Freud is referring to the case of the 'Wolf-man'; see below, *Inhibition, Symptom, and Fear*, note 20.]

9. [*aus den Quellen seines Verdrängten.* Freud's key term *das Verdrängte* is not easy to render in English: the direct translation is 'the repressed', but substantivized past participles tend in English to refer to *people*, not to things or to abstracts ('the damned', 'the defeated', 'the oppressed' etc.). The traditional 'techno'-translations of Freud have long since established 'the repressed' as the English jargon-word, but in many contexts the term would not be readily comprehensible to the non-specialist reader, and is therefore generally avoided in this present volume.]

10. [*Dämmerzustände.*]

11. [Here – as also in the penultimate sentence of the preceding paragraph, and on numerous other occasions throughout these essays – Freud uses the term *Motiv.* The *Standard Edition* routinely translates this as 'motive', but this is potentially misleading: whereas 'motive' commonly refers to the *purpose* of an act, i.e. the end result envisaged by its perpetrator ('the killer's motive was money'), *Motiv* in Freud's usage almost invariably seems to be a quasi-scientific, not to say mechanistic term meaning 'motive force', thus relating to the *generation* of an act or event, not to any supposed aim or purpose. See also *Inhibition, Symptom, and Fear*, Ch. IX, and the corresponding note 57.]

12. [The inverted commas are Freud's.]

Beyond the Pleasure Principle

1. [The terms 'economic', 'dynamic' and 'topical' are all used by Freud in a special sense within the context of his 'metapsychological' system. Cf. the opening paragraphs of Chapters II and IV of *The Unconscious*.]

2. [See below, note 27.]

3. [The 'reality principle' – one of Freud's central notions – may be defined as 'the regulatory mechanism that represents the demands of the external world, and requires us to forgo or modify gratification or postpone it to a more appropriate time. In contrast to the pleasure principle, which ... represents the id or instinctual impulses, the reality principle represents the ego, which controls our impulses and enables us to deal rationally and effectively with the situations of life.' (*The Longman Dictionary of Psychology and Psychiatry*).]

4. [*Organisation*. See below, *The Ego and the Id*, note 10.]

5. [*Addition 1925*:] The essence of the matter is presumably that pleasure and unpleasure, being conscious sensations, are tied to the ego. [See the first few paragraphs of Chapter II of *Inhibition, Symptom, and Fear* – which Freud wrote in the same year in which he added this footnote.]

6. [Freud uses the word *modifizieren*, and clearly intends the less common meaning that occurs in both languages, and which in the case of English 'modify' is defined thus in the *OED*: 'To alter in the direction of moderation or lenity; to make less severe, rigorous, or decided; to qualify, tone down, moderate'.]

7. [First World War.]

8. Cf. *Zur Psychoanalyse der Kriegsneurosen* [*Psycho-Analysis and the War Neuroses*]. With contributions by Ferenczi, Abraham, Simmel and E. Jones (1919). [Freud wrote the Introduction to this volume.]

9. [The original words are respectively *Schreck*, *Furcht* and *Angst*. The distinctions that Freud draws are lexically somewhat specious – particularly the purported distinction between *Furcht* and *Angst* – and this speciousness is duly reflected in the translation. See also *Inhibition, Symptom, and Fear*, Chapter XI, Addendum B: 'Fear: Supplementary Remarks'.]

10. [*'fixate* ... to cause (a person) to react automatically to stimuli in terms which relate to a previous strong emotional experience; to establish (a response) in this way.' (*OED*).]

11. [The final clause of this sentence (from 'or' to 'ego') was added by Freud in 1921.]

12. This interpretation was then fully confirmed by a further observation.

One day when the child's mother had been absent for many hours, she was greeted on her return with the announcement 'Bebi o-o-o-o!', which at first remained incomprehensible. It soon turned out, however, that while on his own for this long period of time the child had found a way of making himself disappear. He had discovered his reflection in the full-length mirror reaching almost to the floor, and had then crouched down so that his reflection was 'gone'.

13. When the child was five and three-quarters his mother died. Now that she was really and truly 'gone' (o-o-o), the boy showed no signs of grief. However, a second child had been born in the meantime, provoking the most intense jealousy in him.

14. Cf. 'Eine Kindheitserinnerung aus *Dichtung und Wahrheit*' (1917) ['A Childhood Recollection from [Goethe's] *Dichtung und Wahrheit*'].

15. [See Freud's footnote below, note 20.]

16. See *Remembering, Repeating, and Working Through* (1914) [for example pp. 36f. in this volume].

17. ['*das Verdrängte*'; the inverted commas are Freud's.]

18. [Freud radically altered his view on this matter: see below, *The Ego and the Id*, note 40. In this context, it might be noted that this phrase ('especially the part we may term its nucleus') did not figure at all in the original edition of the essay. The rest of the sentence *did* appear, but in somewhat different terms: 'Much of the ego may itself be unconscious, and probably only part of that is covered by the term "pre-conscious".']

19. [Freud will explicitly modify his position in *Inhibition, Symptom, and Fear*; see Chapter XI, Section A, Sub-section (a): 'Resistance and counter-cathexis'.]

20. [*Addition 1923:*] I have made the point elsewhere that the compulsion to repeat is aided here by the 'suggestion effect' in psychoanalytic therapy, that is, by that amenability to the physician that has its roots deep in the patient's unconscious parent-complex. [Compare 'Remarks on the Theory and Practice of Dream-Interpretation' (1923), Chapters VII and (especially) VIII.]

21. Cf. the apt remarks of C. G. Jung in his essay 'Die Bedeutung des Vaters für das Schicksal des Einzelnen' ['The Significance of the Father in the Destiny of the Individual'] (1909).

22. [This sentence is faithful to the original in its less than perfect clarity and logic!]

23. [*Pcpt* represents the 'perceptual system', first proposed by Freud in *The Interpretation of Dreams* (1900).]

24. This is based entirely on J[osef] Breuer's discussion of the topic in the theoretical section of *Studien über Hysterie* [*Studies on Hysteria*; Sigmund Freud and Josef Breuer], 1895.

25. [See *The Interpretation of Dreams* (in the Penguin Freud Library, vol. 4, p. 687).]

26. [*Bahnung* (without inverted commas in Freud's original). The verb *bahnen* (cognate with English 'bane' in its etymological sense of 'strike' or 'wound') means 'to strike a path through (snow, the jungle, a press of people, etc.)'. The *Standard Edition* bizarrely renders the word as 'facilitation'.]

27. [*gebunden*. The verb *binden* (past participle *gebunden*) is a key term in Freud's theory of the psyche – but it is not clear precisely how he visualized the metaphor, and it is therefore difficult to render it in English with any certainty; 'annex' seems the likeliest equivalent, and is generally used throughout this volume (the *Standard Edition* opts for 'bind' and 'attach'). It is notable that in the course of the essay Freud twice feels obliged to enclose the word in inverted commas, suggesting that he himself did not regard the concept as either self-evident or self-explanatory.]

28. *Studien über Hysterie* [*Studies on Hysteria*], by Josef Breuer and Sigmund Freud (1895).

29. Cf. 'Triebe und Triebschicksale' ['Drives and Their Fates'] (1915).

30. [*Angstbereitschaft* – literally 'fear-preparedness'.]

31. [*Angstträume*.]

32. Introduction to *Zur Psychoanalyse der Kriegsneurosen* [*Psycho-analysis and the War Neuroses*] (1919) [see above, note 8].

33. Cf. Chapter VII, 'The Psychology of Dream Processes', in my *Interpretation of Dreams*.

34. [Freud's grammar is quite often slapdash, but in the case of this parenthesis it is garbled to the point of complete obscurity. The translation is therefore conjectural, and has been derived by reference to the penultimate sentence of Chapter II (see also the associated note concerning Freud's use of 'modify').]

35. [This phrase directly renders Freud's mercifully unambiguous German (*zeigen . . . den dämonischen Charakter*); the *Standard Edition*, however, bowdlerizes this into 'give the appearance of some "daemonic" force at work'. See also below, note 37.]

36. [*Wunschphantasie* – yet another example, like 'dream-work' (*Traumarbeit*) in the second paragraph of this chapter, of Freud's zest for creating new words by shunting together two seemingly ill-assorted ones.]

37. [The *Standard Edition* offers another revealing bowdlerization here: Freud uses the plain, no-nonsense words *dieser dämonische Zwang* – but

James Strachey felt obliged to render the phrase as 'this compulsion with its hint of possession by some "daemonic" power'.]

38. I have no doubt that similar suppositions as to the nature of 'drives' have already been expressed on numerous occasions.

39. [*Addition 1925:*] The reader is asked to bear in mind that what follows is the elaboration of an extreme line of thought, which will be qualified and amended later on when the sex drives are taken into consideration.

40. [*Partialtrieb*. The *Standard Edition* routinely renders the *Partial*-element of this term as 'component . . .', but there is no good reason to depart from the straightforward translation 'partial . . .' (cf. such standard technical terms as *Partialbruch*, *Partialdruck* – 'partial fraction', 'partial pressure').]

41. [The phrase 'these guardians of life' presumably refers back to 'the drives' – but this is left unclear by Freud.]

42. [*Addition 1923:*] And yet it is to these alone that we can attribute an inner tendency towards 'progress' and higher development! (See below).

43. [*Addition 1925:*] It should be clear from the whole context that the term 'ego drives' is intended here only as a provisional one that harks back to the original nomenclature of psychoanalysis.

44. Ferenczi arrived at the same potential interpretation, but via a different route: 'If we follow this line of thought to its logical conclusion, we must accustom ourselves to the idea that a tendency to stasis or regression also prevails in organic life, while the tendency to development, adaptation etc. is aroused only by external stimuli.' (*Entwicklungsstufen des Wirklichkeitssinnes* [*Stages in the Development of the Sense of Reality*], 1913, p. 137).

45. [See below, pp. 92ff.]

46. [Freud is quoting from Schiller's dire tragedy, *The Bride of Messina* (I, 8).]

47. Weismann (1884) [August Weismann, *Über Leben und Tod* (*On Life and Death*)].

48. Weismann (1882, p. 38) [August Weismann, *Über die Dauer des Lebens* (*On the Duration of Life*)].

49. Weismann (1884, p. 84).

50. Weismann (1882, p. 33).

51. Weismann (1884, pp. 84ff.).

52. Cf. Max Hartmann (1906) [*Tod und Fortpflanzung* (*Death and Reproduction*)], Alex[ander] Lipschütz (1914) [*Warum wir sterben* (*Why We Die*)], Franz Doflein (1919) [*Das Problem des Todes und der Unsterblichkeit bei den Pflanzen und Tieren* (*The Problem of Death and Immortality in Plants and Animals*)].

53. Hartmann (1906, p. 29).

54. For this and what follows, cf. Lipschütz (1914, pp. 26 and 52ff.).

55. *Über die anscheinende Absichtlichkeit im Schicksale des Einzelnen* [*On Apparent Intentionality in the Destiny of the Individual*].

56. [These two sentences were added by Freud in 1921.]

57. [See *On the Introduction of Narcissism*, above, pp. 24f.]

58. [See *On the Introduction of Narcissism*, note 10, and *The Ego and the Id*, note 45.]

59. *On the Introduction of Narcissism* (1914).

60. [See above, *On the Introduction of Narcissism*, note 20.]

61. [See above, *Beyond the Pleasure Principle*, note 1.]

62. [See above, pp. 79 and 91.]

63. [This sentence and the one preceding it were added by Freud in 1921.]

64. [Although he does not say so, Freud clearly means *ego* drives here.]

65. *Drei Abhandlungen zur Sexualtheorie* [*Three Essays on Sexual Theory*], from the first edition onwards (1905).

66. Cf. *Sexualtheorie* [*Sexual Theory*] and 'Triebe und Triebschicksale' ['Drives and Their Fates'] (1915).

67. These speculations have been anticipated to a very considerable extent by Sabina Spielrein in a paper that is rich in substance and ideas but not, to my mind, entirely lucid. Her term for the sadistic component of the sexual drive is 'destructive' (1912). Using yet another approach, A[ugust] Stärcke (1914) identified the libido concept itself with the theoretically supposable biological concept of an *impulsion to death*. (Cf. also Rank, 1907.) All these efforts, like those in the present text, bear witness to the urgent need to bring to the theory of drives the clarity that has so far proved elusive.

68. Lipschütz (1914).

69. [Barbara Low, *Psycho-Analysis*, London and New York, 1920, p. 75.]

70. [See above, p. 87.]

71. However, Weismann (1892) denies this advantage too: 'Fertilization does not by any means signify a rejuvenation or renewal of life; it would not be in the least necessary for the continuation of life; it is solely and simply *a device for enabling two different heredity streams to merge.*' But he *does* consider increased variability in the organism to be an outcome of such merging.

72. [Plato, *The Symposium*, translated by Christopher Gill (London, Penguin, 1999), pp. 22–4.] [*Addition 1921:*] I am indebted to Professor Heinrich Gomperz (Vienna) for the following suggestions regarding the origins of Plato's myth, which are reproduced here partly in his own words:

I should like to point out that essentially the same theory already occurs in the *Upanishads*. For in the *Brihad-aranyaka Upanishad*, I,4,3, where the emergence of the world from the Atman (the self or ego) is described, we read: 'He, verily, had no delight. Therefore he who is alone has no delight. He desired a second. He became as large as a woman and a man in close embrace. He caused that self to fall into two parts. From that arose husband and wife. Therefore, as Yājñvalkya used to say, this (body) is one half of oneself, like one of the two halves of a split pea. Therefore this space is filled by a wife' [trans. by S. Radhakrishnan, *The Principal Upanishads*, London, 1953, p. 164]. The *Brihad-aranyaka Upanishad* is the oldest of all the *upanishads*, and no competent scholar is likely to date it later than *c.* 800BC. As to the question whether Plato could possibly have drawn on these Indian ideas, even if only indirectly: contrary to current opinion I should not want to dismiss the idea completely, given that in the case of the metempsychosis theory, too, such a possibility cannot really be disputed. If there *were* indeed such a link, mediated in the first instance by the Pythagoreans, it would scarcely detract from the significance of the congruity of ideas, since if any such story *had* somehow percolated through to Plato from the oriental tradition, he would not have made it his own, let alone given it such a prominent role, if it had not seemed to him replete with truth.

In his essay *Menschen und Weltenwerden* [*The Coming into Being of Man and World*] (1913), K[onrat] Ziegler systematically explores the history of this particular notion *prior* to Plato, and traces it back to Babylonian conceptions.

73. We would like to add a few words here in order to clarify our nomenclature, which has undergone a certain degree of evolution in the course of this discussion. We derived our knowledge of 'sexual drives' from their relationship to the sexes and to the reproductive function. We still retained this term when the findings of psychoanalysis obliged us to recognize that their relationship to reproduction was more slender than we had supposed. With our postulation of narcissistic libido and our extension of the libido concept to the individual cell, the sexual drive transformed itself in our scheme of things into Eros, the force that seeks to push the various parts of living matter into direct association with each other and then keep them together, and the sexual drives – to use the common appellation – appeared to be the portion of this Eros that is turned towards the object. We then speculated that this Eros was active from the beginning of life, and, as the 'life drive', pitted itself against the 'death drive', which came into being when the inorganic became animate. We sought to solve the riddle of life by supposing these two drives, and supposing them to have been locked in battle with each other right from the very beginning. [*Addition 1921:*] The

changes undergone by the concept of the 'ego drives' are perhaps less clear. Originally we used this term for all those drives about which we knew nothing except that their *direction* made them distinguishable from the sexual drives directed at the object; and we represented the ego drives as being in opposition to the sexual drives, the manifestation of which is the libido. Later we began to analyse the ego, and realized that one part of the ego drives, too, is libidinal in nature, having taken the ego itself as its object. These narcissistic self-preservation drives therefore now had to be reckoned as belonging to the libidinal sexual drives. The opposition between ego drives and sexual drives changed into an opposition between ego drives and object drives, both libidinal in nature. This, however, was replaced by a new opposition between libidinal (ego and object) drives and others that may be posited in the ego, and which are perhaps evincible in the destruction drives. In the course of our speculations, this opposition changes into the antithesis of life drives (Eros) and death drives.

74. [See above, pp. 46–7.]

The Ego and the Id

1. [See above, *Beyond the Pleasure Principle*, Chapter VI, end of third last paragraph.]

2. [See below, note 6.]

3. [Freud's neologism here is *bewusstseinsfähig* – a word that perfectly exemplifies the terminological difficulties that are posed by almost *all* his attempts to convey his theories of the 'conscious' and 'unconscious', and which are particularly abundant in these opening paragraphs of *The Ego and the Id*. Quite apart from any translation problems, the German itself is intrinsically problematic, for the *bewusstsein* component of the word is used in a wholly idiosyncratic way: in normal usage it can only be a noun (English 'consciousness'), but in Freud's neologism it is a verb + predicate (literally: 'to be conscious', or 'being conscious'); indeed, at the very beginning of the paragraph he actually writes it as two separate words: 'Bewusst sein ist . . .' It seems highly likely that this idiosyncratic meaning is also intended by Freud in his chapter title, 'Bewusstsein und Unbewusstes' – a formulation that in any case can only be paraphrased, not translated. Lurking here is a fundamental problem inherent in any translation of Freud's writings, namely the fact that English 'conscious' and 'unconscious' are ill-fitting and often misleading substitutes for the German words *bewusst/unbewusst*, since the two languages arrive at their concepts from opposite directions, so to speak:

'conscious' (from Latin *conscius*, 'knowing') refers essentially to the *person doing the knowing*, whereas 'bewusst' (originally a past participle meaning 'known') refers essentially to the *thing that is known*. In practice, 'conscious' and 'unconscious' often work well enough, partly because of the pervasive influence of Freud himself, and partly because English has long used the words as transferred epithets ('it was a conscious act', elliptical for 'an act of which the perpetrator was conscious'). But there are many cases where 'conscious' doesn't really work at all – not least at the beginning of the fourth paragraph here: the *Standard Edition* renders 'Bewusst sein ist . . .' as ' "Being conscious" is . . .', but the phrase 'being conscious' can only be read as referring to a *person* in whom there is consciousness, whereas Freud clearly means the *thing* of which there is consciousness, as the next sentence demonstrates beyond question when it remarks that any given psychic element 'is conscious for no great length of time' ('nicht dauernd bewusst ist').]

4. [*Vorstellungen* – a word much used by Freud, but almost always imposs-ible to translate with precision: a *Vorstellung* is 'something that is present to the mind', and the word thus covers a broad spectrum of meanings from 'pure idea' to 'mental picture'. 'Notion' fits tolerably well in contexts such as this present one, but should be understood in a very loose sense. Freud often uses it in association or direct combination with *Inhalt* – an even more teasing word (see below, *Inhibition, Symptom, and Fear*, note 21); and as if this weren't enough, he also confronts us with *Wortvorstellung*: see below, note 17.]

5. [*das Verdrängte*. See above, *Remembering, Repeating, and Working Through*, note 9.]

6. [Freud clearly means the word 'descriptive' (*deskriptiv*) in a special sense, defined thus in the *OED*: 'concerned with, or signifying, observable things or qualities, or what is the case rather than what ought to be or might or must be'.]

7. [*OED*: '*Psychoid* . . . A name variously given to vital forces that appear to direct the functions and reflex actions of the living body.' The word was coined by Hans Driesch (1867–1941), initially an experimental zoologist, but subsequently a professor of philosophy and an ardent proponent of vitalism. Driesch is clearly one of the band of 'philosophers' that Freud repeatedly alludes to in these opening paragraphs of his essay.]

8. [Freud is presumably tilting at vitalism here, a philosophy that had flourished in the early to mid-nineteenth century, and then gained fresh impetus through the teachings of Driesch around the beginning of the twentieth.]

9. In respect of the argument so far, see also 'Bemerkungen über den Begriff des Unbewussten' ['A Note on the Unconscious in Psycho-Analysis'] (1912). A recent development in the critique of the unconscious merits attention at this point. Some researchers who are not averse to acknowledging the facts of psychoanalysis, but are unwilling to accept the unconscious, resolve their dilemma by resorting to the undisputed fact that consciousness too – as a phenomenon – displays a wide range of different degrees of intensity or distinctness. There are processes that are vividly, starkly, palpably conscious, but we also experience others that are only faintly, even barely perceptibly conscious – and according to these researchers it is precisely these faintest of conscious processes for which psychoanalysis seeks to use the supposedly inappropriate term 'unconscious', whereas these processes too, so they claim, are conscious or 'within consciousness', and capable of being made wholly and powerfully conscious if sufficient attention is paid to them.

In so far as reasoned arguments carry any weight in the determination of a question such as this, which depends so heavily on convention or emotion, the following remarks are pertinent here:

The emphasis on the varying degrees of distinctness appertaining to consciousness carries no conviction whatever, and is no whit more cogent than such analogous propositions as these: 'There are countless gradations of brightness, from the harshest, most dazzling light through to the merest glimmer, hence there is no such thing as darkness'; or 'There are varying degrees of vitality, hence there is no such thing as death'. In some way or other these propositions might indeed be deeply meaningful, but in practical terms they are useless, as becomes instantly apparent if one seeks to draw particular conclusions from them, such as '. . . therefore there is no need to turn any lights on', or '. . . therefore all organisms are immortal'. Furthermore, all one achieves by subsuming the imperceptible under the conscious is to undermine the one direct and certain fact that we possess regarding the psychic realm. The notion of a consciousness of which one is not at all conscious certainly seems to me far more absurd than the notion of an unconscious element within the psyche. Finally, in thus attempting to equate the unnoticed with the unconscious, people clearly failed to take account of the *dynamic* circumstances, which decisively influenced the psychoanalytical viewpoint. For in the process, two facts are ignored – first, that focusing sufficient attention on an unnoticed element of this sort is very difficult and requires enormous effort; second, that even when this has been achieved, the previously unnoticed element is still not acknowledged by the conscious mind, indeed is often regarded by the latter as wholly alien and antithetical, and rejected out of hand. Repudiation of the 'unconscious' in favour of the 'scarcely noticed' or the 'unnoticed' thus turns out after all to be cousin to the prejudice that unshakeably regards the psychical as being altogether identical with the conscious.

10. [Before acquiring its more modern senses, the word 'organization' (*Organisation* in Freud's German) related chiefly to 'organ', 'organism' etc.; cf. the *OED* entry for 'Organization': 'The action of organizing, or condition of being organized, as a living being'; 'An organized structure, body, or being; an organism' (etc.).]

11. [*Instanz.*]

12. Cf. *Beyond the Pleasure Principle* [Chapter III, third paragraph].

13. [*Tiefenpsychologie*. Freud appears to use the term as a synonym for 'psychoanalysis' (cf. *OED*: 'depth psychology').]

14. [Cf. the 1921 example of the term 'pathological' quoted in the *OED*: 'The pathological method . . . traces the decay or demoralization of mental life instead of its growth.']

15. See *Beyond the Pleasure Principle* [Chapter IV, fifth paragraph].

16. 'Das Unbewusste' (1915) ['The Unconscious'; see Chapter VII].

17. [The terms of Freud's argument here are likely to prove baffling unless the reader refers back to the relevant passage in 'The Unconscious' (see preceding footnote), where he asserts inter alia that as subjects we entertain a dual notion of objects: a 'thing-notion' (*Sachvorstellung*), and a 'word-notion' (*Wortvorstellung*). A *conscious* notion includes both 'thing-notion' and 'word-notion'; an *unconscious* notion consists solely of a 'thing-notion'; a *pre-conscious* notion consists of a 'thing-notion' potentiated by direct association with the corresponding 'word-notion'. Matters are further complicated by the fact that Freud's terminology is even more difficult to translate than usual: as noted earlier, it can often be difficult to know precisely what Freud means by *Vorstellung* – but the neologism *Wortvorstellung* is likely to perplex even the most sophisticated German reader, and any English rendering of it can be little more than an approximation (the term 'word-presentation' used in the *Standard Edition* is a particularly bizarre and misleading concoction).]

18. [See above, *Beyond the Pleasure Principle*, Chapter IV, second paragraph, and the associated note 23.]

19. [In his very early treatise on aphasia, *Zur Auffassung der Aphasien* (1891) (*On Aphasia*), Freud asserts that for the purposes of psychology 'the word' is the basic unit of speech-function, and as such is a complex entity or 'notion' compounded of four distinct elements: a *sound* image; a *visual* image; a *dynamic* image of *spoken* language; a *dynamic* image of *written* language.]

20. [According to the aphasia treatise, the development of our dynamic image of spoken language is dependent on our first learning to speak.]

21. [See J. Varendonck, *The Psychology of Day-Dreams* (London and New York, 1921). Freud provided the Introduction to this volume.]

22. [See *Beyond the Pleasure Principle*, above, pp. 67f.]

23. [See *Beyond the Pleasure Principle*, Chapter I, second paragraph.]

24. [*ein quantitiv-qualitativ Anderes*. The *Standard Edition* incomprehensibly chooses to ignore Freud's notion of 'otherness', and instead turns *ein Anderes* into 'a "something"'.]

25. [*Empfindungen*. Throughout this volume the words *Gefühl* and *Empfindung* are rendered as 'feeling' and 'sensation' respectively – though it might be noted that Freud appears to use the words more or less interchangeably.]

26. [See below, note 40.]

27. G[eorg] Groddeck, *Das Buch vom Es* [*The Book of the Id*] (1923).

28. ['Ego' and 'id' are rather fancy, rather opaque Latinisms, whereas Freud's own terms *das Ich* and *das Es* are plain and forceful, being simply noun forms of the personal pronouns 'I' and 'it'. The 'I' is self-explanatory, but the 'It' perhaps less so. What is implied is clearly the *impersonal* form of the pronoun, as in 'It's raining'. In German, this impersonal usage is not only very common, but can also convey an unnerving sense of a particular and yet unidentifiable, unbiddable presence or force that can assert itself both within us and in the world around us. Where in English one might say 'There was a sudden knocking at the door' or 'I shudder when I think of it', German can more ominously say '*Es klopfte plötzlich an der Tür*', '*Es schaudert mich, wenn ich daran denke*'. It is this potentially menacing order of things that Freud is referring to in his Groddeck-inspired image of 'unknown and uncontrollable forces' at the very heart of our existence. See also below, *Inhibition, Symptom, and Fear*, note 5.]

29. [The unshakeably well-established terms 'ego' and 'id' are retained throughout the present translation – but the real force of this particular sentence can only be appreciated by substituting the direct English equivalents of Freud's own terms: we are essentially an 'it', and on top of this 'it' sits our comparatively puny 'I'.]

30. [The *Standard Edition* alleges that this 'its' means 'the ego's' – but both logic and the grammar of Freud's German suggest that he means 'the id's'.]

31. [See above, note 14.]

32. [See *Beyond the Pleasure Principle*, above, p. 65f.]

33. [See above, *Beyond the Pleasure Principle*, note 3.]

34. [*Das Ich ist vor allem ein körperliches, es ist nicht nur ein Oberfläch-enwesen, sondern selbst die Projektion einer Oberfläche*. There are surely few statements in Freud's work at once so laconic and enigmatic. The original (1927) English translation sought to clarify things with a footnote (duly reprinted in the *Standard Edition*) that was allegedly 'authorized by Freud' – but which arguably puts a slant on his words that he never intended. The sentence itself is translated thus: 'The ego is first and foremost a bodily ego; it is not merely a surface entity, but is itself the projection of a surface'; the footnote then comments: 'I.e. the ego is ultimately derived from bodily sensations, chiefly from those springing from the surface of the body. It may thus be regarded as a mental projection of the surface of the body, besides, as we have seen above, representing the superficies of the mental apparatus.' The main clue suggesting that Freud meant something rather different lies in the word 'projection' (*Projektion*), which he surely uses in the modern neurophysiological sense defined thus in the *OED*: 'The spatial distribution, in the brain . . . , of the points to which nerve impulses go from any given area or organ; . . . also *concretely*, a tract of projection fibres.' (See also the sample quotation dated 1938: 'the cerebral cortex . . . gives rise to a vast extrapyramidal projection passing to many sub-cortical levels'.) Thus in saying that the ego is not a 'surface entity' but the *projection* of a surface, Freud is surely arguing that it is not merely two-dimensional, but is *spatially* and hence three-dimensionally embodied within us. On this interpretation, Freud's 'körperlich' does *not* mean that the ego is 'bodily', i.e. 'derived from bodily sensations', but that it is *itself* 'corporeal' or 'body-like'. This reading is supported by the 'cerebral homunculus' analogy that Freud proceeds to offer by way of illustration: the anatomical representation now best known as 'Penfield's homunculus' depicts the cortex surrounded by a (decidedly grotesque) human figure, in order to demonstrate that neural processes in the brain are organized somatotopically, that is, mapped in such a way that they mimic the locations of the organs and tissues that they serve (see the following note). In the end, however, it has to be acknowledged that Freud simply does not explain himself at all clearly . . .]

35. [The search terms 'cerebral homunculus' and 'Penfield's homunculus' yield numerous helpful sites on the internet.]

36. Precisely such a case was reported to me only recently – as a counter to my description of 'dream-work'.

37. [*ein Körper-Ich*. This must surely qualify as one of the very weirdest of all Freud's compound-noun concoctions.]

38. [*modifiziert*; see above, *Beyond the Pleasure Principle*, note 6.]

39. 'Zur Einführung des Narzissmus' ['On the Introduction of Narcissism'

(1914)]; *Massenpsychologie und Ich-Analyse* [*Group Psychology and the Analysis of the Ego* (1921)].

40. The only thing that seems erroneous and in need of correction is my contention that this super-ego is responsible for 'reality-checking'. It would entirely fit in with the ego's relationship to the world of perception if it turned out that reality-checking had remained one of its own particular tasks. – I should also like to take this opportunity to correct various rather vague statements that I have made in the past concerning the 'nucleus of the ego': only the *Pcpt-Cs* system can properly be regarded as the nucleus of the ego.

41. 'Trauer und Melancholie' ['Mourning and Melancholia' (1917)].

42. The substitution of identification for object-choice has an interesting parallel in the belief of primitive peoples – and the taboos associated therewith – that when an animal is eaten, its qualities accrue to the eater and become part of his own character. As is well known, this belief also contributed to the emergence of cannibalism, and continues to play a part in the whole gamut of successive totem-meal customs, right through to Holy Communion. The results that are supposed – according to this belief – to flow from orally asserting control over the object really *do* apply when it comes later on to sexual object-choice.

43. [*Ichveränderung*. Needless to say, this is another of Freud's special compounds, and does not exist in any parlance other than his own.]

44. [*Charakterveränderung*.]

45. Having now drawn a distinction between the ego and the id, we must acknowledge the *id* as the great reservoir of the libido that we spoke of in our 'Narcissism' essay [see above, *On the Introduction of Narcissism*, note 10; see also *Beyond the Pleasure Principle*, note 58]. The libido that flows into the ego as a result of the identifications described above occasions its *secondary narcissism*.

46. [*Triebentmischung*. In inventing this important term, Freud borrowed from chemistry: *entmischen* is the standard German word for 'dissociate', i.e. 'To separate the elements of (a compound)' (*OED*). However, since he frequently (as here) uses *Entmischung* in tandem with *Mischung*, it seems wise to adopt a similar word-pair in English – hence 'merge'/'de-merge' throughout this present volume (in preference to 'fuse'/'defuse', the word-pair adopted in the *Standard Edition*).]

47. It would perhaps be wiser to say 'with the parents', for a child does not esteem its father and its mother any differently until it has become fully aware of the difference between the sexes, namely lack of a penis. Listening to the story of a young woman recently, I discovered that once she had noticed her own lack of a penis, she didn't assume that *all* women were devoid of this organ, but only those she considered inferior. She continued to believe that her mother possessed one. As it will make it easier to present my argument, I shall deal solely with identification with the father. [The *Standard Edition* curiously converts the 'young woman' (*eine junge Frau*) into a 'young <u>married</u> woman'!]

48. [See *On the Introduction of Narcissism*, above, pp. 16ff.]

49. Cf. *Massenpsychologie und Ich-Analyse* [*Group Psychology and the Analysis of the Ego* (1921)].

50. [See above, p. 120.]

51. [The woolliness of expression is Freud's own: it makes little apparent sense to say that a 'simple Oedipus complex' represents 'a simplification'.]

52. [This may seem confusing, but it faithfully reflects Freud's German. His terms 'mother-object' and 'father-object' (*Mutterobjekt/Vaterobjekt*) appear to be shorthand for 'object-cathexis in respect of the mother' and 'object-cathexis in respect of the father'.]

53. [The *Standard Edition* incorporates two notable alterations in this sentence – alterations that were already included in the original 1927 English version, allegedly at the specific behest of Freud (although no authograph revisions have ever materialized, and the relevant sentence remained unchanged in subsequent German editions): (i) in place of 'two . . . biological factors', the *Standard Edition* prints: 'two . . . factors, one of a biological and the other of a historical nature'; (ii) in place of 'which we have of course attributed to', the *Standard Edition* prints: 'the repression of which we have shown to be connected with'.]

54. [The hypothesis was Ferenczi's. See also *Inhibition, Symptom, and Fear*, below, p. 223 and the relevant note (63).]

55. [Freud's word here is *Seelenleben*, literally 'life of the soul'. Normally in this volume the word is translated as 'psychic life', 'life of the psyche' or simply 'psyche' – but its essentially *religious* origins are highly pertinent in this particular context.]

56. [See below, *Inhibition, Symptom, and Fear*, note 10.]

57. We are leaving science and art aside at this point.

58. [Freud's word here (as also in the second sentence of the closing paragraph of this chapter) is *Bewältigung*, from the verb *bewältigen*, which derives from *Gewalt* (power, force, violence), and means 'to deal with [a challenge etc.] by deploying sufficient energy/force/staying power'; thus one can *bewältigen* a difficult task, an arduous journey, an enormous meal. A frequent and important word in Freud's vocabulary, it is normally rendered in this volume as 'control', 'assert control over' – but in this particular case 'overcome' is more apt, given Freud's oft-repeated emphasis on the ultimate 'dissolution', 'destruction' etc. of the Oedipus complex. In the *Standard Edition* the term is routinely and somewhat misleadingly rendered as 'master'.]

59. [The *Standard Edition* speaks of 'a superstructure built upon impulses of jealous rivalry' – but this is a serious misreading of Freud's German (*Überbau über die . . . Rivalitätsregungen*). The strikingly unusual grammar (*über* + accusative, not dative) means that the phrase unquestionably does *not* describe some static edifice 'built upon' a foundation of jealous feelings, but a construct actively, purposely built out over and above them in order to disguise or – in effect – to sublimate them.]

60. Cf. *Massenpsychologie und Ich-Analyse* [*Group Psychology and the Analysis of the Ego* (1921)], and 'Über einige neurotische Mechanismen bei Eifersucht, Paranoia und Homosexualität' ['Some Neurotic Mechanisms in Jealousy, Paranoia and Homosexuality', (1921)].

61. [See the opening paragraphs of Chapter III.]

62. [Freud's word for 'its' is ambiguous: grammatically it can refer to 'the ego' *or* to 'the Oedipus complex'. The *Standard Edition* questionably resolves the ambiguity by altering the formulation to 'cathexis of the latter', that is, of the Oedipus complex.]

63. [According to legend, warriors slain in the course of the Romans' defeat of Attila the Hun in the mighty Battle of Châlons continued the fight even in death, and Kaulbach's painting duly depicts not only the battle on the ground, but also the battle in the heavens.]

64. [See *Beyond the Pleasure Principle*, above, p. 92.]

65. [See *Beyond the Pleasure Principle*, above, p. 89.]

66. [See also *Inhibition, Symptom, and Fear*, below, p. 181.]

67. [The triple use in this sentence of the word 'object', though unavoidable, masks the fact that in the first two instances Freud uses the technical term *Objekt*, whereas in the third he uses *Gegenstand* – the everyday word for e.g. 'the *subject* of his novel' or 'the *object* of our interest'. Regarding the general topic of identification in homosexuality, see above, p. 127, and Freud's references to his own publications in the relevant note (60).]

68. [Freud's grammar is such that in purely linguistic terms the following interpretation is equally possible: '. . . in the process of overcoming the hostile feelings of rivalry that lead to homosexuality'. In the context of Freud's actual *argument* here, this reading is far less plausible – but the *Standard Edition* opts for it none the less.]

69. [Freud's relative pronoun is unambiguously 'who', not 'what'; he presumably meant it as a personification implying 'which bit of the psyche?']

70. [The notion of an unpleasurable build-up of libido is also mentioned in the *Narcissism* essay; see above, pp. 13–14.]

71. [This tale clearly tickled Freud's fancy: he cites it not only here, but also in the final chapter of *The Joke and Its Relation to the Unconscious* (1905) and in the eleventh of his *Introductory Lectures on Psychoanalysis: New Series* (1916–17).]

72. [See *Beyond the Pleasure Principle*, Chapter V, second paragraph.]

73. [See above, pp. 120–21.]

74. [Freud would appear to be pointing here to the hypothesis he advances in the last paragraph on p. 144.]

75. [Freud is clumsily elliptical here: it is of course not the narcissism itself that has been 'withdrawn from objects', but rather its libido; see *Beyond the Pleasure Principle*, above, pp. 89f. It might also be noted that this remark of Freud's bears on a crucial and problematic ambivalence in his position concerning the true source of the libido; see *On the Introduction of Narcissism*, note 10.]

76. On our understanding of things, the destruction drives directed towards the external world have of course been diverted from the individual's own self through the intervention of Eros. [See above, p. 132.]

77. [See *Beyond the Pleasure Principle*, above, pp. 46f.]

78. [See *Beyond the Pleasure Principle*, above, p. 85.]

79. [The *Standard Edition* has a particularly damaging error here, rendering Freud's unambiguous phrase *sich . . . dem Ich entgegenstellen* as 'stand[ing] apart from the ego'.]

80. [See above, p. 126.]

81. One might say that the psychoanalytical or metapsychological ego stands on its head just as the anatomical ego, the 'cerebral homunculus', does [see above, p. 117].

82. [See below, *Inhibition, Symptom, and Fear*, note 16.]

83. The fight against the obstacle presented by this unconscious guilt-feeling is not made easy for the analyst. Attempts to tackle it directly are doomed to failure; as for indirect means, the only available option is to slowly lay bare the unconsciously repressed reasons for its existence, in the process of which it gradually turns into a *conscious* guilt-feeling. One stands a particularly good chance of influencing it if this *Ucs* guilt-feeling is a 'borrowed' one, i.e. the result of identification with some other person who was once the object of an erotic cathexis. A guilt-feeling that has been adopted in this way is often the sole remaining vestige of the abandoned love-relationship, and barely recognizable as such. (The similarity between this and the process that occurs in melancholia is unmistakable.) If one manages to uncover the erstwhile object-cathexis that lies behind the *Ucs* guilt-feeling, this often brings spectacular therapeutic success; failing that, the outcome of one's therapeutic endeavours is decidedly uncertain. The key factor determining the outcome is the *intensity* of the guilt-feeling, in as much as the therapy is often unable to counter it with anything of equal force. The outcome may also depend on whether the personality of the analyst is such as to enable the patient to substitute him for his ego-ideal, although there is a temptation here for the analyst to present himself to the patient in the role of a prophet, a redeemer, a saviour of souls. As any such deployment of the physician's personality would run directly counter to the ground-rules of psychoanalysis, we must honestly admit that this constitutes a new barrier to the effectiveness of psychoanalysis, the purpose of which is of course not to render pathological reactions impossible, but to give the patient's ego the *freedom* to decide one way or the other.

84. [Freud's Kafka-like vision of the psyche's subjection to an implacably punitive regime is vividly reflected in the language here (see above, *On the Introduction of Narcissism*, note 32).]

85. This proposition is only superficially paradoxical. It simply says that in its capacity for good and evil alike, the nature of man far exceeds what he himself believes to be possible, that is, what his ego is aware of on the basis of conscious perception.

86. [See above, pp. 111f.]

87. [*Inhalte des Über-Ichs*. For a note on Freud's use of the word 'Inhalt', see below, *Inhibition, Symptom, and Fear*, note 21.]

88. [See above, p. 121.]

89. [*Entladungen*. Freud uses the same term in *Inhibition, Symptom, and Fear*: see below, p. 178.]

90. [*Ichgestaltungen* – another of Freud's more inscrutable compounds. The *Standard Edition* offers 'ego-structures'.]

91. [See *Beyond the Pleasure Principle*, above, p. 89.]

92. [This statement signals the beginnings of an important shift in Freud's concept of fear. See *Inhibition, Symptom, and Fear*, below, pp. 160, 280, and especially 229f.]

93. ['Consciential' is defined in the *OED* as both 'rare' and 'obsolete' – but no apology is tendered for its revival here, since without it Freud's teasing neologism *Gewissensangst* is practically untranslatable. Freud expands on his notion of *Gewissensangst* in *Inhibition, Symptom, and Fear*; see below, p. 214, and the relevant footnote.]

94. [Freud is alluding to Wilhelm Stekel, *Nervöse Angstzustände und ihre Behandlung* (*Nervous Anxiety States and their Treatment*, Berlin and Vienna, 1908), p. 5.]

95. [For definitions of 'objective fear' and 'neurotic fear', see *Inhibition, Symptom, and Fear*, Chapter XI, Section B: 'Fear: Supplementary Remarks'.]

96. [Freud's term is *Sehnsucht-Angst* – *not* a compound noun in which one component is attributive of another (like *Gewissensangst*, see above, n. 93), but an equal conjunction of the two component nouns. In *Inhibition, Symptom, and Fear* Freud will dwell at length on the combination of longing and fear that afflicts infants in the absence of the mother; see below, pp. 205f.]

Inhibition, Symptom, and Fear

1. [The word 'inhibition' (like its German equivalent *Hemmung*) owes its primary modern meaning as well as its prevalence entirely to Freud, and exemplifies the spectacular impact of his ideas on our vocabulary and perspectives. Here, as in so many other cases, however, it is necessary to look beyond the Freud-inspired accretions of meaning and recognize that his own use of the term is essentially *pre*-Freudian. In fact he took the word directly from the prevailing terminology of science, particularly physiology, where it had a straightforward mechanical/technical meaning – as is clearly reflected in his comment here (cf. the definition cited in an *OED* quotation dating from 1883: 'By inhibition we mean the arrest of the functions of a structure or organ, by the action upon it of another, while its power to execute those functions is still retained, and can be manifested as soon as the restraining power is removed').]

2. [The *Standard Edition* re-jigs the syntax here and makes Freud say explicitly that 'positive' = 'symptom' and 'negative' = 'inhibition'; there is no such explicit linkage in the original.]

3. [Freud's word *Angst* has always been something of a shibboleth for translators. James Strachey and his colleagues followed the lead of their early predecessors and opted for 'anxiety' in almost all cases, and as a result 'anxiety' has long since established itself as a specialist term with a meaning quite distinct from its meaning in ordinary language (see the relevant *OED* entry); thus, for instance, 'anxiety neurosis' is now the inescapable translation for Freud's term *Angstneurose*. But the fact remains that in the great majority of cases Freud uses the word *Angst* in its normal sense – which corresponds very closely to English 'fear', and which does *not* cover 'anxiety' in the ordinary sense of the word (indeed, when Freud *means* 'anxiety' he uses the standard word *Ängstlichkeit:* see p. 163 and note 14, and p. 220 and note 61). For this reason, 'fear' is the word generally used throughout this present translation.]

4. [*Trauer*. The *Standard Edition* routinely renders this term as 'mourning' (most notably in the title 'Mourning and Melancholia' ('Trauer und Melancholie')) – but 'mourning' is much too closely associated with death and the grief of bereavement to fit Freud's use of the word *Trauer*.]

5. [Freud's language is particularly revealing in this sentence in which the 'ego', the 'super-ego' and the 'id' are all adduced: whereas both the ego and the super-ego are personified, the id is conspicuously not; unlike the other two it seems to be visualized not as a purposive agent, but rather as a kind of space within which dark forces hatch their plots. See above, *The Ego and the Id*, note 28.]

6. [*unliebsam*. The *Standard Edition* curiously and incorrectly translates this word as 'reprehensible' (and a little later as 'undesirable').]

7. [*Formation*.]

8. [Freud defines this phenomenon elsewhere (in the context of hysteria) by reference to people 'in whom any cause of sexual excitement provokes feelings consisting mainly or wholly of unpleasure' ('Bruchstück einer Hysterie-Analyse' ('Fragment of an Analysis of Hysteria (Dora)', 1905).]

9. [See above, *Beyond the Pleasure Principle*, note 23.]

10. [This formulation is recondite, but no more so than Freud's own coinage *Triebrepräsentanz*, which reflects his hypothesis that drives as such inhere in the soma, and are accordingly only 'represented' rather than actually present within the psyche – a hypothesis clearly signalled in his reference to 'the notion serving as the vehicle of the disagreeable impulse' in the opening paragraph of this Chapter (see also the Editor's Preface to 'Instincts and their Vicissitudes' in *Standard Edition*, vol. 14). The *OED* entry for 'representamen' offers an illuminating quotation (dated 1846): 'The representation, or, to speak more properly, the representamen, itself as an . . . object exhibited to the mind.']

11. [See *Introductory Lectures on Psychoanalysis: New Series* (1933), Lecture 7: 'On the question of a *Weltanschaung*'.]

12. [*OED*: 'Any of the series of guide-books issued by Karl Baedeker (1801–59) at Coblenz, or by his successors; also applied loosely to any guide-book.' The word entered English quite quickly: the earliest attestation in the *OED* is 1863. It acquired notoriety in the Second World War: in the 'Baedeker raids' the *Luftwaffe* bombed cities rated with three stars in the Baedeker guide to Britain!]

13. [This oxymoron is another of Freud's sardonic little jokes at the expense of philosophers.]

14. [*Ängstlichkeit*. See above, note 3.]

15. [See above, *The Ego and the Id*, note 10.]

16. ['Illness-gain' is a bizarre construction – but no more bizarre than Freud's own neologism *Krankheitsgewinn*. For Freud's theory that neurotics take refuge in illness because of the 'gain' that it brings them, see, for example, his *Introductory Lectures on Psychoanalysis* (1916–17), Lecture 24.]

17. See 'Analyse der Phobie eines funfjährigen Knaben' ['Analysis of a Phobia in a Five-year-old Boy', 1909].

18. [*Angstentwicklung*. The term mimics standard scientific expressions such as *Gasentwicklung* ('evolution/generation of gas'), and as such is plainly meant to denote a distinct and specific process within the psyche. This is demonstrated particularly clearly in the first sentence of Chapter IX below.]

19. ['refuse' and 'refusal' in these two sentences both render the verb *sich versagen* – a crucial term in Freud's vocabulary, and one that is well exemplified here. See also above, *On the Introduction of Narcissism*, note 23.]

20. 'Aus der Geschichte einer infantilen Neurose' ['From the History of an Infantile Neurosis', 1918].

21. [This lengthy phrase ('the particular *notions* attaching to the individuals' fear') is a rendering of Freud's laconic neologism *Angstinhalte* – and reflects a nasty crux that repeatedly faces the translator throughout this essay. The problem lies in Freud's special use of the word *Inhalt* (plural *Inhalte*). In ordinary usage the word simply means 'content(s)', as in a book or a jar of marmalade. 'Contents', however, connotes something *objective*, whereas Freud almost invariably uses the term to denote the subject's *reading* of their psyche, the subjective notions or 'meanings' that we attach to psychic phenomena – in this case fear. Freud's thinking here is clearly all of a piece with his idea of the 'representamen' (*Repräsentanz*): see above, note 10; see also the penultimate paragraph of this essay.]

22. [*Realangst*. This term of Freud's has always given translators a headache; 'objective fear' does not capture it precisely, but seems a better fit than the woolly phrase 'realistic fear' used throughout the *Standard Edition*. See also Freud's comments on the matter, below, pp. 235f.]

23. [See above, *On the Introduction of Narcissism*, note 20.]

24. [*Ich-Angst*. See above, p. 229.]

25. ['It is not clear'; formerly a standard term in both English and German judicial usage: 'a verdict given by a jury in cases of doubt, deferring the matter to another day for trial' (*OED*).]

26. [See above, *Remembering, Repeating, and Working Through*, note 3.]

27. [*Entladung*. See above, p. 145.]

28. See 'Die Disposition zur Zwangsneurose' ['The Disposition to Obsessional Neurosis'; the case in question is discussed at the very beginning of the work, which was first published in 1913.]

29. [See *The Ego and the Id*, above, pp. 131f.]

30. Cf. Reik, 1925, p. 51 [Theodor Reik, *Geständniszwang und Strafbedürfnis*].

31. [See above, *On the Introduction of Narcissism*, note 23.]

32. [Freud's graphic term is *das Ungeschehenmachen*: rendering something 'un-happened' that has in reality already happened. 'Obliteration' is not ideal, being less a translation than a paraphrase – but a serviceable one, especially given that 'obliterate' originally meant 'blot out of remembrance' (*OED*). (The *Standard Edition* skews the concept by rendering the phrase as 'undoing what has been done': nothing at all is 'undone', but is simply made 'invisible' – as Freud goes on to explain.)]

33. [Freud's phrase (*motorische Symbolik*) is easy to translate – but not so easy to understand.]

34. [The word is Freud's (*fakultativ*); see the relevant *OED* definition: 'Used by scientific and philosophical writers for: That may or may not take place, or have a specified character.']

35. [See Chapter IV of *The Unconscious*.]

36. [See also below, note 46.]

37. [Freud's wording here is *Lebens- oder Todesangst*. The latter term is straightforward: *Todesangst* simply means 'fear of death'. *Lebensangst*, on the other hand, is problematic. In normal psychiatric usage it means 'neurosis caused by fear of not succeeding in life' – but this can scarcely be the meaning Freud intended here in the context of '*traumatic* neurosis' often involving a 'life-threatening danger'. Just for a change, the *Standard Edition* comes to a similar conclusion, and offers 'fear of death (or fear *for* life)'.]

38. [See the penultimate paragraph of Chapter II; see also *The Ego and the Id*, Chapter V.]

39. [First World War.]

40. [See the closing paragraphs of *The Ego and the Id*.]

41. [See below, Chapter XI, Section C, 'Fear, Pain, and Sorrow'.]

42. [But see above, p. 160, where Freud puts this argument more cautiously.]

43. [*Angstbereitschaft*. See above, *Beyond the Pleasure Principle*, note 30.]

44. [*Erinnerungsbild*. The *Standard Edition* characteristically uses a recondite formulation, viz. 'mnemic image' – but this is misleading as well as arcane: Freud is not alluding to the phenomenon of 'mneme' (defined in the *OED* as 'The capacity which a living substance or organism possesses for retaining after-effects of experience or stimulation undergone by itself or its progenitors'); he simply means the image of the mother retained by the baby.]

45. [The phrase 'the . . . subject's perceptions' is yet another attempt to capture the meaning of Freud's deceptively simple term *Inhalte*; see above, note 21.]

46. [Here, as in the similar reference on p. 196, Freud seems on the face of it to imply that 'consciential fear' and 'social fear' are synonymous terms; a few pages later, however, he describes them as distinct sub-sets, one endogenous, the other exogenous: see below, p. 214, and the corresponding note (56).]

47. [This curious formulation is Freud's own – and is no less odd in German than it is in English.]

48. [*Todes-(Lebens-)Angst*. In this instance Freud seems to mean the word *Lebensangst* in its normal sense: see above, note 37.]

49. [Here, as at the end of the previous chapter, Freud sees our relationship with our super-ego as the sole element in our fear of death – but his dualistic vision of the super-ego is epitomized by the fact that it is figured here as a kind of Nemesis, whereas earlier it was represented as the direct opposite – as a kind of guardian angel.]

50. [Freud's term here is *Instanz* – and he used the same key term in the preceding paragraph, in the phrase rendered as '[parental] voice'. See above, *On the Introduction of Narcissism*, note 32.]

51. [See *The Ego and the Id*, above, p. 147.]

52. [See above, *The Ego and the Id*, note 10.]

53. Differentiating the ego and the id inevitably also reawakened our interest in the problems of repression. Up until then we had been content to focus on those aspects of the process that bore on the ego – withholding from consciousness and from motor activity, formation of surrogates (i.e. symptoms); as for the repressed drive-impulse itself, we assumed that it remained unchanged in the unconscious for an indefinite period of time. Our interest having now shifted to the fate of the repressed drive-impulse, we suspect that it is by no means routine, indeed perhaps not even common, for things to remain thus unchanged and unchangeable. The original drive-impulse was certainly inhibited and deflected from its goal by the repression process. But did it none the less remain within the unconscious in rudimentary form, and prove resistant to those influences in life that tend to change and diminish things? Do those old wishes thus still endure whose earlier existence we know of through psychoanalysis? The answer appears both obvious and irrefutable: the old, repressed wishes *must* still exist in the unconscious, since their offshoots, namely symptoms, are palpably still at work. But this answer is insufficient, for it does not allow us to determine which of the two available possibilities is the correct one – that is, whether the erstwhile wish now makes itself felt solely through its offshoots, having transferred its entire cathectic energy to them, or whether it is also still present and active itself. If the fate that it suffered was to be entirely used up in cathecting its offshoots, then a third possibility presents itself, namely that it was reactivated by regression in the course of the neurosis, however inappropriate to the prevailing circumstances it might happen to be. These are by no means idle considerations: numerous aspects of psychic life, both normal and abnormal, seem to call for such questions to be raised. I became aware of the difference between the mere repression of an old wish-impulse and its actual eradication while writing my paper 'Der Untergang des Ödipus-Komplexes' ['The Dissolution of the Oedipus Complex', 1924].

54. [See 'Einige psychische Folgen des anatomischen Geschlechtsunter-schieds' ('Some Psychical Consequences of the Anatomical Distinction Between the Sexes', 1925).]

55. [The *Standard Edition* has a footnote by the editor asserting that Freud means a close connection between fear and *neurosis* – but the whole thrust of the passage makes it clear that he means fear and *symptom*; see especially the third sentence of the fourth paragraph of this chapter!]

56. [Freud considerably helps us to understand his otherwise problematic concept of 'consciential fear' (*Gewissensangst*) by defining it here as 'endo-psychic', and differentiating it from 'social fear' (*soziale Angst*). The *Standard Edition* seriously distorts this important notion by variously rendering it as 'moral fear' and (even more dubiously) 'fear of conscience': *Gewissens-angst* is not derived from society's *mores*, nor is it fear *of* conscience, but an endogenous form of fear arising directly *out of* that indwelling (and mysterious) form of knowingness that we term 'conscience', *Gewissen*.]

57. [This context demonstrates Freud's use of the word *Motiv* with particular clarity ('woher kommt die Neurose, was ist ihr letztes, das ihr besondere Motiv?'). See above, *Remembering, Repeating, and Working Through*, note 11.]

58. [This strikingly allusive epithet is Freud's own (*unangetastet*).]

59. ['Simplicity is the seal of truth.']

60. ['Catharsis' in its psychotherapeutic sense is defined in the *OED* as follows: 'The process of relieving an abnormal excitement by re-establishing the association of the emotion with the memory or idea of the event which was the first cause of it, and of eliminating it by abreaction.' See also the opening sentences of *Remembering, Repeating, and Working Through*, and the relevant note.]

61. [*Ängstlichkeit* – this being the standard German word for 'anxiety' (see above, note 3).]

62. [See the explanatory passage in *Beyond the Pleasure Principle*, above, p. 65.]

63. [The 'momentous event' that Freud is alluding to is the ice age. The idea derived originally from Ferenczi. See also *The Ego and the Id*, above, p. 125.]

64. [See *On the Introduction of Narcissism*, above, p. 28.]

65. [*Gegenbesetzung*. The *Standard Edition* misleadingly renders this as 'anticathexis'.]

66. [See the *OED* quotation from a 1927 English translation of Laforgue: 'In an earlier work I have defined scotomization (or the forming of mental "blind spots") as a process of psychic depreciation, by means of which the individual attempts to deny everything which conflicts with his ego.']

67. [See *The Ego and the Id*, above, pp. 108f.

68. [See *The Ego and Id*, Chapter V, opening pages.]

69. [See 'Die Abwehr-Neuropsychosen' ('The Neuro-Psychoses of Defence', 1894).]

70. [See above, *Beyond the Pleasure Principle*, note 9.]

71. [See *Beyond the Pleasure Principle*, Chapter II, closing paragraphs.]

72. [See above, p. 219.]

73. [See above, pp. 207f.]

74. It may well quite often happen that in a danger situation that is quite correctly perceived as such by the subject, his objective fear is compounded by an element of fear relating to his drives. In such an event the drive whose demands the ego so fearfully shrinks from gratifying is probably a masochistic one, namely the destruction drive directed against the subject's own person. Perhaps it is this additional element that accounts for those cases where the fear reaction ends up being excessive, counter-purposive and paralysing. Phobias with regard to height (windows, towers, precipices etc.) may well have the same origin. Their covert feminine significance is closely related to masochism.

75. See 'Trauer und Melancholie' ['Mourning and Melancholia', 1917; see especially the opening paragraphs of the essay].

76. [Freud discusses this in rather more detail in *Beyond the Pleasure Principle*, Chapter IV.]

77. [This, too, is more amply discussed in *Beyond the Pleasure Principle*, Chapter IV.]

78. [See the opening pages of 'Trauer und Melancholie' ('Mourning and Melancholia', 1917).]